"Nowadays, nearly every educator-pundit, Wall Street tycoon, and Hollywood mogul has his or her recipe for education in the 21st century. It's high time to learn the views and recommendations of a thoughtful young person. And what high school student Nikhil Goyal has to say, on the basis of his research, interviews, and reflections, is well worth pondering."
— **HOWARD GARDNER**, Professor Of Cognition and Education at the Harvard Graduate School Of Education

"What a wonderful book! I nominate Nikhil Goyal for U.S. Secretary of Education!"
— **DIANE RAVITCH**, former Assistant Secretary of Education and *New York Times* bestselling author of *The Death and Life of the Great American School System*

"Nikhil Goyal is a leader among young people who are changing the world of education. Once you read this book, you will never view education the same way. Goyal represents the future — which looks nothing like the past."
— **MICHAEL ELLSBERG**, bestselling author of *The Education of Millionaires*

"Don't read this book only for the novelty of hearing a student perspective. And don't read it just because it nicely articulates how the current school system privileges empty efficiencies and test-taking over creative and critical thinking and the joys of learning. Read it because it puts into words pretty much every critical thought you yourself have ever had about education — your own, your students', or your children's — and lays out some innovative ways to overhaul the system. You'll come away realizing you're not alone, and that change is possible. Not a bad place to start."
— **HOLLY OJALVO**, former editor of the *New York Times* Learning Network blog, founder of News 101, LLC, and a veteran teacher with a decade of experience

"This unique book gives you a student's view to school and education reform unlike any volume written by academic scholars. It is fresh, inspiring and awakening. Simply a must read for anybody interested in today's schools and how they should look like tomorrow."
— **PASI SAHLBERG**, Director General of CIMO, Finland and author of *Finnish Lessons*

"A wonderful read; full of ideas, proposals and examples to fruitfully mull over — some new, some old — all from a fresh perspective."
— **DEBORAH MEIER**, Senior Scholar at NYU Steinhardt School of Education

"It's amazing that education is the dominant force in our young lives, yet in this fast-paced, ever changing world, it's barely moved an inch forward. With a driving intellectual curiosity and a desire to see real change, Nikhil Goyal grabs a shovel and digs in. It's about time we took a fresh look at how to upgrade our education system, and in this book Goyal truly takes us there."

— **JEFF HOFFMAN**, Co-Founder of ColorJar and Serial Entrepreneur at Priceline.com and Ubid.com

"Pay serious attention to the frustration of this precocious high schooler, as we are far past the point of the 'canari in the goldmine.' You may not agree with every single recommendation, but Nikhil Goyal says it candidly as he sees it, and he is not alone as a Millenial to consider that the system is failing them. Teachers, administrators, and parents should listen carefully."

— **CHARLES FADEL**, co-author of *21st Century Skills: Learning for Life in our Times* and founder of Center for Curriculum Redesign

"In our ongoing debates about educational policy, among the voices rarely included are those of students. As this remarkable book by Nikhil Goyal demonstrates, our students are capable of addressing what they want and need from our public schools. You may not agree with all of what Goyal writes — I did not. But you will find this book perceptive, thoughtful and more than a little persuasive. Those involved with the making of educational policy would be well advised to read and ponder what he has written."

— **KENNETH J. BERNSTEIN**, 2010 *Washington Post* Agnes Meyer Outstanding Teacher and nationally known blogger ("teacherken") on education

"This book is a clear-eyed view of the education crisis from a source we usually never get to hear from — a student who's actually on the frontlines. Nikhil Goyal's book takes the reader inside today's schools to reveal what's going wrong, and how we might design a better model. It's a real eye-opener, and an inspiring manifesto for change."

— **WARREN BERGER**, author of *Glimmer: How Design Can Transform Your Life, Your Business, and Maybe Even the World*

"While a first book might appear early to proclaim Nikhil Goyal an emerging voice of his generation, it's not an overstatement to say that he is. From the eyes of a student, a consumer of education, and am emerging critic of a shattered education system, Goyal's voice will resonate across literal and figurative borders. This book is a great read for those who want to wade through what education should haver been yet perhaps never was."

— **ARON SOLOMON**, Founder of Smartswise and former CEO of THINK Global School

"We hear a great deal from educators, politicians, and parents about the shortcomings of the American education system today. We're told that these are the key stakeholders, but the largest stakeholders are the students themselves. With *One Size Does Not Fit All*, Nikhil Goyal gives the students a voice, and it's a voice backed by a far greater amount of research and insight than we typically see in discussions regarding education."
— **RICHARD RUSCZYK**, founder of the *Art of Problem Solving*

"*One Size Does Not Fit All* is thoughtful, extremely well-researched, and poignant look into one of the most important topics of our generation. Nikhil Goyal's fearless curiosity, his laser focus on this generation's future prospects, combined with his meticulous research make this book a must- read for parents, educators, employers, and students. It will make you think, and as a parent, it will change the way you see your child's education."
— **TONY CHEN**, Founder/CEO of Savvy Daddy and Co-Founder of MOVEMENT121

"Nikhil Goyal is remarkable among young people: he cares deeply about education. But he does more than care. He is moved to think, research, and write about the huge problems besetting American education. His work demands our attention. The future of American education will inevitably be the future of America itself."
— **PAUL VON BLUM**, Senior Lecturer in African American Studies and Communication Studies at UCLA

"Traditional education is a product of the age of empires and the industrial age. Aristotle's school produced Alexander in Greece, Chanakya's school in India produced Chandragupta who drove Alexander's generals away. The Victorians created a schooling system to run their Empire, a system that would produce identical people. The captains of the Industrial age adopted it happily — to produce assembly line workers. But the empires have gone and the manufacturing is going from the West. The products of the victorian schooling system are obsolete, as it the system itself. What shall we do? Read Nikhil Goyal's book…"
— **SUGATA MITRA**, Professor of Educational Technology at Newcastle University, UK

"Maybe it will take a 17-year-old, someone who has recently lived and breathed the American education system from the user end, to finally grab the attention of the policymakers who continue their joyless folly of standardizing and mechanizing the teaching/learning process in our schools. Nikhil Goyal asks us all to see education as an emancipatory process, one that frees the individual to be creative, innovative and daring, exceeding pre-determined limits imposed by an oppressive bureaucracy of rules and

compliance. No less than the souls of our youngsters and the future of our nation are at stake. We would do well to listen carefully to the wisdom found in *One Size Does Not Fit All*."
— **ARNOLD DODGE**, Chair, Educational Leadership and Administration Department Assistant Professor of Education at Long Island University

"Like democracy, public education is reserved only for those willing to fight for it. What if more 17-year-olds fought as hard as Nikhil Goyal?"
— **JOE BOWER**, author of the popular, "For the Love of Learning" blog and teacher at a local hospital in Alberta, Canada

"*In One Size Does Not Fit All*, Nikhil Goyal does more than simply diag- nose the problem; he offers a roadmap to transform our schools. Every parent, every teacher, every policymaker, and every citizen should read this book."
— **LAWRENCE BOCK**, founder of the USA Science & Engineering Festival

ONE SIZE DOES NOT FIT ALL: A STUDENT'S ASSESSMENT OF SCHOOL

Printed in the United States.
ISBN: 978-0-9745252-1-1

Published by:
Alternative Education Resource Organization I AERO
417 Roslyn Road Roslyn Heights, NY 11577 I *educationrevolution.org*

Design and layout by Josh Cook I *hetalkedofplacesineverheardof.com*

One Size Does Not Fit All

A STUDENT'S ASSESSMENT OF SCHOOL

by Nikhil Goyal

"The greatest pleasure in life is doing what others say you cannot."

— Walter Bagehot

*To the millions of children whose
voices are not heard*

CONTENTS

FOREWORD

BY DON TAPSCOTT

When looking at how society will change in the 21st century, most people focus on the effects of digital technologies, particularly the Internet. But it is the confluence of these technologies with a new generation that will shape the institutions of society for decades to come. The Net Generation is coming of age. Born between 1977 and 1997, these teenagers and young adults have grown up surrounded by digital devices and media. In 2010, the eldest of the generation turned 35. The youngest turned 15.

Today's youth are the first generation to grow up "bathed in bits," and as a result their brains are actually different. How young people spend their time during extended adolescence 8-18, is the number one predictor what their brains will be like. This is the time when the human brain gets built. Wiring and synaptic connections of the brain, and if you spend 24 hours a week staring at a television, like my generation did, you get a certain kind of brain. If you on the other hand spend an equivalent amount of time with digital technologies being the user, the actor, the collaborator, the initiator, the rememberer, the organizer, that gives you a different kind of brain.

In the book *Grown Up Digital*, I describe the typical Net Generation as having eight distinctive attitudinal and behavioral characteristics, or norms, that differentiate them from other generations. They prize freedom and freedom of choice. They want to customize things, make them their own. They're natural collaborators, who enjoy a conversation, not a lecture. They'll scrutinize you and your organization. They insist on integrity. They want to have fun, even at work and at school. Speed is normal, innovation is part of life.

Nikhil Goyal is an outstanding representative of this generation, and *One Size Does Not Fit All* is a great example of the maturity and insight that youth are bringing to today's issues. Around the world young people like Goyal are flooding into the workplace, marketplace, and every niche of society. These youth are bringing their demographic muscle, media smarts, purchasing power, new models of collaborating and parenting, entrepreneurship, and political power into the world.

Today, many of the best examples of innovation in business, in education, society or government, are coming from young people who are using the web to create change. The internet is not about putting a video on YouTube, creating a gardening community online or having a cool website or a government portal. This is a new mode of production emerging. It's beginning to fundamentally change the way we orchestrate capabilities in society, to innovate, to create goods and services, to govern, and to educate.

Consider the impact of the Net Generation and digital technologies on universities. There is a widening gap between the model of learning offered by many big universities and the natural way that young people who have grown up digital best learn.

If someone frozen 300 years ago miraculously came alive today and looked at the professions — a physician in an operating theater, a pilot in a jumbo cockpit, an engineer designing an automobile in a CAD system — they would surely marvel at how technologies had transformed the knowledge work. But if they walked into a university lecture hall, they would no doubt be comforted that some things have not changed.

The old-style lecture, with the professor standing at the podium in front of a large group of students, is still a fixture of university life on many campuses. It's a model that is teacher-focused, one-way, one-size-fits-all and the student is isolated in the learning process. Yet the students, who have grown up in an interactive digital world, learn differently. Schooled on Google and Wikipedia, they want to inquire, not rely on the professor for a detailed roadmap. They want an animated conversation, not a lecture. They want an interactive education, not a broadcast one dating back to the Industrial Age. These students are making new demands of universities, and if the universities ignore them, they do so at their peril.

In the industrial model of student mass production, the teacher is the broadcaster. A broadcast is by definition the transmission of information from transmitter to receiver in a one-way, linear fashion. The teacher is the transmitter and student is a receptor in the learning process. The formula goes like this: "I'm a professor and I have knowledge. You're a student and you lack knowledge. So get ready, here it comes. Your goal is to take this data into your short-term memory and through practice and repetition build deeper cognitive structures so you can recall it to me when I test you."

True, this broadcast model is enhanced in some disciplines through essays, labs and even seminar discussions. And of course many professors are working hard to move beyond this model. However, it remains dominant overall.

Many of the problems with today's universities apply equally to the K-12 school system. But there is cause for hope. Consider a pilot project I recently saw where all the seven-year-olds in a grade two class were given laptops. It was the most exciting, noisy, collaborative classroom I have ever seen.

The teacher directed the kids to an astronomy blog with a beautiful color image of a rotating solar system on the screen. "Now," said the teacher, "Who knows what the equinox is?"

Nobody knew.

"Alright, why don't you find out?"

The chattering began, as the children clustered together to figure out what an equinox was. Then one group leapt up and waved their hands. They found it! They then proceeded to explain the idea to their classmates.

These kids loved learning about astronomy. They were collaborating. They were working at their own pace. They barely noticed the technology; it was like air to them. But it changed the relationship they had with their teacher. Instead of fidgeting in their chairs while the teacher lectures and scrawls some notes on the blackboard, they were the explorers, the discoverers, and the teacher was their helpful guide.

This classroom showed that digital technologies – in this case, giving kids laptops -- can free the teacher to introduce a new way of learning that's more natural for today's digital natives.

It is also far more satisfying for teachers.

The old broadcast model is suffocating and stifles creativity, not just in education. For my generation, it was true of every aspect of life. We received our daily dose of television, not to mention being broadcast to as children by parents, as students by teachers, as citizens by politicians, and when then entered the workforce as employees by bosses. But young people who have grown up digital are abandoning one-way TV for the higher stimulus of interactive communication they find on the Internet. In fact television viewing is becoming a background media — akin to Muzak. Sitting mutely in front of a TV set — or a professor — doesn't appeal to or work for this generation. They learn differently best through non-sequential, interactive, asynchronous, multi-tasked and collaborative processes.

Growing up digital has changed the way young peoples' minds work in a manner that will help them handle the challenges of the digital age. They're used to multi-tasking, and have learned to handle the information overload. They expect a two-way conversation. What's more, growing up digital has encouraged this generation to be active and demanding enquirers.

The professors who wish to remain relevant will have to abandon the traditional lecture, and start listening and conversing with the students — shifting from a broadcast style and adopting an interactive one. Second, they should encourage students to discover for themselves, and learn a process of discovery and critical thinking instead of just memorizing the professor's store of information. Third, they need to encourage students to collaborate among themselves and with others outside the classroom. Finally, they need to tailor the style of education to their students' individual learning styles.

Because of technology this is now possible. But this is not fundamentally about technology per se. Rather it represents a change in the relationship between students and teachers in the learning process. *One Size Does Not Fit All* is an exceptionally eloquent *cri de coeur* for change.

Don Tapscott
Toronto, Canada
August 2012

INTRODUCTION

Why the hell are you reading a book written by a 17-year-old kid? Beats me. If you want to know the truth, here it is. I'm a high school student in a public high school in New York. For thirteen years, I've been told to shut up and sit down and listen. I've been ignored. I've been left on the sidelines. Not just me, but millions of students around the country and the world. I will not be silenced any longer. Enough is enough.

In the education conversation, we have the adults' table and the kids' table. At the adults' table, adults are making decisions regarding the very people sitting a table away. Kids do not deserve to be stuck at the kids' table. Not when the future of this country is on the line.

School is really screwed up. Thirteen years of being in the system annihilated my creative potential. When I was younger, I loved to learn. I was fascinated with the world around me. I loved reading. I read hundreds of books a year from the *Magic Tree House* series to the *Harry Potter* classics. My mother says that I was always seen walking around with a book in hand. The library, for me, was like a candy store and an ice cream parlor, rolled into one kid paradise. I can only imagine the sight of me as an eight-year-old struggling to carry tens of books from the library. Those were the glory days.

I also loved to write. My love for reading and writing go hand in hand. After reading the first *Harry Potter* book, I grew quite jealous of author J.K. Rowling. I wanted to be as good a writer as she was. I was taken away by her writing, her dexterity to reign the reader into the narration, and her utter fluidity of language flow.

At age eight, I decided that I was going to write a book and show the world what I could do.

My book was the story of a boy and his trip to the Natural History Museum in New York City. It was roughly fifty pages. When it was finally finished, I had a undying urge to publish my masterpiece. I do recall a conversation I had with a prospective publisher.

Publisher: Sir, how old are you?

Me: Eight years old.

The rest was history. Unfortunately, the book deal never played out. Today, the book remains just a document on my computer.

Furthermore, I was enthralled with the concept of making money.

I called myself an entrepreneur. Selling things was a passion. At age nine, even though I couldn't convince my parents to host a garage sale, I swayed them into allowing me to sell items on Amazon and eBay. After reading books that I had bought, I would list them for "Brand New" on Amazon at particular prices.

After awhile, I got a knack at setting prices, printing shipping labels, communicating with potential buyers, and settling disputes. I learned more about business, marketing, and entrepreneurship than I could have ever dreamed of learning in school. Incidentally, my ventures at Amazon led to my discovery that Santa Claus was not real. One day, while using my father's account, I scrolled to his past orders. There they were, unfolding before my eyes, my Christmas present history for the past five years. Talk about a letdown for a nine-year-old!

School stunted my creative prowess. In elementary school, I was a straight-A student. I wanted to be an engineer or a scientist when I grew up. That was mainly piqued by my science classes in school. In second grade, I was consumed by delightful projects and laboratory exercises. For one science class, I grew tadpoles and caterpillars as well as a plant that I named Bo (after Bo Bice, the runner-up in the fourth season of American Idol). Then third grade rolled around. A lot changed.

Two dilemmas emerged: First, science was largely cut from the curriculum. When it was taught, I was just aimlessly filling in worksheets and hearing dull lectures. Second, a new test called the TerraNova was unleashed to all the third graders in the state of New York, assessing math and reading comprehension. I breezed through the humdrum math section, but I was slightly stumped and dumfounded by the reading section. I could not understand how such an eloquent, alluring language was being boiled down to filling in bubbles on a Scantron. It did not make any sense to me.

After sitting for the TerraNova, I came to the realization that I was seen not as a human being, but a test score. Reading and math were the only things that mattered, because they were only subjects assessed on the state tests. While I was in school, I did not fully understand what was actually going on. I still had this preconceived notion that good test scores equaled intelligence. That's the dogma most kids are brought up with.

Soon after, middle school arrived. I began to delve into the subject of geography and participated in the National Geographic Bee. My passions started to blossom.

I started to love politics. Since elementary school, I have been keenly intrigued by it, commencing with the 2004 presidential election, when I was in fourth grade. Then in eighth grade, my interests spiked during the 2008 presidential election, after reading then-Senator Barack Obama's manifesto, *The Audacity of Hope*. I was in an epiphany-like state of mind where everything seemed to coalesce.

The most important things I learned was that you need to have guts to be successful at something and that changing the world was damn hard.

At that point, I discovered what I love.

After middle school, over the next few years, my passions snowballed. I collaborated with young people at institutions around the nation, debating politics, education reform, and current affairs. Together, we voiced similar opinions on how the future of country was being slowly chiseled away. We all agreed to stay in touch.

When I was 15, I went on a trip to India to visit some family members. Fueled by pure curiosity, I spoke to a plethora of Indian students and parents on their experiences in the education system. Prior to these discussions, I had always believed that the Indian school system was far superior to America's system, because students were tested more, received much more homework, and were in school many more days than American students. I had the corporate reformer mindset. At the end of the trip, I soaked in all the knowledge I accumulated from these conversations, put them in the back of my head, and didn't think more of it.

Meanwhile, that summer, my family and I also moved from Bethpage, New York to Syosset, New York, a wealthier community known for its high-ranking and hyper-competitive schools. I was the driving force for this decision, because I had the belief that the Syosset schools were "better" than others. How did I arrive at this conclusion? I obsessed over the *Newsweek* rankings that parents, administrators, and real-estate agents hold as gospel.

After being assimilated into the Syosset High School ecosystem, I noticed that I was bored as hell in class and absolutely nothing I was taught was relevant to real life. I was being trained to be a cog in the machine. Outside of school, I was engaged with fascinating projects, having conversations with brilliant people, and enjoying life.

One day, I had an 'Aha' moment. The dots were connecting backwards. My conversations with the Indian students and parents, my boredom in school, and my personal hatred for standardized tests, were all finally making sense. My move to Syosset and the lack of learning in school prompted me to take action. My prior opinions were dead wrong. Testing, more homework, and memorization did not equate to true learning.

I thought to myself: Was this happening at other schools around the country? I went on a quest. I spoke to students from California to Massachusetts and observed common frustrations with the education system.

I realized that I was on to something. That's when this book began.

How many times have you awakened feeling empowered to do something remarkable? As Tony Robbins says, "There is a powerful, driving force inside every human being that, once unleashed, can make any vision, dream, or desire a reality." I found my vision and set out to make it a reality.

I decided that students cannot be ignored any longer. We needed a voice. Writing a book to document my views and showcase the student voice was the best way to do it. None of my successes in writing, media, or speaking have been a result of my schooling. I learned how to navigate through it outside of school via the Internet, my mentors, conferences, and my travels.

So how did I write this book? There wasn't a secret sauce or formula nor did I have any family connections. In the summer of 2011, I started conducting research for the book. After reading a piece on something in the realm of education, I would put the name of the author and the names of the people quoted, if applicable, on a list. I then searched or often times guessed the person's email and cold emailed them saying I wanted to interview them for my book. In the process, I have interviewed over 100 people. For the interviews, I recorded them on a Skype recorder or on my iPhone. The costs were minimal. Interestingly, I was well received by my interviewees. Most were thrilled that a student was finally writing about education. I cannot count how many times a parent, an educator, an administrator, or a policymaker has written a book on education.

We are not looking for a quick-fix, back room deal. We need a bold plan. A plan to make our schools great. A plan to make America the most innovative and powerful nation in the 21st century and beyond.

I'm attempting to do that with this book.

*

Why the rush on transforming education? The jobs market is forcing us to act swiftly. Decades ago, you were able to find a decent paying middle class job with the skills you learned in school. Not anymore; the world has flip-flopped in the past decade.

In the fall of 2008, the Great Recession collided head-on with globalization. While we were snoozing, the world's economic playing field was being leveled. Thanks to the "flat world" Thomas Friedman, in his manifesto *The World is Flat*, writes, "A global platform allowed more people to plug and play, compete, connect, and share knowledge and work, more cheaply and powerfully than anything we have ever seen in the history of the world." In a nutshell, the world has shrunk from a size small to a size tiny. So far, we've seen Flat World 1.0 and 2.0. Flat World 1.0 was about producing goods and services on the new global field; Flat World 2.0, however, is Flat 1.0 plus a little extra — the ability to generate and share ideas on this platform. We are currently in Flat World 2.0 — a hyper-connected world. In a column, Friedman writes:

> The connected world was a challenge to blue-collar workers
> in the industrialized West. They had to compete with a big-

ger pool of cheap labor. The hyper-connected world is now a challenge to white-collar workers. They have to compete with a bigger pool of cheap geniuses — some of whom are people and some are now robots, microchips and software-guided machines.

This is not a magic show. Most of the 7.9 million jobs lost ain't coming back. The magician isn't going to pull millions of jobs and a rabbit out of his hat.

We were hit by g-force — Flat World 2.0. More and more jobs were outsourced, automated, and digitized. The recession should serve as a wake-up call to American workers. This is your worst nightmare, folks. Everything you were taught about the labor market is no longer relevant. Everything has turned upside-down, changing the nature of the economy forever.

The Old American Dream that once animated settlers, gold miners, farmhands, and our parents is now extinct. The narration went something like this: If you worked hard in school, didn't make too much trouble, and sucked it up, you would be lavished with modest prosperity. For a long time it worked. Not anymore. The New American Dream involves a new bargain — one that leverages creativity, imagination, and passion, rather than passivity, conformity, and submission. School has failed to harmonize with the New American Dream.

The moral of the story is: Invest in yourself. You need to be young and agile. You are the CEO of your life.

The economy is now down to three types of jobs. The first are jobs that are personal, face-to-face, and local. These services cannot be delivered electronically, so no foreigner, robot, or computer can replace them. An Indian from Calcutta will not be fixing Mr. Smith's toilet in San Francisco. I will guarantee that. Many of these jobs do not require many years of post-secondary education. These include the barber who cuts your hair, the waiter at your favorite restaurant, the police officer who gave you a ticket for speeding on the highway, and the taxi driver who drove you home from the police station. You see these people every day. Without that necessary personal, face-to-face ingredient, their jobs would be extinct.

The second category includes routine jobs that can be broken down to an algorithm, digitized, or a set of rules. Since those tasks can be described in rules, they can be easily programmed for a computer. These jobs are the most vulnerable to being outsourced, automated, or digitized. Some examples include accountants, clerks, cashiers, and even high paying and high-skill occupations like radiologists and lawyers.

Princeton economist Alan Blinder says that we are currently in a Third Industrial Revolution. Blinder tells me, "The nature of economic activity transformed from a country where almost everyone earned their living through agriculture to a country where a substantial portion earned their living through manufacturing. The Second Industrial Revolution moved from manufacturing into services. Now, we're undergoing the Third Industrial Revolution, where the number of potentially offshorable jobs may be in the 30-40 million range, of which perhaps 10-12 million are in manufacturing and 20-28 million are in the various non-manufacturing sectors."

What you call the "tradable" side of the economy is exposed to the threat of outsourcing and fueled by give-away bargains on the other end of the globe. Between 90 and 95 million low-skill workers, or 2.6 percent of the global workplace will not be needed by employers by 2020.

If you are in job where your employer spoon-feeds you exactly what to do, like your days in school, he or she will find someone cheaper and more efficient than you to finish the task. Plain and simple.

A billboard that sat along the 101 Highway in Silicon Valley in 2009 put it bluntly: "1,000,000 people overseas can do your job. What makes you special?" The people in the third and final category have successfully answered this question. These are people doing non-routine jobs, including some types of lawyers and doctors, professors, innovators, artists, designers, musicians, scientists, financiers, pilots, professional sport athletes, and authors. When competing against the forces of globalization, they are the cream of the crop. No matter how hard companies try, these jobs will never be prone to outsourcing, automation, or digitization. This would apply to names like Stephen Hawking, Jessica Alba, Chesley Sullenberger, and J.K. Rowling.

The key to thriving in this new age is figuring out how to become a "black-collar workers," a term coined by economist Philip Auerswald and inspired by Steve Jobs' black turtleneck. He writes:

> Black-collar workers are the factory workers of the present day. They're wearing spotless lab-coats, not grimy overalls. Instead of leaning over an assembly line, they are programming multi-million dollar manufacturing machines.

> Black-collar workers are after purpose, not pensions. They're not seeking lifetime employment; they're seeking lifetime learning. They don't have secretaries or bosses; they have teammates. They don't punch in at 9, and they don't time out at 5. They connect, create, contribute, and collaborate whenever and wherever it makes sense. They try to minimize their spending in order to maximize their flexibility.

Being average does not cut it anymore. Jeff Bezos says that at Amazon "it's always day one." The ability to re-engineer and re-imagine separates the best from the average.

When I asked Daniel Pink, author of *A Whole New Mind: The Right Brain Rising*, about the change in the types of workers, he replied, "We have progressed from a society of farmers to a society of factory workers to a society of knowledge workers. And now we're progressing yet again — to a society of creators and empathizers, of pattern recognizers and meaning makers."

All the rules are gone. We have failed to convey the severity of the situation to our children. We have lied directly to their faces.

School is not working. The system is living in a snow globe, unaffected by the events outside. And it's like a Snuggie — one-size-fits-all.

In the chapters ahead, a number of questions will guide us:

- What if school wasn't school anymore?
- How can we tailor education to every single child?
- Why is the testing regime dangerous and inappropriate?
- How can creativity be taught?
- How can we reinvent the teaching profession?
- What if students' voices were heard and seen as human beings, not numbers in a spreadsheet?

The Onion, a satirical newspaper, published a story last year with the headline, "Nation's Students to Give American Education System Yet Another Chance." The piece went on to assert, "Saying they would 'probably kick themselves later' for deciding to enroll once more in a system that has let them down time and time again, millions of American children agreed to put up with their schools' insufficient funding and lack of adequate arts and science programs in hopes that administrators might finally start providing a nurturing, or at least tolerable, environment in which to learn."

It sounds funny, but it's very true. Why are school and life distinguishable? The world should be our school.

Now is our prime opportunity to cultivate — holistically and whole-heartedly — our forces of imagination and creativity within a different paradigm of human purpose. As Adam Braun, founder of Pencils of Promise, said, "Education is the most stupidly solvable issue of our time." We will continue to get burned by the system year after year after year if we sit back and do nothing. John Dewey once said, "If we teach today as we taught yesterday, we rob our children of tomorrow."

Absolutely every facet of the school system must be questioned. I cannot watch another child's ingeniousness be extinguished before my very eyes. We have been victims of our schooling for far too long.

My goal, by the time you are finished with this book, is for you to rethink education in a new light and maybe conclude that the claims of a disgruntled, but optimistic teenager are justified. Just maybe. If you're willing to drop some preconceived notions and biases and begin viewing education as a means for navigating the world, the journey to the birth of a learning transformation will be easier. Reforms will not cut it. Only a revolution will suffice. Let's get started.

CHAPTER 1

STOP SUPPRESSING CHILDREN

"When I was 5 years old, my mother always told me that happiness was the key to life. When I went to school, they asked me what I wanted to be when I grew up. I wrote down 'happy'. They told me I didn't understand the assignment, and I told them they didn't understand life."

JOHN LENNON

When Nick Perez was a child, he was fascinated by technology. He played with video games, learned how to use his old DOS PC, and started coding at just nine-years-old.

Then school began. Instead of staring at his computer screen, Perez was staring at the clock, waiting to get home to learn "interesting things and code." He attended the Westfield School District in Union County, New Jersey. There, he was observed by a "child study team."

"I underwent a psychological evaluation and was diagnosed with ADD," says Perez. "I was placed in a 'supplemental' class where I could do my homework during school hours, and was placed on Adderall at nine-years-old. When Adderall failed to make me care about school, they decided to try more drugs. Wellbutrin gave me a seizure. Prozac made me irritable and hostile. One day, while on Effexor XR, I experienced a dangerously rapid heart-rate, turned pale, and couldn't stop vomiting."

Long story short, the drugs didn't help; it made things worse. So for Plan B, the "child study team" at his school decided to have a paraprofessional follow Perez around all day to keep him on top of things.

"That's when I really started to believe that there was something truly wrong with me, and I didn't belong in society," says Perez. Fortunately, someone came to save him. His talents in technology didn't go unnoticed. When Perez was ten-years-old, his aunt paid for him to attend a computer camp during summer vacation.

"I was completely in awe of the realization that I could use my mind to build things for others to use," recollects Perez. "When I got home from camp with all of my new books and knowledge, my journey in independent education truly began. I knew that if I put enough effort into learning how to code, I could change the world." But school wasn't going to help him get there. He was miserable thinking of all the time he was wasting in school that could have been devoted to building his dreams.

After graduating from middle school, Perez moved onto high school, but he wasn't allowed to partake in the true high school experience. After a psychological evaluation, the school concluded that Perez was "emotionally disturbed." He was placed into a program called "The Bridge," isolating him in a room with roughly five to 20 students, where he spent his days filling out worksheets.

"I wanted to do real work and I didn't want to be isolated from my peers," says Perez. "So I started skipping school and I was left back for a year. With legal threats, the school desperately tried to bring me back. And I realized it was too late. For my entire school life, I was denied the right to exist normally. My school had wasted my time until there was no time left."

That was it for the kid. He couldn't take it anymore. At age 17, Nick Perez dropped out of school.

In America, every nine seconds a student drops out of school. Contrary to popular belief, a study found that most of the dropouts, 70 percent, were confident that they could have graduated, and 81 percent recognized that graduating from high school was essential to their success. So, what is the primary reason for those students to drop out? Like with Perez's school experience, nearly half of the young adults explained that they dropped out because their classes were uninteresting. Furthermore, 81 percent said they would not have dropped out if the subjects were more relevant to real life. The startling surge in the number of high school dropouts is a serious $3 trillion epidemic in America.

Ultimately, after dropping out, Perez spent his days the same way as the days when he skipped school — composing music, learning how to code in a dozen languages, and discovering the subjects of 3-D modeling and Internet security. With some gusto, Perez said to me, "I'm proud of every moment of schooling that I missed."

He adds, "I finally had control. I could decide what I wanted to learn next." Over time, he started working at startups with entrepreneurs in technology, music, media, and marketing. And no one has ever asked him whether he finished high school.

When I caught up with Nick Perez, he was walking home from the train station after a 45-minute commute from his job at a marketing analytics firm, where he's worked almost a year as a software developer. He's 23 years old now. He's had five jobs and has written hundreds of songs, coded hundreds of thousands of lines, and loved every second of it. Perez couldn't be happier with himself and still would have dropped out if he could do it all over.

*

Why do kids hate school? This question has prompted a firestorm debate among policymakers, Nobel Laureates, educators, and parents. Yet, very few actually get it. The answer is obvious — for kids, school is irrelevant and boring as hell. It sure is for me.

I wonder if some teachers and parents ever pondered whether their student's and children's regular claims and complaints about their schooling were justified, respectively. The problem we face in changing the school system is the fact that since it has always functioned in this manner, people assume it must be working. Take teachers. Most teachers are veterans of these schools; this is how they were educated. Similar-minded people continue to be filtered into these positions. Why change it now? Take parents. Like teachers, they too were pushed through the system. There is a minority of teachers and parents who have witnessed or personally experienced an education system any different.

All of us have taken the red pill at some point in our lives — most of us during the period we were born until our formal education commenced.* When we are young, we act like sponges. We soak in knowledge. We engage with our environment. We manipulate our parents. We laugh. We cry. We discover. Suddenly, around age five, everything changes. Our formal education begins. Knowledge is assumed to be delivered differently to us, by textbooks and lectures. It takes kids a long time to get accustomed to this peculiar style of learning. Some, fortunately, never get it.

Kids literally get arrested and get thrown into this prison-like system. Prisons and schools are actually strikingly similar. In both cases, you are told what to do and when, your schedule is dictated by bells, attendance is compulsory, social media is banned, and you are cut off from the rest of society.

Too often we neglect to mention the chronicle of American public schools. Who started them? Where did the ideas come from? And when? The history of schooling in America prior to the 1830s is checkered with elitism — only the wealthy children went to school. After the Civil War, the Industrial Revolution went into full flight. Factories were rigorously looking for

---

* The term "red pill" is derived from the 1999 film *The Matrix*. The main character Neo is offered the choice between a red pill and a blue pill. The blue pill would allow him to remain in the Matrix, a fictional computer-generated world. The red pill would lead to his escape out of the Matrix and into the "real world."

more hands to produce more products. Meanwhile, an influx of immigrants arrived on our shores and cities' populations were mushrooming.

Ding, ding, ding! Mr. Opportunity is knocking! The answer that our *brilliant* thinkers of the time schemed was a mass education system — push millions of kids through school to prepare them to ultimately man the factories.

How were they going to accomplish that? It all started long, long ago in a faraway and magical land known as Prussia. I kid. It was anything, but magical.

After Prussia's humiliating defeat by Napoleon in 1807, King Frederick William III reinforced a national school system. Children aged seven to fourteen were forced to attend school and parents who did not comply would have their children snatched from them. As the German philosopher Johann Gottlieb Fichte, a key influence on the system, said, "If you want to influence [the student] at all, you must do more than merely talk to him; you must fashion him, and fashion him in such a way that he simply cannot will otherwise than what you wish him to will." Thus, a stockpile of obedient Prussian soldiers were made.

Then, Horace Mann came along. Mann was six years into his tenure as the Secretary of Education of the state of Massachusetts. On his honeymoon he took a peek at the Prussian system, sitting in classrooms. Mann returned home anxious to share what he had witnessed. In the seventh of his legendary "Annual Reports" on education to the Commonwealth of Massachusetts, he touted the benefits of a national system and cautioned against the "calamities which result... from leaving this most important of all the functions of a government to chance."

Education crusader John Gatto says the American education reformers imported three major ideas from Prussia. The first was that the purpose of state schooling was not intellectual training but the conditioning of children "to obedience, subordination and collective life." Second, whole ideas were broken into fragmented "subjects," and school days were divided into fixed periods "so that self-motivation to learn would be muted by ceaseless interruptions." Third, the state was posited as the true parent of the children.

The class clash may point to this education scheme. Woodrow Wilson, then president of Princeton University, said the following to the New York City School Teachers Association in 1909: "We want one class of persons to have a liberal education, and we want another class of persons, a very much larger class, of necessity, in every society, to forgo the privileges of a liberal education and fit themselves to perform specific difficult manual tasks." It may also stem from fear. We didn't want millions of kids roaming the streets.

So, if you really think about it, public schools aren't technically American institutions; they are Prussian in nature.

The great H. L. Mencken wrote in *The American Mercury* in April 1924:

> The aim of public education is not to fill the young of the species with knowledge and awaken their intelligence... Nothing could be further from the truth. The aim... is simply to reduce as many individuals as possible to the same safe level, to breed and train a standardized citizenry, to put down dissent and originality. That is its aim in the United States... and that is its aim everywhere else.

Even though the statement hinted at sarcasm and Mencken was infamously known as a satirist at times, the remark was on the nose. Schools became detention camps and in many terms, still are.

Along with prisons, we can notice some significant parallels between factories and schools, even to this date. First, there is blatant age segregation. When I entered school, the age groupings didn't make any sense to me. Why am I being batched with kids with different abilities than mine?

Dr. Deborah Ruf, founder of Educational Options, writes, "Grouping kids by age for instruction makes about as much pedagogical sense as grouping them by height!" In the factories, the youth worked side by side. Second, school bells mark the transition from subject to subject. Factory bells identified the break between certain operations. Third, in schools, classrooms are compartmentalized into specific subjects. To master greater efficiency, each factory worker was responsible for a specific task he or she could master. Finally, it is no coincidence that the language used in the factory came to penetrate into education. The name "superintendent" derives from the factory floor, as does jargon such as "production and productivity," "outcome and output," and "performance and success rates."

Why do you think Americans are such rabid consumers and drone-like workers?

There really should be a sign planted in front of my high school and many others that reads: We prepare tomorrow's factory workers by imparting docility and submission into our graduates. Every one of them leaves this school having learned how to think our way, follow directions, and consume information passively. Attention Ford, all the low hanging fruit — our standardized minds — is here for your taking. Get 'em while they are hot.

Countries that adopted the industrial school system in the 20th century raced ahead of countries that didn't. However, today, there are few to no relics of industrialism in America other than in our schools.

The always sharp foreign-policy thinker Walter Russell Mead posed this crucial question, "Has the Fordist factory system and the big box consumerism that goes with it now become our ideal, the highest form of social life our minds can conceive?" Maybe it was back then, but not anymore.

Do we really want to teach our kids to color within the lines, follow all the rules, and dot all their "i"s and cross their "t"s?

Schools tell kids early on that they aren't good at things, so they become repressed and stop doing them. John Gatto, in a video, once compared students to fleas. If you let fleas free, he says, they will leap instantaneously in their own directions. In order to stop them, they must be held in a sealed container. They will keep trying to escape, but over time, they become discouraged. After awhile, if you open the container, they won't try to escape. School is the container. The fleas are our children.

Our society has also incorrectly defined "intelligence": High SAT scores and GPAs and Ivy League pieces of papers. Do you know what that means? The person did exactly what he or she was told to do. Rebecca Chapman, literary editor of a new online journal called *The New Inquiry*, puts it perfectly to the *New York Times*, "My whole life, I had been doing everything everybody told me. I went to the right school. I got really good grades. I got all the internships. Then, I couldn't do anything."

I have gotten high grades in school, but how do I differ from a kid who didn't perform as well. My schooling has been training me to work in a cubicle for the rest of my life. How the hell would I be able to function in the chaotic place we call the world?

The question we need to pose to students, policymakers, teachers, administrators, and parents is: How can we reinvent education from the ground up? We can't fix education, because that implies the right model was once in place. We can't practically shut down the public education system as futurist Alvin Toffler has argued for. What do we do? Spit it out. We must replace the model of education.

Sheik Ahmed Zaki Yamani, the larger-than-life Saudi oil minister during the 1970s, said, "The Stone Age didn't end for lack of stone, and the oil age will end long before the world runs out of oil."

I am not here to clash over the energy crisis, but to acknowledge that in school, kids must learn how to face a world no one can predict. According to Cathy N. Davidson, co-director of the annual MacArthur Foundation Digital Media and Learning Competitions, 65 percent of today's grade-school kids may end up doing work that hasn't been invented yet.

Why don't we start with the most straightforward ways to transform education? First, let's end grade levels. The virtue of grouping kids by skill level is that it's not about re-enforcing the sense of meritocracy, but rather it is sending a candid message to kids to help them understand what their talents are and what they need to improve on. This is really a no brainer.

When I explain this proposal to people, they insist that it will cost too much money and waste time. Why should the convenience of school districts favor what's right for children?

Second, let's recreate the "classroom." Outside of school, I have never sat in a desk in a row listening to someone ramble. We cannot clump students in brick-and-mortar classrooms and expect them to learn. John le Carré once quipped, "A desk is a dangerous place from which to view the world." Let's shift classrooms into "life-long learning incubators" — student-centered and well networked with a level of spontaneity. I once participated in a Lean Startup weekend workshop where with three other prior unknown people, we created a Minimum Viable Product, by pivoting as well as making and verifying assumptions. During the workshop, the organizers were screaming at the teams, "Get out of the building." In other words, go on the street and talk to your customers. Likewise, we need to "Get out of the classroom." The world is our school.

Third, and perhaps most importantly, let's ensure the public is aware of the situation. I have had plenty of conversations with all types of parents.

I ask them the question, "Are our schools failing?"

Most answer, "Yes."

If so, I ask them, "Why do you think they are failing?"

Their answers were faulty. I have heard responses ranging from: "On international tests, American students perform poorly in comparison with other countries...There is a lack of science and math...My kid does not get enough homework (immigrant parents)..." Rarely do I hear complaints about excessive testing or not enough play and creativity.

Parents are just resigning themselves to the idea that the school system has always been like this and there's nothing that can be done about it. We need parents to get onboard.

School is like Las Vegas — what happens in school, stays in school. End this nostalgia of industrialism. As the pioneering progressive educator John Dewey noted, "Education is not preparation for life; education is life itself." Why are we preparing kids for factory life? I was certainly not born a factory worker or a Prussian for that case. It's time to bend all the rules.

16,000 HOURS

In every year, new fashion crazes hit society. They constantly change. The 1960s saw the arrival of go-go boots, culottes, and box-shaped PVC dresses. Today, excessive tanning, plaid shirts, skinny jeans, and Ugg boots are the typical fads. Over time, they too will fade away. But, some trends never change. Black is always in style. Likewise, information can go obsolete next season, but skills are always chic. Since the amount of information is doubling every two years, half of what you learn in your first year of study could very well be outdated by your third year of study.

If you asked employers a few decades ago what they looked for in a prospective employee, most would reply that a strong grasp of the the 3 R's are the norm: reading, 'riting, and 'rithmetic.

However, when you ask hiring executives at major corporations this question: "Are students prepared for the 21st century workplace?" The answer is that they frankly aren't.

Why is changing education so urgent? Why can't we push it off for a few more years or let the next generation solve it? The skills crisis will not let us. Students graduating from post-secondary education terribly lack basic skills as well as hard-core 21st century skills that I will mention shortly. They also seem to be missing out on teaching "discovery skills," described in the book *The Innovator's DNA* by Jeff Dyer, as associating, questioning, observing, experimenting and networking. In addition, author Tony Wagner explained to me, "Our graduates are not 'jury ready' — able to analyze an argument, weigh evidence, and detect bias."

Why? Our schools fail to foster them. I am ratting on all schools, even the highest performing ones. At my high ranking high school, very few if any graduates leave with these skills intact.

A virtually unanimous 99 percent of voters agree that teaching students a wide range of 21st century skills is critical to our country's future economic success. And an overwhelming 80 percent of voters say the skills needed today are radically different from the skills needed 20 years ago.

The 21st century skills gap is costing businesses quite a lot of money. Some estimate that well over $200 billion a year is spent worldwide in finding and hiring scarce, highly skilled talent, and in bringing new employees up to required skill levels through costly training programs.

What are the 21st century skills? In a conversation with me, Charles Fadel and Bernie Trilling, co-authors of *21st Century Skills: Learning for Life in Our Times*, said they include the 4C's: critical thinking, creative thinking, collaboration, and communication. I would particularly highlight imagination and curiosity, taking risks, and overcoming failure as well.

1. CRITICAL THINKING

Critical thinking, in schools, is often just a buzz phrase. Very few know what it means. In a study of 140 professors at 66 public and private universities in California, researchers discovered that while an overwhelming majority claimed that critical thinking was a primary objective of their instruction, only a small portion could give a clear explanation of what critical thinking was. From the respondents' answers, the researchers concluded that only nine percent were teaching with a view toward critical thinking on a typical day in class. If the professors that are actually teaching the subject don't know, how is anyone else possibly supposed to define critical thinking?

Progressive education theorist John Dewey defined critical thinking in his book *How We Think*, as "reflective thought" — to suspend judgment, maintain a healthy skepticism, and exercise an open mind. These three activities call for the active, persistent, and careful consideration of any belief in light of the ground that supports it. Dewey's definition suggests that critical thinking has both an intellectual and an emotional component. Thus we view critical thinking as the intellectual and emotional ability to go beyond the known without "falling to pieces." Dewey writes, "Examine a problem, find a solution, think about why you were or were not successful, and learn from your successes and failures. Students must be taught to examine, poke, question, and reflect on what they have learned. Skepticism, questioning, and reflection are essential." In sum, critical thinking involves students producing things and reflecting on them. It is all about dissecting the arguments in front of you and making sense of them.

A survey revealed that critical thinking was regarded as the most important skill employees could contribute in helping their companies to grow. At the heart of critical thinking is the Socratic method, wielded by Socrates two millennia ago. He believed that probing questions and answers that people could not rationally justify equated to utter knowledge.

I know, for one thing, the answer to our critical thinking deficits isn't prescribing more textbooks. Throw them out. Kids need to be taught to never take anything at face value. Examine. Interrogate. Investigate. In the real world, the solution isn't a cute, neat answer at the back of the textbook.

2. CREATIVE THINKING

Creative thinking and critical thinking go hand and hand. For an idea to be deemed creative, James C. Kaufman, professor of psychology at the California State University, San Bernardino, said to me, "it must be new, original, and appropriate."

We all have a natural capacity for creativity, but we are schooled out of it as we get older.

Aristotle once said, "For the things we have to learn before we can do them, we learn by doing them." To the contrary, schools require kids to sit quietly in their seats and shut up. In the process, they are sapping kids who have an affinity for daydreaming and thinking out-of-the-box.

The people who are creative are those who are intrinsically motivated — ultimately enjoying a task. They are creative if they enjoy doing a task. Kaufman adds, "Giving people choice increases creativity. You can increase it by simply allowing it."

But don't tell someone to be creative. Such an order hinders the creative process. However, according to the University of Georgia's Mark Runco, there is a suggestion that works successfully: "Do something only you would come up with — that none of your friends or family would think of." When Runco gives this advice in experiments, he sees the number of creative responses double.

How do we teach creativity? Creativity is learned by doing; there's no shortcut around it. You can't have a powerpoint presentation with steps on how to be creative — x, y, and z. It's much more complicated and personalized than that. A deeper analysis will be offered in chapter seven.

The world will soon no longer belong to the "people who can reason with computer-like physiques of logic, speed, and precision" writes Daniel Pink. It "belongs to a different kind of person with a different kind of mind" — a creative, right-brain individual. "Scientists have long known that a neurological Mason-Dixon line cleaves our brains into two regions — the left and the right hemisphere," writes Pink, author of *A Whole New Mind*. Logic is governed by the left brain and creativity is governed by the right brain. As we transform into the Age of Creation, not just left or right brainers, but both types will rule.

3. COLLABORATION

There's a well-known saying: Great minds think alike. It should be retooled to: Great minds think together.

If you look at any movement or company or invention in the world, it is always the combination of the blood, sweat, and tears of countless stakeholders. In my endeavors, I have never been able to succeed at anything by myself. Ever.

Many companies are throwing their hands up and evolving their workplace from stuffy, claustrophobic office cubicles to open spaces where horizontal interaction is seamless. For instance, at Google, every inch is consumed by spaces to collaborate, interact, and discuss. There are ping-pong tables, pristine tanks to watch the fish, sleek gaming chairs, and an industrial slide. At Facebook, every room has a unique twist to it, mirroring contemporary America. A survey conducted in 2008 by Gensler concluded the best companies spend 23 percent more time collaborating, 40 percent more time learning, and 16 percent more time socializing than average companies. Open conversations are the underpinning of these companies' gospel. This is the essence of synergy — the whole is greater than the sum of its parts.

The former president of Harvard University Lawrence Summers writes in the *New York Times*, "One leading investment bank has a hiring process in which a candidate must interview with upward of 60 senior members of the firm before receiving an offer." While you would probably think they would be looking primarily for candidates with high college G.P.A.s or test scores, they aren't. The most important attribute? Summers reveals, "The ability to work with others."

Classrooms need to become synergy stations.

4. COMMUNICATION

Communication is the act of relaying information clearly from one being to another. It may be through written, oral, or presentation communication. In business, you must be able to pitch a solid idea to potential investors, scribe a professional and convincing email, and pen a plan. In medicine, you must be able to supply patients, doctors, and nurses with feedback and utilize information. If you're a doctor, you must be able to break bad news to patients and their families. And if you decide to publish your research, chances are that you will need to speak at a medical conference. In law, if you're a courtroom lawyer, you must must be able to present a logical case to the jury and communicate well with your clients. That is just a snapshot of some careers, but strong communication skills are a necessity for success in almost every profession.

However, most students get out of school largely devoid of these skills. First, there are enormous deficits in employees' writing skills in the workplace. The College Board discovered that a third of all workers fell short of employers' expectations in written communication skills.

Who are the people that write and what do they write during their daily tasks? According to that aforementioned survey, writing is a regular part of the job for two-thirds of all employees. Employees who cannot write well cost their companies plenty of money each year. The Commission estimates that remedying deficiencies in writing costs American corporations as much as $3.1 billion annually. Sending a single worker for remedial training in writing can cost more than $3000.

Indeed, the "R" is taught terribly or is neglected in schools. Writing in any medium — blogs, speeches, articles, etc. — should be a requirement in every year of school and adequate time must be allotted to it.

Another form of communication is public speaking. This may mean presenting a research paper at a neurobiology conference, sharing ideas with the world at the TED conference, or addressing the millions of Americans with the State of the Union address. Public speaking is a prominent mode of communication in modern culture. Big-shot speakers can get paid thousands of dollars for keynotes and talks. For example, groups will cough up $100,000 to hear Virgin Group's Richard Branson speak, to more than $1 million to hear Donald Trump himself.

American culture is driven by a person's ability to communicate effectively, clearly, and persuasively. Yet, we're spending less and less time teaching young people the very subject to assist them in circumnavigating the world. No wonder 70 percent of the U.S. population report experiencing communication apprehension. Watching my fellow classmates give speeches publicly is painful. There is a minority of students, often only those in the National Forensics League, that have the ability to speak with purpose, speak persuasively, and speak in public. However, I don't know a teenager who doesn't like to argue or debate. Why isn't speech and debate in the curriculum?

As Bob Dylan once said, "I'm speaking for all of us. I'm the spokesman for a generation."

5. CURIOSITY

Young children are naturally curious. The world is a mystery as soon as they come out of the womb. When they start babbling and develop a word bank, they will ask a million questions a day. Is the tooth fairy real? When is Santa coming? Are we there yet? Imagination is instrumental for contemplating reality, distinguishing between what is real and what is not. It allows them to ponder the future. And questions are the heart of this. My mere curiosity with how the education system functioned led me to writing this book. I started by asking a few simple questions. Imagine if someone muzzled that skepticism early on. You would not be reading this book.

Look at four-year-olds. They constantly nag their mothers, curious about the nuts and bolts of the world. As a child, I wouldn't shut up. To some parents, it's extremely irritating, so asking questions may be discouraged. Then, when kids are fully assimilated into kindergarten, they quickly learn that teachers value the right answer rather than stimulating questions. If graphed, the number of questions asked by kids from childhood to adulthood, would demonstrate a sharp downward slope. Curiosity, like creativity is drummed out of kids. In school, kids are encouraged to seek the answer, rather than formulate a good question.

Innovators, however, were raised in an atmospheres that were sustained by people who cared about discovery and experimentation. They asked countless numbers of questions and weren't told to shut up. And they have never stopped. Studies have confirmed that it is indeed innovators that never lose that childhood inquisitiveness. Eric Schmidt, CEO of Google, once noted, "We run this company on questions, not answers." Breakthroughs are often born with someone simply asking, "What if....?" It's the questions, stupid! Even Albert Einstein once said that if he only had an hour to solve a problem, he'd spend 55 minutes thinking about the problem and five minutes thinking about solutions.

This raises an interesting you-know-what. Author Warren Berger points out to me, "If we can see that questions are linked to innovation and problem-solving, why are so many of us reluctant to ask them?" A University of Michigan study found that people in business generally loathe raising questions, primarily because they fear that anyone who asks questions will be deemed incompetent or uninformed. Most of the time, questions are far more pivotal than answers.

Nobel Laureate physicist Isidor Isaac Rabi, once quipped to *Parents Magazine*, "My mother made me a scientist without ever intending to. Every other Jewish mother in Brooklyn would ask her child after school: So? Did you learn anything today? But not my mother. "Izzy," she would say, "did you ask a good question today?" That difference—asking good questions — made me become a scientist." There are no stupid questions.

In the globalized world we live in, you will always be at an advantage if you have the curiosity to delve into anything. Doc Searls, senior editor of the *Linux Journal*, writes in it, "Work matters, but curiosity matters more. Nobody works harder at learning than a curious kid." Curious kids are self-motivators, willing to go to infinity, and beyond.

It is time to bring the spirit of imagination and wonder back into our lives and our schools.

The future belongs to the curious.

6. RISK-TAKING

If there is one sector in the country that is not feeling the after-effects of the recession, it is technology. The startup culture is booming from New York to Boulder to San Francisco. Who are the people piloting the way? Folks in their 20s and 30s. After recovering from their education that told them risk-taking was taboo, many are branching out and attending Lean Startup workshops, startup bootcamps, and programming classes to start or join companies. Risk-taking isn't limited to just the technology sector, it is a core-skill in the age of work.

This book is a risk in and of itself. I am allowing my ideas be prone to criticism and debate.

Taking risks within the curriculum boosts learning, enabling kids to experiment with various ideas and approaches. Most students are conservative learners, too caught up in worrying about grades, and in turn "playing it safe." Material is presented without second thoughts or a degree of skepticism.

This is widespread for instance in the scientific field. A study uncovered that, in general, as students get older they become less likely to take intellectual risks, such as sharing their tentative ideas when learning science. Risk-taking coincides inevitably with experiencing failure. Thus, risk-taking in highly stimulated atmospheres can allow students to experience it without having damaging emotional consequences.

We shy away from experiences that take us out of our comfort zones, but that's exactly what offers you a greater potential to be acquainted with something you could never have experienced before. Don't hesitate to introduce yourself to a stranger on the train or a person scouring the bookshelves at Barnes & Noble. Imagine how many people you could meet, how many stories you could exchange, and how many lives you could touch. O.K., you get rejected or ignored, so what. Shake it off and move on.

Ask yourself: "What's there to lose?"

7. OVERCOMING FAILURE

It would take me too long to count how times I have been rejected by literary agents, publishers, and conferences. I could moan and groan for hours or days on end, but what's the point? Thus, I try to live by the 15-minute-rule. For 15 minutes you can complain and whine as much as you want. When the 15 minutes are up, suck it up and move on. Gaining the skill of overcoming failure is one of the most important things you will need in your lifetime.

Watch a child learn to walk. They battle and stumble. Seconds later, they're right back up, attempting to walk again. Children aren't afraid to fail. It is society that implants this fear.

Malcolm Gladwell, in his book *Outliers*, brings up the example of the band, the Beatles, who performed live in Hamburg, Germany alone over 1,200 times over a stretch from 1960 to 1964, amassing more than 10,000 hours of playing time. Needless to note, 10,000 hours of practicing includes failing over and over again, recovering, and keeping your eyes on the target.

Through a process of experimentation, that's when the true innovations blossom. For some executives, failure is celebrated. Thomas D. Kuczmarski, a Chicago new-product development consultant, even proposes "failure parties" as a way of glorifying well-designed experiments that ultimately failed. This will be discussed in greater detail in chapter five.

Never stop failing.

From kindergarten to twelfth grade, by my calculations, kids spend roughly 16,000 hours in school. Author Malcolm Gladwell also writes about the "10,000-Hour-Rule," in which he states that the key to success in any field is largely a matter of practicing a specific task for a total of around 10,000 hours. His theory isn't perfect, but students graduate from high school unable to critically think, solve problems, communicate, and collaborate.

Adults make kids jump through ever so many, pre-determined scholastic hoops. It has come to a point where people find it dangerous to stray from the path — do something other than the norm. Unless we shift the maxims in our society, where every kid gets a trophy and a ribbon and success is determined by test grades and acceptances to prestigious universities, nothing will change.

In my experiences, I have observed too many kids sucked into this "race to nowhere." Gerald Celente, editor of the *Trends Journal*, said it best in the documentary *The College Conspiracy*: "You have to have a certain kind of brain to understand the dead language that they write in textbooks. But they brainwash you from a little kid up so that you'll buy into the system. You get good grades and you study hard and you become a member of the system. No freedom. You don't know how to think, because they told you how to think their way."

We shelter kids from the real world. After post-secondary education, we say 'Go survive on your own!' Most kids drown. Saddled with bundles of debt, many college graduates move home to live with their parents.

It frightens me when I hear students say they don't know what they love to do. For their entire lives, they never thought beyond what they were taught in school. That's one of the biggest problems in the world. Compliance is the shortcut to success.

I was one of the kids who did exactly what my parents, teachers, and peers told me to do. I got the straight A's. I did all my homework. I studied for all my tests. I took the SATs in middle school for admission into the John Hopkins Center for Talented Youth, for pete's sake. Looking back in retrospect, I was misguided. None of those great scores mean anything in the real world.

In the book *The Millionaire Mind*, Dr. Thomas J. Stanley conducted an extensive survey of over 1,000 millionaires in the United States. He approximated that the average collegiate GPA for a self-made millionaire is 2.76. I bet those kids were pissed off they were called stupid by their teachers and parents and set out to prove everyone wrong.

When we are young, very few of us dream of becoming anonymous middle managers or pencil pushers for the rest of our lives. Come on — what kind of sane person wants to spend their life sitting behind a desk in a cubicle, nine to five, five days a week? That's no fun.

Look at this study of high school students by Jacob Halpern:

"When you grow up, which of the following jobs would you most like to have?"

1. The chief of a major company like General Motors
2. A Navy SEAL
3. A United States Senator
4. The president of a great university like Harvard or Yale

5. The personal assistant to a very famous singer or movie star

Among girls, the results were as follows: 9.5 percent chose "the chief of a major company like General Motors;" 9.8 percent chose "a Navy SEAL;" 13.6 percent chose "a United States Senator;" 23.7 percent chose "the president of a great university like Harvard or Yale;" and 43.4 percent chose "the personal assistant to a very famous singer or movie star."

Notice that almost a majority of girls were happy with being the assistant of a powerful person rather than a powerful person themselves.

A lot of young boys dream of becoming the next Michael Jordan or the next Derek Jeter. Most won't end up like them, but there's nothing wrong with dreaming about it. Teach kids to create a Plan B in case Plan A fails. But NEVER discourage a child. The last thing you want to do is extinguish the dreams of someone who could very well reach those heights.

The bottom line is that we have created a million-dollar monster that crushes dreams. To the natural equilibrium of school, dreamers are a predator. They are impatient. They are always on the go. They are the "square pegs in the round holes — the rebels, the misfits, the troublemakers."

Dreamers look at the status quo and say: "I will not stand for this. Let's do something about it." Instead of following all the little rules, be something that author Seth Godin calls a "sheepwalker." Every once in a while, Godin says, someone stands up and says "Not me."

Let's bring back the dreamers. Recollect the 1960s and '70s. People imagined a world of flying cars and robot maids. Venture capitalist Peter Thiel remarked, "We wanted flying cars and we got 140 characters."

What happened? We have stopped asking "What if?" We have to rediscover that spark. Creativity expert Sir Ken Robinson in his book *The Element* writes:

> Most of the brilliant, creative people didn't do well in school: most really didn't discover what they could do, and who they really were, until they'd left school and recovered from their education. Too many graduate or leave early, unsure of their real talents and equally unsure of what direction to take next. Too many feel that what they're good at isn't valued by schools. Too many think they're not good at anything.

Too many never find their element. Robinson explains:

> The element is the place where the things you love to do and the things that you are good at come together. It is the meeting point between natural aptitude and personal passion.

Featuring aptitude and passion, the conditions are attitude and opportunity. The sequence goes something like this: I get this; I love it; I want it; Where is it?

Too often in school, we sacrifice learning what we love for what is prescribed by the curriculum. We're bombarded with four years of English, four years of social studies, three years of science, and three years of mathematics. We force kids to learn subjects in high school that are largely irrelevant to the rest of their lives. By the time, most reach high school, they have a fair idea of their interests, but very few people ask them.

No one ever asked me what my passions are. Do you understand how screwed up that statement is? It is ludicrous to toil through 12 years of primary and secondary schooling without asking kids what they love to learn. They then go on to post-secondary education and the real world without having an idea what to do with themselves. Why do you think so many people in their 20s go through life crises?

There is a saying that inside every fat man is a thin man dying to get out. Inside every child suppressed by our schools is a creative and ingenious human being crying to be released. Teachers, parents, don't tell me that your child can't find it. Try harder. Dig deeper. Every child loves something. Discover that passion today.

WON'T SOMEBODY PLEASE THINK OF THE CHILDREN?

Almost every child in America, leave out a handful, should be suing their schools for the education they receive. We are victims. We are being set up to fail later on in life and they don't even know it. This top-down approach to education has not and will never work. In parallel, Dov Seidman, the CEO of LRN and the author of *How*, put it best to the *New York Times*, "The days of leading countries or companies via a one-way conversation are over. The old system of 'command and control' — using carrots and sticks — to exert power over people is fast being replaced by 'connect and collaborate' — to generate power through people."

We have to start holding kids to adult standards. Larry Rosenstock, principal of High Tech High in San Diego, says, "If you treat kids like adults, then they will behave like adults." Let them act like professionals, scientists, authors, engineers, singers, and historians.

In many classrooms around the country, the philosophy of teaching is based on pedagogy which literally means the art and science of educating children. More accurately, it exhibits a teacher focused education. We need to shift towards a learning style called andragogy — adult-leading. It was theorized by educator Malcolm Knowles. Here are the basics:

1. Experience including error provides the basis of learning activities.

2. Adults need to be responsible for their decisions on education and involvement in the planning
and evaluation of their instruction.

3. Adult learning is problem centered rather than content oriented.

4. Adults respond better to internal versus extrinsic motivators (passion versus reward)

The children in the Hole-in-the-Wall experiments dabbled with andragogy and what unfolded was nothing short of remarkable. In 1999, Sugata Mitra and his colleagues dug a hole in the wall bordering an urban slum in New Delhi, installed an Internet-connected PC, and just left. Kids from the slum who couldn't read, write, and had never used a computer before, fiddled with the devices and soon taught themselves and their fellow peers how to use and learn from them.

I spoke to Mitra, professor at Newcastle University in the United Kingdom, who construed, "Even in the absence of any direct input from a teacher, an environment that stimulates curiosity can cause learning, the emergent phenomenon." He calls this "minimally invasive education." Mitra added, "If you let a group of 18-year-olds in a room with robots, parts, computers, what reason would there be if they didn't build one?" What his experiments have validated is that children are not empty vessels, waiting to be fed information; curiosity is innate.

Adults, now is the time to stop covering your ears and screaming "la-la-la I can't hear you." The solution is simple and quite glorious — let children control their education. When children have an interest, only then does education happen.

*

We need to ask: What if school wasn't school anymore? Imagine if we approached learning through debate and tinkered with ideas by bringing back French salons from the 17th century. Imagine if schools were dynamic social engines and the birthplace of life-long learners and global citizens.

Right now, schools are like the citadels of ancient times. Let's bridge the gap between school and the community and the world.

Can you imagine a child wanting to learn more when the end of the school day is over? That's when we will know the system is finally working.

Alvin Toffler once remarked, "The illiterate of the 21st century will not be those who cannot read and write, but those who cannot learn, unlearn, and relearn." To reinvent our institutions, we must divorce industrialism once and for all and heed the words of our children. When you stop learning, you stop living. Stay thirsty, folks.

I asked high school dropout Nick Perez the question, "If you could create a school your younger self would attend, what would be the important part of it?"

"Freedom," he replied.

We missed our chance to fix the system decades ago. Today, our sole option is to start anew.

CHAPTER 2
LET MY COUNTRY AWAKE

Where the mind is without fear and the head is held high
Where knowledge is free
Where the world has not been broken up into fragments
By narrow domestic walls
Where words come out from the depth of truth
Where tireless striving stretches its arms towards perfection
Where the clear stream of reason has not lost its way
Into the dreary desert sand of dead habit
Where the mind is led forward by thee
Into ever-widening thought and action
Into that heaven of freedom, my Father, let my country awake.

RABINDRANATH TAGORE

President Obama warned of a "Sputnik moment." Secretary of Education Arne Duncan said it was an absolute wake-up call for America. And Chester E. Finn Jr., a former Assistant Secretary of Education, said it was like the U.S. was getting attacked by a foreign country.

What are policymakers so riled up about? We got our asses handed to us in the Program for International Student Assessment, known as PISA, a test given to 15-year-old students by the Organization for Economic Cooperation and Development (OECD) to the world's major industrial powers. The scores, which were released on Pearl Harbor Day 2010, put the United States at 17th in reading, 23rd in science, and 31st in mathematics. These numbers were on par with students in Poland, France, Norway, and Belgium. Shanghai (China) wiped the competition clean, topping the charts in all three subjects.

The following are the charts with the PISA rankings from 2010:

	READING			MATH			SCIENCE	
	OECD Average:	493		OECD Average:	496		OECD Average:	501
1	Shanghai (China)	556	1	Shanghai (China)	600	1	Shanghai (China)	575
2	South Korea	539	2	Singapore	562	2	Finland	554
3	Finland	536	3	Hong Kong (China)	555	3	Hong Kong (China)	549
4	Hong Kong (China)	533	4	South Korea	546	4	Singapore	542
5	Singapore	526	5	Taiwan	543	5	Japan	539
6	Canada	524	6	Finland	541	6	South Korea	538
7	New Zealand	521	7	Liechtenstein	536	7	New Zealand	532
8	Japan	520	8	Switzerland	534	8	Canada	529
9	Australia	515	9	Japan	529	9	Estonia	528
10	Netherlands	508	10	Canada	527	10	Australia	527
17	United States	500	31	United States	487	23	United States	502

I don't miss a talk show or an education debate where someone mentions this data as an indicator of America's decline in the world — that countries with higher scores will out-compete us in the future. It's easy to pull these scores and draw conclusions. They make great soundbites and snappy headlines. However, the PISA rankings are absolutely erroneous.

The first pitfall is evaluating the American education system with the rest of the world based solely on test scores. Major socio-economic and GDP discrepancies exist between nations. For example, it sounds ridiculous to compare the United States, a country with a population of roughly 300 million with Finland, a tiny Scandinavian state home to just five million.

The second pitfall, especially for policymakers, is to believe that the panacea to this PISA embarrassment is to copy the methods that Shanghai and other "top education systems" implement. What they don't seem to realize is that high test scores in the PISA exam come at a cost for many of these countries, often sapping the love of learning and the joys of creativity and imagination out of the children. China is one example.

Lastly, the third pitfall is that we are disregarding some crucial data at hand. There is a weak, non-significant, or negative correlation between ranks on international tests and ranks on the World Economic Forum's Globalization Competitiveness Index (GCI) for countries that ranked in the top 50 percent on the GCI, meaning more developed countries. The GCI scores a country for the quality of its institutions, infrastructure, macro-economy, health and primary education, higher education and training, market efficiency, technological business sophistication and innovation. Albeit, Finland is an exception.

The point is, rather than obsessing over international test data, we should be relaying our attention to the catastrophe we have at home.

In this chapter, we will deconstruct the nuts and bolts of the education systems of to-be superpowers China and India and draw lessons from the Scandinavian country of Finland. Understanding how other systems educate their children is imperative for two reasons: first, we need to figure out what's working effectively and second, we need to ensure we do not fall into the same traps.

Like many of these policymakers, I was under the impression that the Indians and the Chinese would eventually rule the world, because the students go through an insane schooling process. The amount of homework, testing, and pressure is outrageously high. As we will see in this chapter, I was wrong.

Let's begin with China — the newest poster child of great education.

"NO PEASANT LEFT BEHIND"

As dusk fades over Beijing on an average Monday in April, bevies of Chinese students end classes for the day and hurry to their next destination. Some go straight home. Some get transported to cram school for more hours of studying. And some just pass out from the exhaustion. If you go to a Beijing neighborhood in the evening or on the weekend, you will find few to no children frolicking in the streets. Required to "pump iron," kids will continue to study endlessly into the pitch black of the night.

Welcome to the Chinese education system! Students do not have lives. Fun is just another three letter word for them to memorize. From diapers, Chinese kids are groomed to be testing warriors in preparation for Judgement Day — the most important day of their life — the *gaokao*, the national college entrance exam. There is no time for the jubilations and solaces of childhood.

It's no wonder that the addictive testing culture may indeed explain those mind blowing PISA exam results. For the record, Chester Finn Jr., we were not attacked by China on Pearl Harbor Day 2010. Stop being, in your own words, so "melodramatic." No one should be stunned by the scores. It's like it's China's job to grind out outstanding test takers. Interestingly, this hasn't been major news in China, a nation known for showboating their international achievements. Xinhuanet.com, the official web portal for *Xinhua News Agency*, China's state-controlled media organization, failed to acknowledge the accolades. China Daily, another puppet of the government, glossed over the PISA scores, brushing off the view that Chinese-style parenting and learning is superior.

Simply put, China has the worst education system in the world. High test scores comes at a detrimental cost. Students are carbon copies of one another. There is absolutely no creativity in schools. Bai Hua said to the *New York Times*, "Our education system is like ancient Sparta. Not physically, but mentally. Our children learn how to calculate fast, play the piano, to do everything well. They have a lot of skills. But when they grow up they are lost, because no one ever asked them to think about what they want."

To comprehend the ramifications of Chinese pedagogy, consider the example of Solomon Shereshevskii, a Russian journalist born in 1886, also known as "The Man Who Remembered Everything." David Brooks, columnist for the *New York Times*, writes in his book *The Social Animal*:

In one experiment, researchers showed Shereshevskii a complex formula of thirty letters and numbers on a piece of paper. Then they put the paper in a box and sealed it for fifteen years. When they took the paper out, Shereshevkii could remember it exactly...Shereshevkii could remember, but couldn't distill. He lived in a random blizzard of facts, but could not organize them into repeating patterns. Eventually, he couldn't make sense of metaphors, similes, poems, or even complex sentences.

Shereshevkii was constantly distracted by his memories and unable to control them. Like many Chinese students today, he could easily experience and recollect in fine detail, but he could not be in sync with his emotions.

Why is copying and memorization so highly admired in China? I reached out to Didi Kirsten Tatlow, a talented columnist for the *International Herald Tribune* stationed in Beijing, who explained, "Since ancient times, copying has been a fine art in the country. As an artist, you were taught to reproduce material to keep traditions going and show respect for your teacher. In addition, the only way to learn the character-based language has been to simply copy the characters over and over again to build motor memory. It's not like learning English, where words correspond to definite sounds, making them easier to learn (if you don't know a Chinese character, you can't even say it out loud, so you're really stuck) and where the sound segments represent an abstraction that may push children towards a more flexible way of thinking."

In Chinese classrooms, learning can parallel full-blown indoctrination. Independent thinkers are suffocated. Kids who raise questions and think beyond the textbook are branded as troublemakers. There is also, not surprisingly, a mad culture of plagiarism. One foreigner who taught eighth graders wrote in *The Atlantic*, "I... got an enormous number of segments taken word-for-word from their books or newspapers; news items read directly from something they printed out or a magazine article, etc."

For Chinese parents, a world-class education for their child is everything. There is a stigma that if their child fails school, they will fail life as well. I had a chance to speak with Tatlow's nine-year-old son, Frederick Tatlow-Coonan, about his experience in school. He said, "There is an expectation that you need to do very well on tests." Everyone is yelling: "Produce. Produce. Produce." However, too many students cannot cope.

A survey by an international education evaluation group in 2009 shows that of 29 countries, Chinese children's calculation ability ranks first in the world, while their imagination ranks last, and their creativity ranks from the bottom.

Only 4.7 percent of Chinese primary and secondary school students think they have curiosity and imagination and 14.9 percent of them hope to have imagination and creativity.

After years of primary education, in high school, a student must choose a path, either a technical field in mathematics and sciences or a humanities field in literature, politics, history, and art. Make a stupid decision and you're stuck for life. You get what you get and you don't get upset. How can the Chinese entrust their youth to make such life-altering decisions?

The system is an international embarrassment. The underbelly of a rising China is that schools are breeding students that can conquer any formulaic problem, but falter when a spontaneous conundrum is presented to them.

SAT ON STEROIDS

China would not be what it is today if it wasn't for its hellish examination system. The civil service exam's primary intention was to skim off the best performing students on the exam and churn them into civil officials. Thus, the meritocratic strategy was mimicked by Britain and France in the 19th century when they needed public servants for their imperial outreaches.

From my research and conversations with a number of Chinese students, I will concede the success of the system in terms of leveling the playing field and offering an opportunity for the lower and middle class to climb the social ladder to prosperity, but what has unraveled today is a literal nightmare. The civil service exams were centered on the Confucian Five Classics. They were just a test of the person's ability to memorize the classics. That was it.

Though long extinct, the spirit of the civil service exam haunts us today in another form, the *gaokao*, which is the national college entrance examination.

While it was trimmed down to a nine hour exam from the civil service exam's length of 72 hours, the *gaokao* is still a living hell. The current system was adapted from Soviet allies in the early 1950's just after the founding of the People's Republic. In 1952, Mainland China adopted a unified, national college entrance exam. Then due to the political calamities of the Cultural Revolution, schools were shut down, and scores of students were assaulted as "enemies of the state." When Deng Xiaoping came into power after Mao Zedong's death in 1976, he realized that in order to narrow the education gap between China and other countries, reinstituting the *gaokao* was imperative.

The *gaokao*, offered only once a year typically in June, is the ultimate gauge of academic achievement. And "because of its life-determining nature," says Yong Zhao, professor at Oregon State University, to me, "the *gaokao* has become the 'baton' that conducts the whole education orchestra." Through a collectivized effort, students, parents, and teachers work together to produce the best possible score. The pressure to score high is uncanny. In Sichuan Province in southwestern China, students studied in a hospital, hooked up to oxygen containers, in hopes of improving their concentration. Some girls take contraceptives so they will not get their periods during the exam. At Xioagang High School in Hubei province, students were hooked up to IV drips as an energy booster. As one observer put it, "Students are not sick; society is sick."

Chinese teenagers have given themselves the nickname: The Damaged Generation. The typical response from a Chinese student is: "I have no freedom. I'm not happy! My life is the *gaokao*."

Here's a depressing anecdote: In 2011, one 44-year-old man, Liang Shi, from Chengdu, took the *gaokao* again for the 15th time. The *gaokao* can change people's lives.

Consequently, the $85 billion plus private education market or Chinese cram school operators, is very lucrative. The government's one-child-policy has induced a fervent demand for a child's education by thriving on the widely known "little emperor" phenomenon, where children gain excessive attention. Thus, parents pay an arm and a leg on after-school tutoring services.

In some respects, Chinese education is like running a marathon. At some point, you will "hit the wall."* Some hit the wall head-on, others conquer the wall. The wall is the *gaokao*, ultimately leading to post-secondary education. The ones who soar to the top have a sound memory, stalwart logical ability, little to no creativity, and no appetite to question authority.

On the day of the *gaokao* in June, the country literally stops. Roads near testing centers are closed down. Construction work is postponed. And police personally escort children that are late to the test. For parents, it's almost a religious belief to do everything humanly possible to support your child through the *gaokao*.

When the results of the examination are released in late June or early July, the Chinese media has an annual practice of transforming the highest scorers into celebrities. However, too many take for granted that the highest test-scorers on the *gaokao* are on a trajectory to success. A survey confirms that reality shows otherwise.

Keeping track of more than 1,000 top scorers from 1977 to 2008, a study found that none of them stood out in the field of academics, business, or politics, failing to fulfill people's expectations. The super-scorers called *zhuangyuan*, like Li Taibo, who took first place in all of Beijing for the

---

* "Hitting the wall" in a marathon means that you have exhausted all of the glycogen in your body.

science section of the exam, often fail to cultivate the traits for success in the real world. What's more, a list that tracked China's young and wealthy, determined that none of the wealthiest people born after 1980 graduated from Peking University or Tsinghua University, China's top two universities. About two-thirds of the rich 32-year-olds-or-younger graduated from non-prestigious universities, including vocational colleges.

One Chinese saying compares the *gaokao* to a stampede of "thousands of soldiers and tens of thousands of horses across a single log bridge." In the stampede, a student's individual health and well-being are not spared. More than 30 million people younger than 18, about 1 in 10, are suffering from depression and behavioral problems. And 84 percent of high school students reported feeling depressed and under stress. Nearly 50 percent of elementary school students said they felt shame and anger after being criticized by parents or teachers. Suicide is the biggest killer among Chinese ages 15 to 34. There were three separate deaths of college exam takers in 2010, including a male student who failed the exam. China's suicides are up 60 percent in the past 50 years. The *gaokao* was implemented in 1952. Coincidence or not?

The dilemma is, as Yichao Cen, a student at Syosset High School and a recent immigrant from China, frankly told me, there's no way to escape. Terrible *gaokao* scores, he says, often equals no future. Luckily for Cen, he got out of the system. Others aren't as fortunate.

THE ANT TRIBE

The "college bubble" is well and alive in China. I bring to your attention a stunning *New York Times* piece on China's army of college graduates two years ago:

> Liu Yang, a coal miner's daughter, arrived in the capital this past summer, with a freshly printed diploma from Datong University, $140 in her wallet and an air of invincibility. Her first taste of reality came later the same day, as she lugged her bags through a ramshackle neighborhood, not far from the Olympic Village, where tens of thousands of other young strivers cram four to a room. Unable to find a bed and unimpressed by the rabbit warren of slapdash buildings, Ms. Liu scowled as the smell of trash wafted up around her.
>
> "Beijing isn't like this in the movies," she said.

Liu's story, like many others, are a similar tale in modern China. These college graduates dream of success in the big cities, but then reality slaps them hard. For the time being, Liu has joined the ranks of the "ant tribe" — the millions of China's post-1980 generation of low income college graduates, who crowd the slums in China's booming cities and toil for chump change. The term "ant tribe" was coined by Lian Si, a professor who penned a book with that title.

"They share every similarity with ants," says Lian Si to the *New York Times*. "They live in colonies in cramped areas. They're hardworking, yet anonymous, and underpaid."

China has witnessed a surge in the number of college graduates in recent years, thanks in large part to an enrollment boom that has seen the university student population swell as much as 30 percent year-to-year over the last decade. The predicament is that the unemployment rate for graduates is 30 percent, failing to demonstrate a sign of improvement. In all, this is the Great Chinese Squeeze.

We must ask the question: Is the Chinese college degree worth anything? "It is if you want to shovel excrement in Wenzhou," notes Gordon Chane, author of The Coming Collapse of China, in the *New York Times*. "The prosperous city in Zhejiang province this year advertised for college graduates to fill eight spots collecting 'night soil.' More than 1,100 of them applied for the jobs." Skipping college to become a migrant worker may strangely be more economical. China's college graduates on average make only 300 yuan, or roughly $44, more per month than the average Chinese migrant worker. If you go beyond post-secondary, a degree (Master's, Ph.D) is worth less than what a nanny makes.

In fact, it was reported by China's Ministry of Education that the country now plans to phase out college majors that consistently produce unemployable graduates. So, any program in which 60 percent of the graduates failed to find work for two consecutive years would face funding reductions until supply was brought back into sync with demand.

Bill Frezza, a fellow at the Competitive Enterprise Institute, argues in *RealClearMarkets*, "The Chinese hand may not be invisible, but it would be one that Adam Smith would recognize. Isn't it amazing that even self-identified communists are figuring out that markets only work when adjustment mechanisms act to reduce surpluses and shortages? Destroy those mechanisms and unemployable college graduates pile up as fast as unsold electric cars."

Subsequently, what some describe as a "herd-like mentality" develops where students flood into studying particular subjects, pressured by society and family, rather than a subject they love. Humanities and social science majors now account for a quarter of all graduates compared to one in five in 2000, while engineering graduates have remained the same at 36 percent of graduates. Meanwhile, the country is producing five times as many science graduates compared to 2000. The college bubble is on the brink of bursting.

China's dilemma is two-fold. On one hand, the ranks of "ant tribe" members have blown up. On the other, companies cannot find people with adequate skills to work in such environments. The McKinsey Global Institute (MGI) concluded that fewer than 10 percent of Chinese job candidates, on average, would be suitable for work in a foreign company. A *McKinsey Quarterly* study found that 44 percent of the executives in Chinese companies reported that insufficient talent was the biggest barrier to their global ambitions. Why? Because these people were shaped by an education system that never polished their inventiveness or critical thinking dexterities.

A professor experienced this first-hand in his class of Chinese MBA students. Documenting his struggles in a piece for the *Los Angeles Times*, Randy Pollock, a former USC lecturer, who consults with companies on communication and management issues in China, writes that he once challenged his students to brainstorm "two-hour business plans." Then he divided them into six groups, giving them detailed instructions and an example: "a restaurant chain."

"The more original their idea, the better, I stressed — and we'd vote for a prize winner," writes Pollock. "The word 'prize' energized the room. Laptops flew open. Fingers pounded. Voices roared. Packs of cookies were ripped open and shared. Not a single person text-messaged. I'd touched a nerve." In the end, however, five of the six groups presented restaurant chains. The sixth proposed a catering service. The point is as Pollock reveals, "Why risk a unique solution when the instructor has let it slip he likes the food business?"

The fact is that his students weren't recent college graduates; they were middle managers, financial analysts, and marketers from state-owned enterprises and multinational corporations. I spoke to Pollock, who explained, "There's a skills shortage, not a talent shortage. A talent is something one is born with a natural ability. For example, Michael Jordan was born with talent, but he also worked very hard to develop that skill. That is what separates the good from the great. People in China have the hardware (natural ability), but the software (cultural and political and educational mindsets imposed by growing up and living in Mainland China) put on that hardware is often not helpful." Thus, their potential is often stunted.

In his two year tenure at the school, Pollock writes that his students posited that copying is a superior business strategy to inventing and innovating. They wanted everything to fit neatly into a box. Or to function like an assembly line where everyone follows directions. That is 20th century work. When students are given public critique, they lose face. It sounds like a personal attack, when it isn't. For their entire lives, they did everything they were supposed to. They memorized everything they needed to, studied their asses off, and may have found a job. However, they have poor English, cannot communicate well, lack practical skills, and are unable to deal with unexpected problems. That's what happens when you teach students how to memorize, rather than how to think.

From early on, Chinese kids are spoon-fed this dogma from their hovering parents: "Do well on the *gaokao*. Get into a good university. Graduate. And you'll be secure for the rest of your life." But folks, the grand bargain is gone. In 1998, years before the aforementioned *McKinsey Quarterly* study, Xiwai's co-founder, Xu Ziwang was hit with this reality when he did Chinese recruiting for Goldman Sachs. He picked three graduates from China's top universities and was impressed that they all scored 100 percent on the exam following the associate training stint in New York — only to be disappointed a year later, when their performance reviews were in the bottom quartiles.

"There's a price," Ziwang concluded to the *New York Times*, "for 12 years of prep for an exam, and that's to always think there's a narrow, right answer. If you give precise instructions, they do well. If you define a task broadly, they get lost and ask for help."

China's labor pool is saturated with millions of lousy job candidates.

Let me take a second and step back from my endless bashing of China. What China embodies and what the United States truly lacks is a steadfast work ethic and a national commitment to education. China has an enormous cultural respect for education, in part from its Confucian ideologies. The premise behind Confucianism is that if you work hard, overcome adversity, you will reap rewards later in life.

Arnold Dodge, professor at Long Island University, when he went on a trip to China, told me that he noticed that the Confucian ideology was embedded into many sectors of the country. He says, "It infuses a spirit of 'I need to succeed. I want to succeed.' into people." Dodge's observations of students reminded him of the contrary attitudes kids and adults have in this country.

We're not going to become Confucians tomorrow, but at least we can elevate education on our list of priorities. There are Confucian ideals we must emulate in this nation.

Why should we also care about China? More Chinese politicians and parents, especially those living in big cities, are realizing the system's deleterious effects on children. So the country is taking baby steps in reforming it. In 2001, the Chinese Ministry of Education proposed a "New Curriculum" that is intended to "change the overemphasis on... rote memorization and mechanical drill. Promote instead students' active participation, their desire to investigate, and eagerness...to analyze and solve problems." Private schools have taken the lead, trumpeting mottos like, "We must put students in the center of learning and focus on cultivation of creativity."

Many Chinese leaders understand that the Chinese education system is in hot water. Unlike most politicians in the United States, the Chinese did not sit down and watch the system crumble; they decided to act. And act decisively.

What resulted was a concrete plan called the "National Outline for Medium and Long-Term Education Reform and Development (2010-2020)." The Education Ministry invited public comment and literally received millions of responses. Overhauling the curriculum is the prime strategy. China's Deputy Director General of Basic Education Wang Dinghua offered some specifics on the plan in a speech, noting:

> For instance, math will de-emphasize response speed and the need to memorize complex and seldom-used formulas. In their place, the curriculum will encourage multiple ways of solving problems, and a deeper understanding of concepts relating to space development, for example. In science, inauthentic demonstrations, calculations, and drills will be replaced with student experiments in real-world applications, including an emphasis on new energy, health, and conservation.

As a whole, its plans will be rolled out to China's 370,000 elementary and secondary schools, affecting the nation's 200 million K-12 students.

This is our wakeup call — our quiet crisis!

I wish Arne Duncan and President Obama would listen. The thing that bothers me is that the United States is headed down China's former path. Jonathan Plucker, a professor of Educational Psychology at Indiana University, narrated a peculiar story to *Newsweek*. He recently toured a number of such schools in Shanghai and Beijing. When faculty of a major Chinese university asked Plucker to identify trends in American education, he described our focus on standardized curriculum, rote memorization, and nationalized testing. "After my answer was translated, they just started laughing out loud," Plucker says. "They said, 'You're racing toward our old model. But we're racing toward your model, as fast as we can.'"

If you look into the United States' crystal ball in terms of education and the labor market, China is somewhat similar to what you will see — a punitive education system based on standardized testing and a glut of college graduates that are unskilled and unable to find work. But there is still time. As Napoleon Bonaparte famously said, "When China wakes, it will shake the world." China has a weak snore and is tossing and turning in its sleep. For China, uprooting a culture that has developed over thousands of years is not the easiest task in the world. Individuality is not an important value in the Chinese culture. The preferred phrase in China is "The first bird out gets shot" — not "the early bird catches the worm." It will be a long time before most people in the world can name a Chinese brand.

Can China dominate when it censors Google and holds an iron fist over media? James Fallows doesn't think so.

"Everything depends on first, an open exchange of ideas, through media, books, and movies, and second, a free flow of people from around the world," says Fallows, author and columnist at *The Atlantic*. "Neither of those is fully possible in China now." He believes it's better than 20 years ago, but nothing groundbreaking has been instituted just yet.

Still, the last thing the United States can do is count China out.

Due to the one-party system, if China wants something to happen, it will get done. From my conversations with a diverse range of people in China, I have drawn the conclusion that they hope one day they too, will be the designers, the innovators, and the creators of the world. I would not bet a dime against them. When China socks the *gaokao* and a revamped curriculum is established across the country, America should fire up the red siren, because the giant has awakened.

Lastly, I offer a nugget of advice to Arne Duncan, President Obama, and Chester Finn. Jr., I believe you all have forgotten that America's innovative spirit does not derive from good scores on international tests, but rather from our rebelliousness, our willingness to dream big, and the dexterity to think differently.

Let's move on to the rising superpower, India.

BILLIONS OF IDIOTS

In the summer of 2010, I visited India on a family trip. I spoke with scores of Indian students studying in high school or college. For one high school boy, school was hell. He studied mathematics, science, English, history, and Hindi. His class had 39 students. School was five days a week with alternating Saturdays. The student began school bright-eyed, bushy-tailed at 7:30 in the morning and left at two in the afternoon.

I asked him, "What is the purpose of school?" He replied: "To prepare for college." I then asked him, "What is critical thinking? The boy shrugged and said he did not know. I discussed rote learning briefly. Jokingly, he said that after hours of memorizing, he forgot most of the information a week later. The boy's story was a carbon-copy of many students I spoke with.

A few months after that trip, I watched the popular film *3 Idiots*, now the highest grossing film in Indian history, which exposed the holes in the Indian education system. The story revolves around three engineering students who share a room in the Imperial College of Engineering. Farhan is studying engineering to pursue his father's wishes over his own wish — to become a wildlife photographer. Raju is studying to raise his family's fortunes and get them out of poverty. But, Rancho is studying for his passion in machines. He finds the college to be run like a factory. The environment is toxic and devoid of "new ideas and inventions," where "everybody is in a race." When Rancho raises these concerns with the dean of the college, Professor Viru "Virus" Shahastrabuddhe, his thinking is sneered upon. Virus' favorite student, Chatur "Silencer" Ramalingam spends his days memorizing for exams in his effort to reach corporate and social status. Throughout the film, Rancho repeats a simple message: "Pursue excellence and success with follow. All is well."

The best line in the film was stated by Farhan describing Rancho: "Today my respect for that idiot shot up. Most of us went to college just for a degree. No degree meant no plum job, no pretty wife, no credit card, no social status. But none of this mattered to him, he was in college for the joy of learning, he never cared if he was first or last." Later on, Raju takes a frank approach in an interview for a corporate job, while Farhan finally convinces his parents to allow him to pursue his love of wildlife photography. Both are eventually successful in their undertakings. Their story is framed as intermittent flashbacks from the present day, a decade after Chatur bet that he'd become more successful than Rancho. At the end of the story, Chatur is now a wealthy and successful businessman, who is looking to seal a deal with a famous scientist named Phunsukh Wangdu. Phunsukh Wangdu is indeed Rancho, who has 400 patents and is now a school teacher.

Here, the term *idiot* doesn't refer to a stupid person rather a person who follows his or her dreams and passions.

After my trip to India and after watching *3 Idiots*, it all hit me. All my past intuitions about the Indian education system were shattered.

Education has always been one of the highest priorities in India. The modern education system has its roots from the British colonial period when they introduced a full English system in the 19th century. Rote learning was encouraged, and British curriculum played a prominent role. It was Lord Macaulay, the jurist, who set the agenda for education in India. The English colonial perspective is revealed in the famous speech Minute on Indian Education, presented in 1835 by Macaulay. It denigrated the classics of Sanskrit, Persian, and Arabic as "unequal to that of an English boy." Macaulay was of the view that "a single shelf of a good European library was worth the whole native language of India and Arabia." In perhaps the most famous part of the Minute, he stated his intent for English education in India, to "form a class who may be interpreters between us and the millions whom we govern; a class of persons, Indian in blood and colour, but English in taste, in opinions, in morals, and in intellect." The "class" would then assist governing the indigenous Indian people.

Mahatma Gandhi desired to reject this system and change institutions to chisel the talents of the Indian people. He vented his sufferance of the Macaulay syllabi, before he sailed to England to study law: "I am firmly of the opinion that the Government schools have unmanned us, rendered us helpless and Godless. They have filled us with discontent and providing no remedy for the discontent, have made us despondent. They have made us what we were intended to become clerks and interpreters." So it isn't a coincidence that many of India's progressive thinkers were educated outside India.

Unfortunately, Macaulay's ideas still dominate education in India. Elements of colonialism are present in the authoritarian nature of teachers in the classroom, the passive learning styles, and the stress on rote memorization. India still has a colonial system, designed to serve others. Agrawal O.P. said it best in a book, "The country (India) continues to produce people, who are in the rat race for white collar jobs in the old tradition of British Raj. In short, India's education system is still mentally enslaved to the old pre-Independence pattern and to the imported values of the West."

India needs an Indian education system. Not a British one. Not an American one.

In India, exams are everything — make or break. They reflect a terrible notion of learning. High "marks" are the only thing Indian parents want from their children. Society is literally an exam-ocracy. Anurag Behar of Wipro writes, "In Hindi, the resonance of the two words makes this reality more emphatic, we have a *pareeksha tantra*, not a *shiksha tantra*."

The golden ticket of the education system is acceptance to the im- possibly exclusive Indian Institutes of Technology. Every year, more than 450,000 students take the Joint Entrance Exam, hoping for entry to the noteworthy public engineering institutes spread across India. Slightly more than 13,000 passed in 2010, a 3 percent success. Some students will study full-time for two years just for that one exam, mostly for the IITs but also for other universities and colleges. One college, Shri Ram College of Commerce, flabbergasted the country by requiring some students to score a perfect 100 percent — a score never demanded before — in order to apply for a spot in its Bachelor's of Commerce (Honors) course, a type of undergraduate business degree.

Similar to the Chinese *gaokao*, if a student fails the college entrance exam, he or she will need to wait a whole year before retrying. What ensues is a culture of fear of making mistakes in schools. Students understand that lurking into a new thought, experimenting, or asking questions can result in being ridiculed or sometimes being violently punished by teachers. According to one Bangalorean teacher, "To keep an Indian teacher from hitting her students would be similar to taking an Indian's rice away, and expecting her to simply be content with sliced white bread and butter."

The nation's creative growth is stifled by an educational environment where children cannot learn without fear of physical or verbal abuse. A *Hindustan Times* C-fore survey of 1000 students aged 15-19 from Delhi, Mumbai, Kolkata, and Bangalore, found that over half of the total respondents listed parents and relatives as the set of people causing them maximum stress, a pattern almost uniform across the cities and for both boys and girls. A disconnect between children and parents is a factor. Only 19 percent of students said their parents were comfortable with them pursuing a field they wanted. While 12 percent of students wanted to pursue the arts and humanities, only 5 percent of parents preferred these streams for their children.

When I was in India, a student echoed these concerns saying, "I have seen that people are not focused. Most end up learning something that does not excite them." Students lack a sense of confidence to study a field of their choice and create a niche for themselves in that field. The education system does not build job creators.

A minority of India's 1.2 billion people have been lucky enough to study past high school. Despite its robust economic numbers and explosive young population, India faces a serious skills shortage.

The job market, as *New York Times* writer Anand Giridharadas sees it, is split sharply in two: "With a robust handshake, a placeless accent and a confident walk, you can get a $300-a-month job with Citibank or Microsoft. With a limp handshake and a thick accent, you might peddle credit cards door to door for $2 a day."

Very few high school and college graduates can communicate effectively in English, work in teams, solve problems, and deliver presentations. What counts are the right skills.

While an inadequacy in communication skills is fairly obvious, it's much more than that. Teaching emphasizes copying notes and maintaining discipline at the expense of analysis and debate. "The irony is that in India it takes engineers two to three years to recover from the damage of the education system," explains Vivek Wadhwa, an entrepreneur, to me. "They're used to rote memorization."

Companies are feeling the pinch of the skills shortage that has increased much more rapidly than expected. They are sucking on the same pool of talent, but are getting little in return. There isn't a silver bullet to the skills gap. In reality, managers aren't born after a quick training or leadership course. Infosys says that, of 1.3 million applicants for jobs in 2006, it found only 2 percent acceptable. The company spends more than $184 million on training centers.

"When we are raising our children," says Sam Pitroda, an entrepreneur who is chairman of the Knowledge Commission and was an adviser to Prime Minister Rajiv Gandhi in the 1980s, to the *New York Times*, "we constantly tell them: 'Don't do this, don't do that. Stand here, stand there.' It creates a feeling that if there is a boundary, you don't cross it. You create boxes around people when we need people thinking outside the box."

How can India shift the paradigm? It should look back to its rich past.

India has been home to some of the most creative minds in history. It produced the great Rabindranath Tagore, C.V. Raman, and Amartya Sen.

Tagore is certainly India's greatest educator. However, he despised every school he ever attended, and left them as quickly as possible.

The Nobel Laureate in Literature once lampooned the rote learning centered education system in an allegory about traditional education called "The Parrot's Training." A certain Raja has a beautiful bird. He becomes convinced that his parrot needs to be educated. A golden cage is constructed for the bird and Raja summons pundits from all over his empire. They debated perpetually. "Textbooks can never be too many for our purpose!" exclaimed one pundit, as he sat down to educate the bird. The pundits show the Raja the force-fed method of instruction they devised. "The method was so stupendous that the bird looked ridiculously unimportant in comparison...As for any complaint from the bird itself, that simply could not be expected. Its throat was so completely choked with the leaves from the books that it could neither whistle nor whisper."

One day the bird dies. No one knew how long ago that happened. The Raja's nephews come to report the fact that the bird's education has been completed, since it no longer flies, hops, or sings. The story ends with Raja poking the bird's body with his finger, only hearing the rustling of its inner stuffing of book-leaves.

At Tagore's school in Santiniketan, students were faced with a radically different situation. For Tagore, developing the senses was on the same level of importance as developing the intellectual mind. Drawing on his home life at Jorasanko, Rabindranath tried to create an atmosphere in which the arts would become instinctive. One of the first areas to be emphasized was music. Rabindranath writes that in his adolescence, a "cascade of musical emotion" gushed forth day after day at Jorasanko. "We felt we would try to test everything," he writes, "and no achievement seemed impossible...We wrote, we sang, we acted, we poured ourselves out on every side."

Tagore taught students how to think, rather than blindly accept or *kowtow* to authority. That's the philosophy modern Indian schools are in desperate need of adopting. As Indian graduate student Davita Maharaj writes, "Only when our education system begins to encourage students to think for themselves, question, debate, and form their own opinions, will education become truly liberating, empowering, and socially reforming."

India can draw a lesson from Tagore and emulate his wisdom. They can begin by scrapping or reforming exams. In some optimistic news, the board exams, given to students in 10th and 12th grade, were terminated recently. In December 2011, speaking at the inaugural ceremony of the Ramanujan 125 year celebrations, the Minister for Human Resource Development, Kapil Sibal, announced that they would do away with examinations at the end of the year, replacing them with Comprehensive and Continuous Evaluation (CCE) system in a bid to de-stress children. This was a step in that direction. Striking a fine chord, Sibal spoke of "potential Ramanujans" whom the system may not recognize. "They may well be sitting in this hall." The Ministry thus sought to construct an education system that promotes creativity, freedom, joy, and an awareness of cultural heritage. "It will help our children to retain their sense of wonder, to develop a spirit of enquiry, and to nurture the joys of learning," he said. Improving examinations does not require magic. It's about moving from memorization to 21st century skills.

India must also get over its stigma of failure. In my visit to India, many said society is getting better, but its not fully there yet. For India's iconic Tata Group, innovation is becoming increasingly central to its strategy. So, chairman Ratan Tata has instituted a surprising competition: A prize for the best failed idea! To invigorate innovation and keep the company from avoiding risks, the prize is intended to communicate how pivotal trying and failing can be. "Failure is a Gold Mine!" yells the chairman.

Despite an impressive growth rate of eight percent in GDP since 2004, India's full innovation potential remains unrealized as a World Bank report warns. "The same idea, if it's born in Silicon Valley it goes the distance," said Nadathur S. Raghavan, a investor in startups and a founder of Infosys, one of India's most successful technology companies, to the *New York Times*. "If it's born in India it does not go the distance."

Innovation must be at the top of India's national agenda. As one columnist put it in *India Today*:

> Innovation is not natural to students whose only goal in life is to grab a plum job in an MNC. The crop of IITians we are producing lacks a critical link with the society and their own surroundings. Their sociological growth is stunted because in their formative years most of them are cut off from society and its problems. The reason: they are preparing for an endless array of entrance examinations from 9th grade onwards. An innovative mind looks for solutions to problems around it.

I picture the Indian education system as a malnourished, yet very talented child, capable of doing great things if nurtured. India's natural advantage is its pool of manpower. But when classrooms are crammed with sweaty, fatigued children incessantly fed information, the potential of this manpower is throttled. India's democracy is in great danger if it fails to take Tagore's legacy to heart. For India to progress, they need citizens who are able to think critically and independently and whose souls are singing 'innovation and creation.' Only the kind of education that Tagore envisioned can equip their citizens to meet the challenges of our modernized, globalized world.

The question is: Can "Incredible India" turn into "Innovative India?" As Sramana Mitra urged India's best and brightest to look at innovation and entrepreneurship as their path forward: "Build products. Build companies. And finally, build fortunes." India needs 1.2 billion *idiots*!

Forget the Chinese and Indians. The Finns are the "rock stars" of education.

FINNISH LESSONS

High school students get less than an hour of homework a day. There are no rankings, competition or tracking. There is little to no standardized testing. Kids don't commence school until age seven.

Yet, in the 2009 PISA results, Finland placed third in mathematics, second in reading, and second in science literacy. Their only real rivals are the Asian education powerhouses China (Shanghai), South Korea, and Singapore, whose drill-heavy teaching methods often evoke memories of the ones used in old Soviet-bloc Olympic-medal programs, *Time*'s Joshua Levine recollects.

I was shocked and I was hungry to learn more. In my research, I came across the brilliant work of Pasi Sahlberg, Director General of the Center for International Mobility (CIMO) in Finland and author of *Finnish Lessons*, and reached out to him for a chat. To my delight, Sahlberg invited me to the Harvard Club in New York City where he and Howard Gardner would be chatting about his new book. On a chilly evening in mid-January 2012, I had a deep conversation with him on the Finnish school system.

Sahlberg puts high-quality teachers at the heart of Finland's education Cinderella story, now an international obsession. "We have systematically made the profession interesting, attractive, and morally purposeful," he notes. "It's more difficult to be admitted into primary school teacher education than law or medicine in Finland." Teachers in schools also have the liberty to customize lessons and activities, which emerged from the fluid national curriculum. As we shall see in the last chapter, an education system will only be as powerful as the quality of its teachers.

An analysis of the Finnish system summarized its core principles as follows:

- Resources for those who need them most
- High standards and supports for special needs
- Qualified teachers
- Evaluation of education
- Balancing decentralization and centralization

Furthermore, uniqueness and creativity is prized. Their approach to pedagogy is far away from the norm. In terms of the curriculum, students learn English, mathematics, science, and Finnish.

Finns love reading. *Wall Street Journal* writer Ellen Gamerman writes, "Parents of newborns receive a government-paid gift pack that includes a picture book. Some libraries are attached to shopping malls, and a book bus travels to more remote neighborhoods like a Good Humor truck."

Math is taught in a practical fashion. For example, at Kallahti Comprehensive School, kids frolic in the snow, arranging various things from nature into shapes and describing them using geometric terms. The teacher had the dexterity to allow her students to do the activity, because it fell under the guidelines of Finland's national curriculum. For math, the national curriculum is just under 10 pages — something we can emulate here in the United States.

For science, a study found that students complete a lot of practical work and class sizes are capped at 16 students.

Besides reading, mathematics, and science, students in grades one through nine spend anywhere between four to eleven periods each week taking classes in art, music, cooking, carpentry, metalwork, and textiles. Exactly. Why would you separate kids who work with their hands and those who don't?

Finns also recognize the value of individualized attention. Nearly 30 percent of Finland's children receive some kind of special help during their first nine years of school. They pinpoint problems early before they get worse when the student is older.

Nevertheless, there is always time for play. The Finns have provided students with 75 minutes of recess a day in elementary schools versus an average of 27 minutes in the United States. There is such a value put into play that the kids will go out even when it's very cold. Principal Timo Heikkinen of Kallahti Comprehensive School said to the *New Republic*, "If minus 15 [Celsius] and windy, maybe not, but otherwise, yes. The children can't learn if they don't play. The children must play."

Perhaps the most eye-popping on the list of what makes Finland's education system so unique than the rest is that the nation has rejected the standardization movement that has gained storm in Asia and of course in the United States. The Finnish National Board of Education concluded that such tests would consume too much instructional time, cost too much to construct, proctor, and grade, and generate undue stress. The Finnish answer to standardized tests has been to give exams to small but statistically significant samples of students and to trust teachers — so much so that the National Board of Education closed its inspectorate in 1991. Sahlberg tells me, "Finnish students only take standardized exams as high school seniors if they desire to go to university."

Thus, students have little angst about getting into the best university, and no worries about paying for it. College is free. Ninety-three percent of Finns graduate from academic or vocational high schools, 17.5 percentage points higher than the United States, and 66 percent go on to higher education, the highest rate in the European Union. One problem is that while there isn't much tracking, ninth grade does become a divider for Finnish students. Students are separated for the last three years of high school based on grades. Under the current structure, 53 percent will go to academic high school, and the rest will enter vocational school. While I am not a fan of this segregation, Sahlberg assures me that these schools are required to promote transferability — students can have access to courses from both academic and vocational schools.

The Finnish schools weren't always so successful. Until the 1960s, the Finns were still emerging from the wrap of Soviet influence. Most children left public school after six years at best. Along with a poor education system, they had a lackluster agrarian economy based on just one product — trees. In 1963, the Finnish Parliament made the bold decision to choose public education as its best shot at economic recovery. Sahlberg conveyed, "There was a clear understanding across the political map that revolutionizing education was the only way for Finland to be a true member of the industrial world."

In the 1980s, Finland scrapped the two parallel education systems that students followed after primary schools, where smart kids went one direction, laggards the other. In its place, a national system was erected. What ensued were concrete reforms, including reductions in class size, a national curriculum, limitations in standardized testing, and perhaps, most importantly, a mandate that teachers hold masters degrees. Lawmakers landed on a fairly simple, but highly effective plan of action that grounded a foundation for years to come. Sahlberg said, "Public schools would be organized into a system of comprehensive schools, for ages seven to 16." There wouldn't be any grade levels. In Finnish schools, Sahlberg says, "Many children build their own learning plan."

Actions, not rhetoric, created the Finnish model for success. Practically speaking, the decisions made by Finnish leaders meant that the objectives to create a renowned education system would not trifle away into rhetoric.

In Finland's devastating economic depression less than two decades ago brought on by the loss of the country's most important markets as the Soviet Union unstitched, politicians once again took control of their future and made oftentimes painful and unpopular decisions. The nation came out of the crisis with an economy that the World Economic Forum in Davos, Switzerland, ranks as one of the most competitive in the world. In the process, they've committed themselves to a strategic investment in research and development. The Finns put 4 percent of their GDP share into R&D expenditure, the highest in the OECD after Sweden and far ahead of the United States (at 2.6 percent).

The United States can draw many lessons from Finland. First, we can start by killing our deep fascination with standardized tests. "Americans like all these bars and graphs and colored charts," Principal Kari Louhivuori teased to *Smithsonian Magazine*, "Looks like we did better than average two years ago," he said after he found the reports. "It's nonsense. We know much more about the children than these tests can tell us." Another Finnish educator chimed in, "If you only measure the statistics, you miss the human aspect." Both are spot on. Second, we can introduce more play into schools. And third, as we shall see in the next chapter, the United States must adopt a national curriculum though we cannot duplicate their exact model. Don't believe anyone who tells you something else. Finland has a minuscule economy, a fairly homogenous pool, a low poverty rate, socialist cannons, and a population of just 5.5 million. Let me reiterate: poverty is what draws the line between America and Finland. Nearly 25 percent of American children live in poverty compared with less than 4 percent of Finnish children. That is what is holding us back.

America has the ripe DNA for a marvelous school system. What are we waiting for?

*

Ignore the PISA rankings. PISA scores are to the quality of education what snake oil is to medicine.

We can look to the points made by Harvard scientist Stephen J. Gould in his book *The Mismeasure of Man*, which was aimed at uncovering the failures of standardized intelligence tests, for some assistance. Gould notes that the first fallacy is "reification," which is "our tendency to convert abstract concepts into entities," referring particularly to IQ and general intelligence factor. The second fallacy is ranking or the "propensity for ordering complex variation as a gradual ascending scale." Both fallacies apply to the PISA exam.

In my conversation with Professor Yong Zhao of Oregon State University, he raised two pinpointed questions: Can't we say the same about PISA and education? Aren't we reducing education to a single number?

Moreover, the Asian tiger education systems tailor their entire curriculum to the PISA exam, teach to the test, and thus garner high scores.

I fell into the PISA trap. Don't make the same mistake as I did. If we extract the best lessons from these school systems, emulate them here at home, and learn from their blunders, we will be just fine. Let's open our hearts and educate for sympathy, creativity, and imagination. We will succeed not by becoming more Chinese or Indian or Finnish but by becoming, as the writer James Fallows once put it, "more like us."

CHAPTER 3

CORPORATE TAKEOVER

As yesterday's positive report card shows,
childrens do learn when standards are high and results are measured.

PRESIDENT GEORGE W. BUSH

I'm no expert in the sphere of education and politics, so I reached out to the experts themselves. In my conversations with some of the brightest education thinkers of our time — Howard Gardner, Diane Ravitch, Deborah Meier, and Alfie Kohn — I tried to absorb every nugget of knowledge. Through these experts, over time, I digested the history of education policy in America. The education wars have been ongoing for years without cease and will likely wage on for many more.

In the various interviews I have done with my book on national television and print and online media, I've been asked to reveal my political stance. On one occasion, I made such a mistake. My political stance has absolutely no effect on my education views. The debate is much more complicated than simply red versus blue. Both Republicans and Democrats, as we will see, have screwed up education in epic proportions. No one has been correct. As a nation when going into such debates, if we understand this, transforming the system will be much easier.

A+ IN MEDIOCRITY

A little over a quarter century ago, a blue-ribbon commission appointed by President Ronald Reagan's administration released a blockbuster report called "A Nation at Risk," (ANAR) a chronicle saturated with hard-hitting jargon on the state of education in the United States.

"The educational foundations of our society are presently being eroded by a rising tide of mediocrity that threatens our very future as a Nation and a people," it warned. "If an unfriendly foreign power had attempted to impose on America, the mediocre educational performance that exists today, we might well have viewed it as an act of war." *New York Times* columnist Russell Baker limited his critique to an analysis of the rhetoric. Examining "a rise of mediocrity," Baker declared that "a sentence like that wouldn't be worth more than a C in tenth-grade English. I'm giving them an A+ in mediocrity." Still, jokes aside, the release of ANAR was a "'shot heard 'round the" country.

ANAR enshrined the idea that in order to adapt to the evolving workplace, radical changes in education would be required:

> Computers and computer-controlled equipment are penetrating every aspect of our lives — homes, factories, and offices. One estimate indicates that by the turn of the century millions of jobs will involve laser technology and robotics. Technology is radically transforming a host of other occupations. They include health care, medical science, energy production, food processing, construction, and the building, repair, and maintenance of sophisticated scientific, educational, military, and industrial equipment.

The report spread like wildfire, making the front pages of many newspapers. As *Edutopia* put it looking at the incident in retrospect, "Reporters fell on the report like a pack of hungry dogs." During the next month after it was released, the *Washington Post* alone ran some two dozen stories about the report, and the buzz kept spreading.

I don't buy the warnings in the report for a second. The indicators of the risk were largely misguided. A lower average achievement of high school students on most standardized tests nor a decline in SAT scores is a reason to fret. It was a golden treasury of absurd, distorted statistics, all cast in terms of test scores. ANAR pioneered the assumption that the best way to improve student performance was to erect rigorous content standards, establish a core curriculum, and increase the number of school days in a year only to shove more material down students' throats.

The late Gerald Bracey, a long-time critic of education policy, comically remarked that ANAR should have been published on April 1, 1983. It was a great April Fool's Day joke on America. Imagine what could have been. The Reagan administration had attempted to employ ANAR as propaganda to coax the public into supporting their education policies grounded in three basic ideas: abolishing the Department of Education, supporting private schools through vouchers and tuition tax credits, and slashing federal education spending. Thankfully, the policies failed to come to fruition. However, in the following decades, we would witness our education system become a nightmare.

NO CHILD LEFT BEHIND: THE BAD, THE WORSE, THE UGLY

A mentally exhausted, but jubilant-appearing President George W. Bush is seated at a wooden desk in the gymnasium of Hamilton High School in Ohio. As he signs the No Child Left Behind Act into law, the president is overlooked by then Senator Edward Kennedy, then Representative John Boehner, and a number of excited children and policy officials. The year **is** 2002, mere days after Bush's inauguration. No one at that time predicted that the next decade would unfold into a disaster of epic proportions.

I've been in school with NCLB from the get-go. I was in the midst of kindergarten when it was signed. The law is really a continuation of policies nurtured under President Bill Clinton with a much more brutal stance on standards and accountability. From the looks of it, NCLB had good intentions — ensuring that all children have an opportunity for a quality education and demanding that all schools are accountable. At its core, it aimed to improve the basic skills of students, particularly poor and minority students. Sounds great, right? When you take a closer peek, NCLB's definition of good education is flawed — decent scores on reading and mathematics tests.

When it came time whether or not to adopt the train-wreck, politicians left and right of the spectrum, overwhelmingly climbed aboard, most likely having never read the bill in entirety which spanned hundreds of pages of dull text.

For one thing, the main goal of NCLB is simply unattainable, which calls for 100 percent of students be proficient in reading and mathematics by 2014, something no education system anywhere on earth has accomplished. Built on the fallacy that standardized testing was the silver bullet to all our educational woes, NCLB caused a national obsession over testing.

Essentially, the American public was just blatantly lied to. The bipartisan piece of junk may have been more appropriately dubbed "No Politician Left Behind." A blogger remarked that it created a monster only Calvin and Hobbes would appreciate.

Along with a heap of politicians that NCLB fooled, then-Assistant Secretary of Education in the Bush administration and now NCLB critic, Diane Ravitch was hoodwinked into supporting the law. As Ravitch argues in her book *The Death and Life of the Great American School System: How Testing and Choice Are Undermining Education*, "No Child Left Behind had no vision other than improving test scores in reading and math. It produced mountains of data, not educated citizens. Its advocates then treated that data as evidence of its success. It ignored the importance of knowledge. It promoted a cramped, mechanistic, profoundly anti-intellectual definition of education."

Knowledge did not matter. First, let's break down the rudiments of NCLB and identify its massive blemishes.

THE SASQUATCH EFFECT

I first began feeling the effects of NCLB in third grade. In previous years, my classes included science, social studies, geography, and music as well as English and mathematics. Now, a majority of my school day was devoted to English and mathematics instruction. Generally, only what's tested gets taught.

A survey concluded that 71 percent of the country's 15,000 school districts had reduced or eliminated the hours of instructional time spent on art, music, social studies, and science to make more time for reading and math. Thomas Sobol, an education professor at Columbia Teachers College and a former New York State education commissioner, exclaimed to the *New York Times*, "Only two subjects? What sadness. That's like a violin student who's only permitted to play scales, nothing else, day after day, scales, scales, scales. They'd lose their zest for music."

Gary Stager, an educator and Executive Director of the Constructivist Consortium, says that in elementary school, art, music, science, and social studies suffer from the Sasquatch Effect — people have heard it exists in other schools, but have never seen it themselves.

Subsequently, teaching to the test has hijacked classroom learning, producing a culture of student passivity and teacher routinization. For instance, on the first day of my chemistry class, my teacher asked us, "What is the goal of this class?" One kid pipped up, saying, "Do well on the chemistry regents"* with my teacher nodding in satisfaction. Folks, that is bureaucratic brainwashing at its finest.

A culture of filling in bubbles has emerged as the dominant force in an era of high-stakes testing. My first run with standardized testing was in third grade when I sat for the Terra Nova exam. From that year onward, I was forced to take the New York State English Language Arts (ELA) exam and the New York State Mathematics exam — two pointless and foolish tests given every year from fourth to eighth grade. Before I even began high school, I started taking the Regents Examinations to complete my high school graduation requirements. I was a test junkie.

I like how Joanne Yatvin, a longtime public school educator, puts it in the *Washington Post*, "Many of the once excellent teachers I know have been reduced to automatons reciting scripted lessons, focusing on mechanical skills, and rehearsing students for standardized tests. The school cur-

* The Chemistry Regents are a New York State standardized test in Chemistry.

riculum has become something teachers 'deliver' like a pizza and students 'swallow' whole, whether or not they like mushrooms." This awful tasting medicine, prescribed and endlessly preached by the corporate reformers, is not the answer. Plain and simple.

In a conversation with educator Milton Chen, he tells me of a colleague who was in India, when an Indian educator questioned her about the American practice of high-stakes testing. As she explained the policy, the Indian educator said simply, "Here, when we want the elephant to grow, we feed the elephant. We don't weigh the elephant."

Testing is the new fad sweeping the nation. Instead of getting kids high on learning, schools have metamorphosed into test-preparation factories with a over-arching stress on drill, kill, bubble fill methods. These tests are only one measure, one snapshot of a student's achievement. They are the make-or-break assessment that determines a school's status with the Department of Education. They are the numbers that are published in major newspapers across the country. They are the scores that real-estate agents tout when verifying a neighborhood's value.

As author Stephen Covey once said, "Reducing children to a test score is the worst form of identity theft we could commit in schools." Students don't deserve to be pelted with Scantrons and No. 2 pencils. We aren't numbers. We are living, breathing, and creative human beings.

THE STANDARDS

Keep a close eye on the standards movement. NCLB forced states to establish their own "challenging" standards of what student should know and be able to do in the core content subjects — reading, mathematics, and science. What transpired were hundreds of standards (presented as mandates) hitting every nut and bolt of the subjects, leaving no autonomy to the students and teachers to create a stimulating and ingenious curriculum. In a piece for *Education Week*, Alfie Kohn, a leading figure of progressive education, nicely summarizes the standards movement:

> Much of the current standards movement is just the latest episode in a long, sorry history of trying to create a teacher-proof curriculum. Alternatively, they may simply assume that more specificity is always preferable. In reality, just because it makes sense to explain to a waiter exactly how I'd like my burger cooked doesn't mean it's better to declare that students will study the perimeter of polygons (along with scores of other particular topics) than it is to offer broad guidelines for helping students learn to think like mathematicians.

Supporting "laundry lists of a bunch o'facts" as curriculum is pure nonsense and dangerous. This model of education has a virtual monopoly in schools.

A common misconception is to believe that all standards magically co-align with all students. Kohn writes that Chester E. Finn Jr. & Co. want states to spell out which books children should read in English class, which individuals and events to study in history, and so on; any other standards are simply "fluff."

When asked what a set of national standards should be like (if we had to adopt them), Harold Howe II, the U.S. commissioner of education under President Lyndon B. Johnson, replied, "they should be as vague as possible."

Look at Finland for aid. As we observed in the previous chapter, Finland has a national curriculum based on very broad objectives and there is no 'script' that teachers must abide by.

Here is an excerpt from the Finnish national curriculum, explaining the objectives for 5th and 6th grade history:

The pupils will:

• come to understand that historical information consists of the interpretations of historians, which may change as new sources or method of examination emerge
• come to understand various ways of dividing history into eras; they will use the concepts of prehistory; history, antiquity, the Middle Ages, and the modern era correctly.
• learn to recognize changes in the history of their own families or home region, and to depict changes, such as the birth of farming, that are seen as having had a fundamental impact on human life.
• learn to identify the continuity of history with the aid of examples.
• learn to present reasons for historical changes.

As you can see, the Finnish curriculum is very "open." Thus, I propose the United States adopt a national curriculum based on lean guidelines. Second, I would call for a national council of students, teachers, administrators, parents, and policymakers to erect these very guidelines. To make these guidelines ubiquitous in this country, we cannot bully states, as NCLB did, into adopting them. Nor can the Race to the Top funding contest be repeated either, where there are winners and losers. If necessary, the right cocktail of incentives can be offered to states to spread these guidelines.

RUTHLESS ACCOUNTABILITY MEASURES

NCLB is congested with bribes and threats to its very core. Through puni-tive measures, the Bush administration shoved the law down the throats of communities across the nation. Educator Diane Ravitch remarked, "NCLB was all sticks and no carrots."

The underpinning of education policy was standardized test-based accountability without a clear and consistent vision of how it would actu-ally help schools. Under NCLB, adequate yearly progress (AYP) is used to determine if schools are successfully educating their students. The law re-quires states to use a single accountability system for public schools to de-termine whether all students, as well as individual subgroups of students, are making progress toward meeting state academic content standards. Progress on those standards must be tested yearly in grades three through eight and in one grade in high school. The results are then compared to prior years. After it is determined whether or not the school has made ade-quate progress towards the 100 percent proficiency goal by 2014 — a forced tread toward an impossible nirvana. It was literally set up to label most public schools as failures.

Schools that fail to meet their target for two consecutive years might offer their students the choice to go to a more successful public school; if they fail the following year, they must provide tutoring to their students. If the school fails for the fourth straight year, internal measures must be enacted including, but not limited to replacing the entire teaching staff and administration, turning the school over to state control, or converting the school into a charter school.

In attempts to raise a school's rating, dropping out is encouraged. A study found that Texas' public school accountability system, the model for NCLB, directly contributes to lower graduation rates, especially for minori-ties. By analyzing data from more than 271,000 students, the study found that 60 percent of African-American students, 75 percent of Latino students and 80 percent of ESL students did not graduate within five years. The researchers found an overall graduation rate of only 33 percent and deter-mined that NCLB is directly contributing to these unusually high dropout rates.

Schools are playing hot potato with the U.S. government, willing to jeopardize children's education for high ratings in accountability mea-sures. Students are not assets or liabilities, however NCLB dehumanized them in that way among school personnel.

Ultimately, another report revealed that more than 43,000 schools, or 48 percent, did not make AYP in 2011. The failure rates range from a low of 11 percent in Wisconsin to a high of 89 percent in Florida. While the findings are below the 82 percent failure rate estimated by Secretary of Education Arne Duncan, the numbers are yet another sign of the failed law.

Congratulations Department of Education! It only took you 10 years to wake up and see that this law isn't working. Your circus act of school closures would only make the Ringling Brothers proud!

*

I'm an NCLB baby — all of my schooling has been during the NCLB era. Let's finally admit that the national testing experiment has not only failed miserably, but has gone haywire. NCLB has earned the reputation of destroying children's love of learning. Spineless politicians who didn't have the wit nor the audacity to fix our education cataclysms indoctrinated the nation with rubbish. NCLB can be summed up by the remarks of Scott Howard, a former superintendent of schools in Perry, Ohio in *Time*, "No Child Left Behind is like a Russian novel. That's because it's long, it's complicated, and in the end, everybody gets killed."

This law cannot be reformed; it can only be repealed. America, it's time to move on.

NCLB 2.0

In January 2009, the Obama administration discreetly slipped $4.35 billion of education funding into the American Recovery and Reinvestment Act without the slightest bit of legislative debate. Race to the Top equals NCLB 2.0. As Arnold Dodge, chairman and assistant professor in educational leadership and administration at Long Island University, suggested to me, "Race to the Top is No Child Left Behind in disguise."

The $4.35 billion competition gives millions to states that best adopt Duncan-based policies. The required, loathsome mandates include requiring states to link teachers' salaries and evaluations to students' achievement on standardized testing, continuing an emphasis on high-stakes testing, implementing assessments for preschoolers, mandating that states sign onto the Common Core standards, and beefing up funding for charter schools. Stir it all up and you get a recipe for disaster.

When James Arnold, superintendent of Pelham City Schools in Georgia, thinks of Race to the Top, it reminds him of an old television show: the 1950s "Queen For a Day." On the show, ordinary women, chosen from a studio audience, each competed and compared their personal sob stories and explained why they believed they should be crowned the "Queen For a Day." Usually, each contestant asked for a merchandise prize such as a washer and dryer. After all the stories were imparted, the audience chose the winner via the "applause-o-meter." The winner received her original request along with a number of lavish gifts, like velvet robes, a jeweled crown, and a scepter. The gifts were expected to transform the winner's life from destitute to instant wealth and happiness. It didn't. Their 15 minutes of fame quickly vanished. And the unlucky contestants went right back to their unfortunate situations.

Similarly, Race to the Top was sold as a silver bullet. States latched onto Duncan's mandates with no other option. The country was in the midst of the worst economic catastrophe since the Great Depression. School budgets were drowning in red ink, thus causing schools to lay off teachers left and right and tighten the amount of money spent on programs and re-sources. *Kowtowing* to Duncan, even as ludicrous as his policies were, was the only way to prevent the termination of schools in the state.

Arnold writes that "Queen For a Day" was never meant to alleviate poverty or the conditions for the contestants, like the Race to the Top waiv-ers are not meant to improve student achievement.

By now, 11 states and the District of Columbia have been awarded money because they had the highest scoring plans. Race to the Top directly impacts 13.6 million students and 980,000 teachers in 25,000 schools. Those are a lot of students, teachers, and schools getting screwed up!

ABRACADABRA

University of North Carolina at Chapel Hill Professor Gregory Cizek was asked by the state of Georgia to scout out signs of a teacher or principal's manipulation of a student's work. He found plenty.

Further analysis along with interviews of educators from flagged schools, led investigators to label some 178 educators, including 38 prin-cipals in 44 of the 56 schools, as participants in cheating. The resulting report, released by the state of Georgia found "systemic misconduct within the district as far back as 2001" and concluded that "thousands of school children were harmed by widespread cheating in the Atlanta Public School System." Data was everything. The 413-page report reads like an Agatha Christie thriller, with stories of teachers holding "erasure parties" and principals publicly humiliating their employees. "A culture of fear and a conspiracy of silence infected the school system, and kept many teachers from teaching freely about misconduct," the report's authors concluded.

The revelations have tarnished Atlanta's Cinderella story of school re-form, an urban school district that for years was hailed as one of the country's most successful due to increased student performance. A Machiavellian figure, Beverly L. Hall, now the former superintendent, ruled with an iron fist. Princi-pals were told that if scores didn't go up, they would be fired. One teacher told investigators the district was "run like the mob." Hall even covered one wall in her office with bar graphs showing the test results of all 100 city schools.

She hit the jackpot. Scores skyrocketed. Not surprisingly, Arne Duncan even hosted her at the White House. To conceal evidence, Hall and her aides buried documents claiming misconduct and wrongdoings. Then everything fell like a deck of cards. But, it wasn't only Atlanta. Add in Washington D.C., Los Angeles, and Houston...

We all thought Michelle Rhee, former chancellor of D.C. public schools, was some All Knowing, All Powerful being with the superpower of singlehandedly doubling test scores. Abracadabra! Rhee was spotted on the cover of *Time* holding a broom (to sweep away "bad" teachers). Diane Ravitch calls her "truly an education celebrity."

But all the coveted and apparent success of the D.C. public schools during her reign is false. An explosive investigative series in *USA Today* in March 2011 documented 1,610 cases of standardized test-score manipulation in six states and Washington D.C. between 2009 and 2010. At some schools, they found the odds that so many answers had been changed from wrong to right randomly were 1 in 100 billion, more difficult than winning the Powerball.

As eager as she is for the national spotlight, Rhee will not appear on camera to address the scandal. She got the easy way out without any scrutiny.

The French Revolution's Reign of Terror has been mimicked in the 21st century, but this time it is in the teaching profession. The fear is real. State against state. School against school. Teacher against teacher. In that aforementioned *USA Today* series, a head of a teachers' union calls it "the education Ponzi scheme: if your test scores improve, you make more money. If not, you get fired."

Don't believe any superintendent or principal who doesn't think cheating exists in the confines of their school. They're in denial or they're naive or both. That'll give you another reason to investigate.

You just have to be a human being to understand the pressures Race to the Top has put on teachers and administrators. When you put people in highly competitive environments, cheating becomes very advantageous.

Where will the next "Atlanta" or "Washington D.C." be?

NO FOUR-YEAR-OLD LEFT UNTESTED

In January 2003, the Bush administration unleashed plans to give 908,000 four-year-olds in Head Start programs nationwide a standardized exam to see how much they were learning. Parents screamed. Psychologists barked. Kids whined. Still, the series of mini-tests called the National Reporting Service, which measured verbal and math skills, went through to the kids.

After much clamoring from early childhood experts, Congress tabled the tests in 2007. Leap four years and guess what you have? The Obama administration is pushing standardized testing into preschool classrooms. Déjà vu. Politicians never learn, do they?

The Department of Education announced the early childhood education portion of the Race to the Top game, promising to dispense a total of $500 million to winners that wow the judges. Here are the shiny-new guidelines released:

> Priority 1: Absolutely Priority — Using Early Learning and Development Standards and Kindergarten Entry Assessments to Promote School Readiness.

> Priority 2: Absolute Priority – Using Tiered Quality Rating and Improvement Systems to Promote School Readiness

> Priority 3: Competitive Preference Priority – Including all Early Learning and Development Programs in the Tiered Quality Rating and Improvement System

> Priority 4: Invitational Priority – Sustaining Program Effects in the Early Elementary Grades

> Priority 5: Invitational Priority – Encouraging Private Sector Support)

As *Washington Post* blogger Valerie Strauss writes, "There is something disturbing about an early childhood education initiative that doesn't seem to take into account how young children learn best." Zilch about playing in the sandbox or exploring new opportunities or engaging in creative activities. Put yourself in the shoes of a four-year-old. How would you like it if a lady took away your blocks and toys and made you sit and take a test? High-stakes standardized tests should not be the yardstick used to assess children and pre-school programs. Please, especially not a four-year-old!

Executive director of the National Head Start Association, an early advocacy group, Yasmina Vinci told *Education Week*, "Assessment is the third rail of early childhood because children develop at very different rates, young children especially. You have to be very careful as to what that would look like and for what purposes. It should not be for the purposes of classifying the children. It has to be observational." If I got a poor score on such an exam, my self esteem and motivation would tumble.

Will we soon have testing in the womb?

THE FIGHT OF OUR LIFE

Charter schools are often lauded as the panacea for failing public schools. To win Race to the Top funds, charter school support was a pre-requisite.

Less than a quarter century ago, in an address to the National Press Club, the late American Federation of Teachers president Albert Shanker proposed the creation of "charter schools" — publicly funded institutions that would be given greater flexibility to experiment with new ways of educating students. Today, Shanker's original intent of charters has gone berzerk. I spoke with Arnold Dodge, professor at Long Island University, who wrote a compelling review on *Waiting for Superman*, the film that rallied behind charter schools. He says, "The problem with charter schools is that they exist because they are specimens. If we could bring the charter school movement to scale and make sure that all students are enrolled in a successful charter school, then we would truly have something 'super.'"

On average, charter schools are producing worse educational achievement results than regular public schools. A landmark study from Stanford University's Center for Research on Education Outcomes discovered that while 17 percent of charter schools "provide superior education opportunities for their students," a whopping "37 percent deliver learning results that are significantly worse than their students would have realized had they remained in traditional public schools." In addition, the National Center for Education Statistics found that charter school students performed significantly worse on academic assessments than their peers in traditional public schools. While I hate using standardized test scores as a yardstick, they are the sole quantitative measure in this case.

The problem is not only their poor performance on standardized tests, but where the charter school's funding derives from. Wall Street tycoons, for instance, have found their 'calling' and a hobby in public school reform by putting their money toward expanding charter schools, thinking of themselves as the crusaders in the 'civil rights movement' of their time. Take Ravenel Boykin Curry IV, the Managing Director at Eagle Capital Management. In an interview in Steven Brill's book *Class Warfare*, Curry IV feels the education cause is both "exciting and fun" and "because so many of us got interested in this at the same time, you get to work with people who are your friends." Isn't that just cute? No.

The Wall Street titans' hold over education reform is destructive. The irony is that these financiers will gladly champion the growth of charters for poor and minority students, while they send their own children to rich, private institutions. Only begin to believe a politician or a billionaire if they will send their own child to an institution they prescribe other children to attend. Curry IV would scoff at such a suggestion.

You probably can't guess the largest charter school network in the United States. With 135 schools and more than 45,000 students enrolled nationwide, the largest charter school network is operated by people associated with the Gulen Movement, a secretive and controversial Turkish religious group. The people are followers of Fethullah Gulen, an alluring Turkish Islamic cleric, who promotes tolerance and education. However, the schools, which focus on mathematics and science, have been the subject of close scrutiny on accusations that the schools have abused a special visa program by bringing in their expatriate employees and that the schools are using taxpayer dollars to benefit the movement. American schools are being taken over by terribly regulated Turkish charter schools.

As noted, the charter school system's lack of oversight has caused tremendous issues. The majority of charter schools are shuttered due to financial mismanagement. For instance, Williamsburg Charter High School in Brooklyn, New York was shuttered after years of poor management by the Believe High Schools Network. And Philadelphia's charter school system has 19 of its 74 charter schools under investigation for fraud, financial mismanagement, and conflicts of interest.

Charters are not only worsening the situation, but they are a mere distraction from transforming schools.

The *New York Times* featured a hard hitting piece titled "Why Don't We Have Any White Kids?" as part of the series "A System Divided." It delves into the racial schisms of Explore Charter School, a K-8 school in Flatbush, Brooklyn. Of the school's 502 students from kindergarten through eighth grade this school year, 92.7 percent are black, 5.7 percent are Hispanic, and a scattering are of mixed race. None are white or Asian.

As more charter schools take over "failed" public schools, the resegregation of New York's public school system has transpired. Consider a report that determined that charters "tend to be more racially segregated than traditional public schools" — and in lots of places, they seem to be openly hostile to children who are poor, who are from minority communities or who have special education needs. Another study identifies that seven out of ten black charter school students are on campuses with extremely few white students. Why as a country are we still stuck on the axiom of separate but equal schools? Was it not overturned by Brown v. Board of Education more than half a century ago? The 2010 campaign by Mayor Michael R. Bloomberg's administration to expand charter schools was dubbed "the fight of our life" in an email released by the city.

Put simply, the city turns a blind eye to the disadvantaged children of the education system. The situation has turned ugly after ten years of Mayor Bloomberg running the show — a billionaire who doesn't have a clue what it means to live on less than a couple of million a year. In parallel, as Arianna Huffington, author of *Third World America*, might put it, New York City is simply becoming a 'Third World' city.

Why can't the billionaires, hedge-fund managers, and politicians comprehend that there is no charter school miracle? Perhaps, in their eyes, charters provide a simple, elegant solution to our "failing" public schools.

Some charters succeed. I respect those schools, without any doubt, but charters are not the "cure-all" for our public education system. We are falling into H.L. Mencken's trap: "There is always a well-known solution to every human problem — neat, plausible, and wrong."

*

In 2012, the Obama administration freed 19 states from the requirements of No Child Left Behind. At first it looks great. While the apocalypse for public schools may have been avoided, when taking a closer look, however, it means that test scores will matter even more in the states granted waivers. Why? The states that won waivers must agree to accept the Common Core State Standards, a very costly and nonsensical national curriculum in mathematics and English. It was developed by Achieve Inc., a company created by the nation's governors and corporate leaders, and has not been field-tested anywhere. After number crunching, California decided not to bother applying for a waiver when they found that complying with the waiver requirements would cost at least $2 billion a year. California State Superintendent of Public Instruction Tom Torlakson likened taking on new federal requirements to owning a home in which "the kitchen is on fire, and someone tells us to go clean up the living room."

Rule of thumb: Never trust anything Secretary Arne Duncan says.

Oddly, in June 2011, the president offered some surprising remarks at the Univision Town Hall:

> We have piled on a lot of standardized tests on our kids. Now, there's nothing wrong with a standardized test being given occasionally just to give a baseline of where kids are at. Malia and Sasha, my two daughters, they just recently took a standardized test. But it wasn't a high-stakes test. It wasn't a test where they had to panic. I mean, they didn't even really know that they were going to take it ahead of time. They didn't study for it, they just went ahead and took it. And it was a tool to diagnose where they were strong, where they were weak, and what the teachers needed to emphasize.
>
> Too often what we've been doing is using these tests to punish students or to, in some cases, punish schools. And so what we've said is let's find a test that everybody agrees makes sense; let's apply it in a less pressure-packed atmosphere; let's figure out whether we have to do it every year or whether we can do it maybe every several years; and let's make sure that that's not the only way we're judging whether a school is doing well.

Because there are other criteria: What's the attendance rate? How are young people performing in terms of basic competency on projects? There are other ways of us measuring whether students are doing well or not.

Then, I almost fainted when I heard this from the president:

So what I want to do is — one thing I never want to see happen is schools that are just teaching to the test. Because then you're not learning about the world; you're not learning about different cultures, you're not learning about science, you're not learning about math. All you're learning about is how to fill out a little bubble on an exam and the little tricks that you need to do in order to take a test. And that's not going to make education interesting to you. And young people do well in stuff that they're interested in. They're not going to do as well if it's boring.

And finally in the 2012 State of the Union Address, Obama declared, "Teach with creativity and passion; to stop teaching to the test; and to replace teachers who just aren't helping kids learn."

I was shaken up.

The president doesn't seem to realize that every single one of his previous statements are antithetical to the policies his very own Department of Education has pursued, including the expansion of standardized testing.

I can only say: Act by your word, Mr. President. Repeal No Child Left Behind and abolish Race to the Top!

THE 800-POUND GORILLA

These days, it seems like everyone in the business and political world has a neat fix to our miserable education system. The corporate education reform takeover is a Trojan horse for privatization. Who are the losers in this mess? Students and teachers.

The loony sugar daddy tribe from the Koch Brothers to the DeVos family do not give a flying fig about how other peoples' children are educated. They simply want to make a killing off of the rise of charters and school vouchers. To most bystanders in the education reform discussions, the debate seems to be dominated by the corporate reformers, who use fear tactics, fancy lingo, and carrots and sticks to push their agenda. Here's a riddle: "Where does an 800 pound gorilla sleep?" The answer: "Anywhere it wants to." The big, bad billionaires and corporate reformers are the 800-pound gorillas marauding public education.

As educator Gary Stager quipped in the *Huffington Post*, "In public education today, unqualified is the new qualified." When you allow celebrities and billionaires to define reform, you get as Stager suggests, Reform™.

Stager adds, "History did not begin with Gates, Klein, Bloomberg, Rhee, Obama, or Duncan. They do not hold the monopoly on the truth."

The corporate reformers have hijacked education with their wealth and celebrity status, while refusing to acknowledge the effects of their fiascos: ultimately pushing children off the cliff.

This is what I want parents to scream to the world: I want my child to go to a great school where his or her curiosity is ignited. I want their teachers paid well and motivated — not by incentives, but by passion. I want their administrators not bought out by corporations trying to obliterate their competition.

ACHIEVEMENT GAP

Stop wasting your time reading the countless reports and articles on the achievement gap. Policymakers have allocated almost all of their energies to this issue at the expense of changing the type of learning in school. In the next two simple paragraphs, I will offer solutions on decreasing the achievement gap — the disparity in education performance between minority and low income students and wealthy, upper class students on standardized tests. It is tightly correlated with poverty and socioeconomic conditions.

Can the gap be closed anytime soon? The short answer is no. As long as we have income inequality in this country, we will always have an achievement gap. I must add that you can't really compare a kid who is malnourished, living with a single parent, and prone to violence with a kid who is well off, has two parents, and lives in a safe neighborhood.

What steps can we take to reduce the gap? Three things: First, we must adequately fund schools regardless of the zip code. Second, we must bring the most intelligent teachers into highly risk-prone schools and pay them even more. Third, we must prevent the entrance of charter schools, which causes significant segregation, in lieu of public schools.

Voilà, hopefully I have saved you the time of reading the thousands of books and articles on the subject. You wonder why nothing has ever been solved.

DRILL, KILL, BUBBLE FILL

World War I was underway. Teacher shortages were looming since men fought abroad and women toiled in factories. The number of public schools increased from about 500 in 1880 to 10,000 by 1910 and the number of students in secondary education increased more than tenfold. Plus, the immigrant population had tripled in the last decade. The country was about to go to hell in a handbasket.

How were we going to process students efficiently? Notice how I use the word "process." Students were goods on a conveyor belt.

Who came to the rescue? Frederick J. Kelly. Folks, this is the son of a gun who invented the first multiple choice exam.

In his doctoral dissertation at Kansas State University in 1914, Kelly outlined his brainchild, the Kansas Silent Reading Test (though I call it Frankenstein). He desired a testing system that was two things — objective and efficient.

Kelly insisted that questions had to be created without any ambiguity. Only right or wrong answers. The format will be familiar to any reader: "Below are given the names of four animals. Draw a line around the name of each animal that is useful on the farm: cow tiger rat wolf."

The instructions continue: "The exercise tells us to draw a line around the word cow. No other answer is right. Even if a line is drawn under the word cow, the exercise is wrong, and nothing counts...Stop at once when time is called. Do not open the papers until told, so that all may begin at the same time."

What attracted people to the test was that it was objective, no longer was a teacher's judgment a variable in how much a child knew.

Years later, however, Kelly foreboded, "This a test of lower order thinking for the lower orders." Still, a form of Kelly's text was adopted by the College Board as the framework for the holy Scholastic Aptitude Test (SAT).

After the war ended, Kelly began to espouse a radically different stance in his own thinking about education. When he arose to the presidency at the University of Idaho, Kelly argued in his inaugural presidential address against the standardization movement that had infiltrated education in the post-World War I era.

"College practices have shifted the responsibility from the student to the teacher, the emphasis from learning to teaching, with the result that the development of fundamental strengths of purpose or of lasting habits of study is rare," President Kelly said, announcing his own blueprint for educational reform. Similarly as in the tale of Frankenstein, Kelly denounced his monster, saying the tests were an appropriate method to test only a tiny portion of what is actually taught and should be abandoned.

The University of Idaho faculty wanted no part of President Kelly's reforms and revolted. Kelly was ultimately asked to step down from his position. Unfortunately, the test lived on. Today, most kids across the United States have taken some variation of the Kansas Silent Reading Test.

Why do most teachers still use multiple choice tests? Two reasons: First, because it is convenient. You push the bubble sheets through the

Scantron machine, hear some dings, and voila, all marked up for you effortlessly. Second, once you get the scores, you can determine passing and failing immediately. No effort required.

As Richard Hersh, co-director of the College and Works Readiness Assessment, argues:

> We do not limit our testing of surgeons, pilots, or architects to short-answer and/or essay tests — we ask them to perform across a wide variety of real tasks they will face on the job and for tasks they will rarely face but must be ready for in case. Their assessments are not limited to paper and pencil tests — none of us would ever consider flying with a pilot who has not been fully tested on take-offs and landings, or being operated on by a surgeon who had not been trained in operating rooms, or living in a building designed by an architect who had not had sufficient supervised practice and testing in the design and construction of such edifices.

If alive today, Kelly would probably burst out into rage saying, "What kind of idiot still uses this type of testing. For crying out loud, if you haven't noticed, this isn't the Industrial Revolution, people."

Albert North Whitehead warned in *The Aims of Education and Other Essays* that an education gorged with inert ideas, "ideas that are merely received into the mind without being utilized, or tested, or thrown into fresh combinations," is not only useless, but dangerous. Without applying knowledge, students cannot connect the dots and make sense of what they're learning. In schools, we hand kids silly fill-in-the-bubbles tests.

Paul Krugman, a Nobel Prize Laureate in Economics and a columnist at the New York Times, repeatedly invokes the confidence fairy, the idea that slashing government spending and employment in the face of a deeply depressed economy would actually create jobs, when criticizing Republican proposals in his columns. In schools, we have a fairy. It's called the rote learning fairy, the axiom that more memorization, regurgitation, and drilling helps students learn. However, it's a complete myth that schools have incidentally championed. School has evolved into a cycle: memorize, memorize, memorize, spit back, spit back, spit back, forget.

Centuries ago, it was possible to memorize certain facts that elevated a person as an educated one. As Matthew Burns of the *Los Angeles Times* puts it, "The typical English peasant's life accumulation of knowledge amounted to less than one edition of the *Wall Street Journal* today." Rote learning worked well when the Internet was only a pie in the sky. Today, looking up a fact or figure on Google is effortless, only plucking a second or two of our time. Why should we waste precious time storing facts in our heads when all this beautiful technology is at our fingertips? Unless you plan on beating Watson, the IBM supercomputer on Jeopardy, chances are that you won't ever be asked to memorize information in life outside of school.

I spoke with Tony Wagner, Innovation Education Fellow at the Technology and Entrepreneurship Center at Harvard University, who has written extensively on this subject. He said, "If the questions require only factual recall — which is most often the case — then students are probably not being asked to do very much in the way of reasoning, analysis, or hypothesizing — and the primary skill being taught is memorization." Learning is not a sport. Quickness of recall doesn't attest to depth of understanding. The Internet is the fountain of our knowledge now.

PINEAPPLEGATE

This may very well be the perfect time to invoke Charlie Sheen. America's on a drug, and it's called standardized testing. We've become a nation of standardized testing junkies.

Never let a school that flaunts test scores trick you. "If a school boasts about its test scores," says Alfie Kohn, "parents ought to immediately respond by asking what had to be sacrificed from their kids' education in order to make that happen."

If you pass my school, Syosset High School, you will notice a Blue Ribbon sign in front of the school. What does that mean? It literally means that my school cares about telling people that its primary mission is to produce test-takers to ensure its high rankings. That's it. If my school screws up its rankings, house values plummet and school administrators will be under fire. That's what you call the dangerous and inappropriate testing regime.

In the past few years, testing scandals have rocked New York State. First, in 2009, historian Diane Ravitch revealed that the points needed to earn a "Level 2" — the lowest "passing" grade on New York State exams — have dropped dramatically.

Intrigued by her colleague's observations, Diana Senechal conducted a little experiment. With a natural "zero" on the written portion of a sixth grade English Language Arts test, she guessed all the answers on the multiple choice portion. Her multiple choice guesswork earned her 12 out of 39 "raw points" and a scale score of 622 — a solid, passing "2." Repeating the experiment with the 7th grade math test, she once again scored a '2' "without solving a single math problem, or even looking at one." So nowadays, in the words of Senechal, it is possible to "guess your way to promotion."

A second testing scandal shook the state in 2012. For millions of eighth grade students taking the New York State English Language Arts exam in April, a few particular questions unleashed a Pandora's box, leaving many students scratching their heads. It involved an absurd tale of a talking pineapple, who challenges a hare to a race, and the other animals are convinced the pineapple must have a trick up its sleeve and will win. When the pineapple stands still, the animals eat it. The moral of the story: "Pineapples don't have sleeves."

The story originally derived from children's author Daniel Pinkwater's story "The Rabbit and the Eggplant," which had been licensed to Pearson. Pearson altered the characters — changing rabbit to hare, eggplant to pineapple. Pinkwater castigated the questions as "nonsense on top of nonsense on top of nonsense." Take a look for yourself.

One of the disputed questions asked, "Why did the animal eat the pineapple?" The choices included: they were annoyed, amused, hungry, or wanted to. Students were stuck between two of the four choices: they were annoyed or they were hungry; either one seemed to work. Pinkwater in a hilarious interview with the *Wall Street Journal* responded, "They feared socialism. Or they had made an appointment to see their aunt in Minnesota. The next answer is, 'Are you a fool? Animals can't talk.'"

The other controversial question on the exam asked, "Which was the wisest animal?" The choices included: hare, moose, crow, or owl. Some students said that none of the animals seemed very bright, but that a likely answer was the owl, since it was the one that spoke the moral. I definitely couldn't answer this question. Pinkwater said, "There are only two answers for who were the wisest: the author or the publisher who made the test."

I love how Alexandra Petri of the *Washington Post*, put it: "If your eighth grader can comprehend this, this is cause for concern. It is a sign that he is doing serious drugs."

The New York Daily News hunted down *Jeopardy* champion Ken Jennings, who put it mildly when he said, "Is this a joke? The story makes no sense whatsoever. The narrative has no internal logic, the 'moral' is unclear, and the plot details seem so oddly chosen that the story seems to have been written during a peyote trip. (The prose is clunky too, but I hate to pile on)."

After the virtual firestorm rippled from parent blogs to Facebook pages and word broke out that a student even designed a t-shirt reading "pineapples don't even have sleeves," the New York State Education Commission John King responded to the frenzy by saying they would toss out the test questions.

This comes to my main point — we are faced with an unstoppable Pearson-designed classroom. The world's largest for-profit education business, Pearson, was lavished with a $32 million five-year contract to develop New York standardized testing. For Pete's sake, with all that dough, Pearson should have shipped out free pineapples with test booklets. Shame on them.

Even though it's chump change for Pearson, New York State gave them millions for recycled crap. Apparently, Pearson had recycled the same reading passage and associated questions for standardized exams in

Florida, Illinois, Delaware, New Mexico, Arkansas, Alabama, and perhaps other states, causing huge confusion among students for at least the last seven years. In its contract with Pearson, New York spelled out that on tests "the material must have characters that are portrayed as positive role models, have a positive message and be well written." Pearson undoubtedly violated the contract. But, in its statements, Pearson is confident that they did its job. When the story first broke, I was hoping this was a bad April Fool's Day joke by *The Onion*, but in the end, this incident adds more fire to the Opt-Out of Testing crusade.

As we can conclude from PineappleGate, the corporate testing industry regularly messes up. Yet, we also depend on these companies to score the answers. They hold the golden egg — one little screw-up and they change a kid's life forever — derailing college admissions, job prospects, and the chance to sit with his or her peers at graduation. We have put all our eggs in one basket, putting our faith into these companies to deliver perfectly, 100 percent of the time.

Behind the closed doors and the tangled bureaucracy, many people wonder what actually goes on at these scoring centers. In 2002, Amy Weivoda wrote a very provocative piece in *Salon* titled, "We hung the most dimwitted essays on the wall":

> The state of Pennsylvania paid the Minnesota-based test-scoring company I worked for $12 million to score a two-question essay test. Here's what that money bought: Two hundred or so $6-an-hour test scorers for a couple of weeks; photocopying fees to give us all copies of the tests on pink-and-blue paper; overhead costs on a water-damaged building with no air-conditioning that had recently been abandoned by the telephone company. Oh yes, and lawyers' fees, when the test turned out to be mis-scored.

Weivoda reveals that she read hundreds of tests a day, allocating no more than 30 seconds to each question. If a child was particularly funny or dim, the test was posted in the hallway for entertainment.

> Each test was a little different. Kids would either answer questions based on a short, boring reading, to test for comprehension, or they'd get a free-write question that would test writing skills and ability to answer simple questions like "Describe the best gift you ever got." Brains wear out after reading hundreds of identical descriptions of Nintendo games: They really rocked, they were really cool, they were exactly what I'd always dreamed about in my most wildest dream I'd ever had about the best Christmas of my

whole life, so far. That was about all anyone had to say about Nintendo, and very few kids seemed to get anything better or anything different than that. Maybe once a week I'd get a puppy or a bike. We scorers would start out each fresh test eager to give each kid the best score they could reasonably expect.

Here's the most alarming part: "But after a few hours or days or weeks, we'd sleepwalk and skim and assign scores sort of randomly. It was hard not to." And Weivoda discreetly pointed out that some of the scorers had earned their degrees in prison.

Eight years later, in *The Monthly Review,* Dan DiMaggio cited many of the similar issues Weivoda had brought up in *Salon.* He worked at a test-scoring center in downtown St. Paul and a Minneapolis suburb. In test-scoring centers, DiMaggio explains:

> Dozens of scorers sit in rows, staring at computer screens where students' papers appear (after the papers have undergone some mysterious scanning process). I imagine that most students think their papers are being graded as if they are the most important thing in the world. Yet every day, each scorer is expected to read hundreds of papers. So for all the months of preparation and the dozens of hours of class time spent writing practice essays, a student's writing probably will be processed and scored in about a minute.
>
> No matter at what pace scorers work, however, tests are not always scored with the utmost attentiveness. The work is mind numbing, so scorers have to invent ways to entertain themselves. The most common method seems to be staring blankly at the wall or into space for minutes at a time. But at work this year, I discovered that no one would notice if I just read news articles while scoring tests. So every night, while scoring from home, I would surf the Internet and cut and paste loads of articles — reports on Indian Maoists, scientific speculation on whether animals can be gay, critiques of standardized testing — into what typically came to be an eighty-page, single-spaced Word document. Then I would print it out and read it the next day while I was working at the scoring center. This was the only way to avoid going insane. I still managed to score at the average rate for the room and perform according to "quality" standards. While scoring from home, I routinely carry on three or four intense conversations on Gchat. This is the reality of test scoring.

What gives me more chills than the inhumane practices in these test-scoring centers, are the actual student responses to the free-response questions. He goes on to reveal that he read thousands of responses by middle-schoolers to the question, "What is a goal of yours in life?" A grand majority chalked out robotic, cloned paragraphs. Points weren't given for creativity. Students were told what to regurgitate on these tests. DiMaggio writes, "These rote responses, in themselves, are a testament to the failure of our education system, its failure to actually connect with kids' lives and do more than discipline them and prepare them to be obedient workers — or troops."

Any corporate executive or politician who champions high-stakes testing for kids and teachers should take the very same tests and publish their scores publicly. That would make a brilliant *New York Post* front-page story.

At a time of belt-tightening, where K-12 budgets have been slashed by billions, spending on standardized testing seems to be untampered with. After the passage of the No Child Left Behind Act in January 2002, annual state standardized test costs rose from $423 million to almost $1.1 billion in 2008. The cost of grading almost 45 million tests annually, as well as increased tutoring and after school programs for schools with low standardized test scores, have factored in to the $500 million increase in education spending for the city. The annual cost of standardized testing in the United States has been estimated at somewhere between $20 billion and $50 billion, which doesn't even include the cost of remediation for students who aren't up to par.

Can you imagine the impact if we diverted the billions from testing and negative campaign ads to fund more programs, raise teacher salaries, improve school lunches, and reduce class sizes? You would think this would be common sense, but it's not in America.

ABOLISH GRADES!

The kids catch on pretty quickly to the game of school — get good grades and get out as fast as you can. To motivate the students to complete the work, schools dangle carrots and sticks — extrinsic motivators — grades — in front of them, like a cart driver to a mule. The only motivation for me to get good grades is getting the free tokens at Chuck E. Cheese.*

One of the biggest roadblocks to a learning revolution is transforming the way we assess students. Grades are such an artificial motivation.

Grades were first implemented in the United States in the later part of the 19th century. One of the early adopters of the grading system was incidentally the American Meatpackers Association — for grading the quality of meat. Shortly after, the association gave up the system, since they found it too inflexible...even for meat.

My fellow classmates regularly harp, "As long as you get good grades, the learning doesn't matter." An extensive sum of research illustrates that grading is responsible for reducing students' interest in learning itself.

Let's take a lesson from William Fariah who is widely known as the man who invented the grading system. Fariah was a tutor at Cambridge University in the late 18th century. Frustrated by the fact that to become familiar with his students, he needed to engage with them daily, Farish constructed a methodology of teaching that allowed him to process more students in a shorter period of time. Grades were born!

Before this, grades were used to determine the salary of workers based on the quality of shoes produced in factories. In the classroom, grading failed to make students more intelligent or to give birth to contagious learning, but Fariah was given a raise and reduced hours anyways. I mean that's all that matters, right?

John Cage put it best: "I can't understand why people are frightened of new ideas. I'm frightened of the old ideas." Grading is more than two centuries old. This nation is almost as ancient. The grading system is not only old, it's also unreliable. In high school, grade inflation is rampant. A 2009 study revealed that more than 45 percent of that year's college freshmen said they managed to graduate high school with an "A" average.

What's more, grading causes students to be risk-prone. Research has uncovered that students of all ages who have been led to concentrate on getting a good grade were likely to pick the easiest possible assignment if given a choice. For example, children who were told that they would be graded on their solution of anagrams chose easier anagrams to work on and seemed to take less pleasure from solving them than children who were not being graded.

People often tell me: 'Nikhil, that's cute and all, but if kids aren't graded, how are we supposed to tell if they are learning?' I reply by saying there is no shortcut to this answer.

For instance, badges are an option to replace grades. In dictionary terms, a badge is a special or distinctive mark, token, or device worn as a sign of allegiance, membership, authority, or achievement. It is a way of credentialing the mastery of skill-sets and knowledge in informal and peer-to-peer learning. Mozilla, the John D. and Catherine T. MacArthur Foundation, and others are working to develop such a system. There are concerns that badges provide extrinsic motivation where learners are solely attracted to learn to acquire badges. However, they can serve as a sign of recognition or a nod of approval.

Performance and authentic assessments are two more options. First, it's important to distinguish between "assessment" and "test." Ac-

---

* Chuck E. Cheese offers free tokens to kids who bring in their latest report card with good grades.

cording to Ruth Mitchell, "a test is a single occasion, unidimensional, timed exercise, usually in multiple choice or short answer form. Assessment is an activity that can take many forms, can extend over time, and aims to capture the quality of a student's work or of an educational program...[it is] a collection of ways to provide accurate information about what students know and are able to do or about the quality of educational programs. The collective assessments reflect the complexity of what is to be learned and do not distort its nature in the information gathering process." Whether called authentic, performance, or portfolio-based assessment, they identify strategies that focus on critical thinking and creativity.

No more spoon-feeding kids answers. No more filling-in-the-bubbles strategies. No more educators stuffing multiple choice tests down students' throats, because they are quick and cheap to grade. Assessment is not an assembly line.

Two distinct types of assessment are authentic and performance. Authentic assessment refers to assessment tasks that resemble the real world. It's as natural as possible. It values the process on the same level as the outcome.

Performance assessment is a term that is commonly used in lieu of, or with, authentic assessment. It requires students to demonstrate their knowledge and skills by creating a response or a product. That means writing articles, creating videos, designing robots, etc. Often it includes checklists and progress reports to document the work completed.

One intriguing facet of a performance assessment is portfolios, structured on how professionals document their accomplishments. In a digital portfolio, written work, journals, logs, books read, movies, peer reviews, self evaluations, audio recordings, interviews, and blog posts can be included. Then students decide how to evaluate the work, an opportunity to reflect on the pieces of work and set goals for the future. Not only does this allow for constant improvement and progress to higher-quality work, but it also gives students the power to shape and mold their learning. Moreover, a teacher may desire to have concrete evidence that a student has sufficient skills in a content area to advance to the next level. In that instance, educators need to develop rubrics with clear-cut criteria and the skill-sets required for a particular project. Obviously, the report would be much more informative than flat-out giving a number grade. But the overarching value of portfolios is not to yield a number; the point is to pin-point exactly where a student is succeeding and struggling. It offers an opportunity for self-improvement. The student is running the show.

In my conversation with educator Deborah Meier, she said that when she was at the Central Park East Secondary School in New York City that she founded, she experimented with judging low-income inner-city students on the basis of collections of their best work and oral examinations. Ultimately, the educators found that if students did well on these alternative assessments, they gained admission to college and tended to do well there. In parallel, in the labor market we are observing that companies are becoming more inclined to hire designers and developers based on the work in their portfolio, rather than their grades in school. If I were an employer, I would hire a high school dropout over a Harvard graduate, if the dropout had a stronger portfolio and more real world experience.

Feedback is at the center of a revolutionary assessment system. Iteration and failure are naturally a part of the process. Joe Bower, anti-grading guru and author of the popular, "For the Love of Learning" blog, offered a clever remark to me: "Assessment is not a spreadsheet — it's a conversation." I propose that classrooms have daily critique sessions where fellow peers constructively criticize each other's work. This is a simple and very attainable solution.

How do these new types of assessment work on a national scale? In most instances, the public agrees that current testing methods sap learning out of kids. However, when they ask 21st century education reformers the question, "What's the alternative?", many respond in abstract mumbo jumbo without a definite, concrete answer.

One alternative that can be used to assess the quality of schools is the College and Work Readiness Assessment, developed by the Council for Aid to Education and spearheaded by Richard Hersh, its director:

> The 90-minute performance assessment evaluates how well high school students are learning how to think critically, reason analytically, solve problems, and write coherently. The assessment administered online, contains a plethora of open-ended questions and performance tasks about a hypothetical but realistic situation. In addition to directions and questions, each Performance Task also has its own document library that includes a range of information sources: letters, memos, summaries of research reports, newspaper articles, maps, photographs, diagrams, tables, charts, and interview notes and transcripts. They often require students to marshal evidence from different sources; distinguish rational arguments from emotional ones and fact from opinion; understand data in tables and figures; deal with inadequate, ambiguous, and/or conflicting information; spot deception and holes in the arguments made by others; recognize information that is and is not relevant to the task at hand; identify additional information that would help to resolve issues; and weigh, organize, and synthesize information from several sources — all fundamentals of a vibrant, active 21st century education.

Some schools sample the student population, but others assess every student. Plus, with a $40 per test price-tag, it's cheaper than the SAT, the ACT, and less than half the cost of an Advanced Placement exam.

Another phenomenal assessment is the iSkills assessment. The one-hour outcomes-based exam measures applied information and communication technology (ICT) literary skills through a range of real-world tasks. This entails real-time, scenario-based tasks that measure an individual's ability to navigate, critically evaluate, and understand the wealth of information available through digital technology. iSkills specifically pinpoints critical and problem-solving skills in a digital environment.

I will gladly sit for these assessments over a multiple choice exam any day. I am sure my peers would as well.

How can we implement them? Instead of assessing every single student, let's sample, similar to what organizations like Gallup do when surveying public opinion. If necessary, we can also turn to portfolios for assistance. Outside readers can evaluate the projects of a number of students to get a sense of the quality of a school as a whole. Via periodic school inspections and relying on classroom-based evidence, the likelihood of schools gaming the system will fade.

The beauty is that you can't even study for these assessments.

We have been carelessly throwing away decades of time and money. We cannot afford to lose another decade. Government policies like No Child Left Behind and Race to the Top have affected all public schools in the country. If we try to change schools one at a time, a few generations would be needed before massive changes occur. That is why we need government to step up and take action. The options are in plain sight. The question is not can we, but will we.

CHAPTER 4

SO YOU WANT TO BE A BARISTA?

You dropped a hundred and fifty grand on a f**kin education you coulda got for a dollah fifty in late charges at the public library.

WILL IN GOOD WILL HUNTING

If cigarette packs are required to have pictures of diseased lungs, college brochures should be required to have pictures of graduates working at Starbucks.

DANIEL LIN

GETTING IN

On April Fool's Day 2012, *National Public Radio* ran a parody about a preschool's new requirement that all applicants submit DNA profiles in order to get a good reading of a child's intelligence. While a joke, it is a fine representation of the berserk preschool admissions process in New York City. In all, the jockeying for acceptance at private preschools smacks of a dog and pony show.

It has become so competitive that it has caused many to mistake it for a kiddie version of "The Apprentice." *Slate* joked that a film crew is coming to New York to document the preschool version of "Survivor."

Tuition at these preschools is mushrooming, knocking on $40,000 a year. Incidentally, the amount of debt parents have accrued from precollege programs has increased 10 percent. A film to document everything was the only thing missing.

The indie documentary Nursery University was born. The *New York Times* hailed Marc Simon's documentary as something that falls between Freddy Krueger and a Barney film on the scary scale. Parents are pulling their hair out to make sure their child is attractive to admissions officers. This dog-eat-dog like competition stems from the theory that if a child is admitted into the "right" preschool, it will dawn a chain effect, ultimately ending with an Ivy League school admission letter many years down the road.

The way these institutions test these kids for admission is at the far end of hypocrisy. First, three-year-olds aren't exactly the easiest age group to pin down and evaluate. Some get skirmish sitting in a chair for more than 30 seconds, some get thrown off when something exciting happens outside, and some get agitated by an afternoon stomachache. You can't expect them to sit in a desk with a No. 2 pencil and take a standardized test.

Second, in the hunt for the perfect preschool, some parents have gone out of their way to submit DVDs of their kids at play and perfect their kids' extensive résumés. For a little more assistance, the helicopter parents sign their kids up for sessions at companies like Bright Kids NYC. Plunking down $145 a session, two to four year-olds receive a few hour-long sessions consumed with filling out dull black-and-white workbooks.

Third, they're trained to listen to questions from complete strangers. Even a slight tangent from the answer spells disaster. No kid enjoys this torture.

Fourth, as part of the application process, kids are told to partake in an observed "play date" session.

In a witty piece in the *Washington Post*, Maral Kibarian Skelsey, a clinical assistant professor of dermatology at Georgetown Medical Center, reveals, "They'll see how he plays with other kids and if he knows what to do with crackers and juice. But mainly they want to know if he's a biter. If, God forbid, you suspect he may have bitten someone, immediately pull the fire alarm and then put your house on the market. Your child will never eat a snack in that town again." In California, one three-year-old refused to share his shovel in the sandbox during a play session and the director confirmed that he hadn't put the child's application to the top of the pile. In sum, if the child fails to sufficiently perform on any segment of the application process, according to countless numbers of admissions directors, his or her future is doomed. Come on.

One Manhattan mother even sued a preschool for jeopardizing her daughter's chances of getting into an elite private school, or one day, the Ivy League, saying the school was "just one big playroom." I marvel at what society has become.

In many cities other than New York, preschools require IQ tests of two-year-olds. It turns out, intelligence tests miss a lot as well. For instance, in the 1920s, Lewis Terman, a professor of psychology at Stanford University, whose specialty was intelligence testing, started a now-famous longitudinal study, "Genetic Studies of Genius," that became his life's work. He collected nearly 1,500 California children with off the charts IQ levels, averaging over 140 and ranging as high as 200. The group of young geniuses came to be known as the "Termites." Afterwards, he tracked their every move, recording, measuring, and analyzing their life events.

Ultimately, Terman's hope was to demonstrate that these "exceptionally superior" children would be destined to be the future elite of the United States. But, as we will see later, Terman didn't realize how little IQ correlated to success. When the Termites made it to adulthood, Terman's error was obvious. A majority of the geniuses had fairly ordinary careers and a startling number ended up with poor, failing careers. Not one of the Termites won the Nobel Prize nor did any accomplish something extraordinary. In fact, two of the elementary students Terman had originally tested — Luis Alvarez and William Shockley — went on to become Nobel Laureates, but were rejected by Terman since their IQs weren't high enough.

Therefore, it is vital for helicopter parents to understand that a less than stellar score on a kindergarten or preschool entrance exam, does not spell Armageddon for their child. Even some administrators who use the exam scores say they're utterly worthless. Quoted in *New York Magazine*, Steve Nelson, head of the Calhoun School in New York City, says, "I want a school full of kids who daydream. I want kids who are occasionally impulsive. I want kids who are fun to be with. I want kids who don't want to answer the questions on those tests in the way the adult wants them to be answered, because that kid is already seeing the world differently." In fact, he adds, after thinking it over for a moment, "I want kids who are cynical enough at age four to know that there's something wrong with someone asking them these things and think, 'I'm going to screw with them in the process!'"

I have a strong intuition that eventually my generation will sue their parents for stealing their childhood.

This trajectory prolongs into the kindergarten years. I can't remember the last time I wanted to go to school. When I unclog my crammed memory, I land in the good ol' days of kindergarten. A bit more than two decades ago, Robert Fulghum published a book of whimsical essays called *All I Really Need to Know I Learned in Kindergarten*. An excerpt that caught my interest was, "Too much high-content information, and I get the existential willies. I keep sputtering out at intersections where life choices must be made and I either know too much or not enough. The examined life is no picnic."

He continued, "All I really need to know about how to live and what to do and how to be I learned in kindergarten. Wisdom was not at the top of the graduate school mountain, but there in the sand pile at school." In Fulghum's mind, kindergarten was a harmonious world of wonder, naps, play, and snacks.

When I was in kindergarten and the early grades of elementary school, I didn't feel the full wrath of No Child Left Behind and the testing regime. That world is now extinct. Elementary school is becoming less like a trip to Mister Rogers' Neighborhood and more like a trip to Mister Scantron.

*

Fast forward roughly a decade and say hello to college admissions. The process resembles the presidential election campaign. Kids are going out of their way to impress admissions officers, even to the point of cheating and bluffing their extraordinary feats. Similarly, the campaign season is flush with Pinocchio politicians. And during the summer before college applications are due, the number of Asian tour groups at Ivy League universities and the forums at College Confidential go mad. Similarly, roughly a year before the presidential elections, the media starts literally going apeshit.

No wonder it's toilsome to follow what's going on in the election cycle and in the college admissions process. Think of the college admissions process as teaching your grandmother how to use a computer. You think she's sort of following what's going on, but in reality, she has no freaking clue what's happening. The frenzy over college admissions has proliferated to levels only test preparation company executives could have dreamed of.

Let's add in the shady selection process. In a *Newsweek* exclusive, an admissions officer reveals, "All in all, we're less selective than some of the elite schools or the Ivy League. But there are still some factors out of an applicant's hands. One night, I got food poisoning at a restaurant in Buffalo. The next day, I rejected all the Buffalo applications. I couldn't stomach reading them." Talk about an abuse of power.

In early 2012, I attended a screening of Vicki Abeles' film *Race to Nowhere*, which has been used as a centerpiece for bringing communities together to spark dialogue on how to best prepare young people to become healthy, bright, and contributing citizens. After it was played, a discussion followed and a panelist asked the general audience if college admissions, back when they were students, were as feverish as it is today? Not a single hand was in the air. I chatted with Abeles who said, "If Harvard receives 35,000 applications for a mere 1,640 freshmen spaces, something is clearly amiss in our value system."

There's a laundry list of books dedicated to helping parents survive the process, from *Admission Matters: What Students and Parents Need to Know About Getting into College* to *Crazy U: One Dad's Crash Course in Getting His Kid into College*. Madness at it's finest.

Abeles further asserts, "Childhood has been replaced with résumé-building, and the *joie de vivre* that has historically inspired imagination has been replaced with Tiger Mom-approved tutors and coaches and lessons."

The figure at the center of this college admissions predicament is

Amy Chua, better known as Tiger Mom. She set off a national parenting style war after her disturbing *Wall Street Journal* piece titled, "Why Chinese Mothers Are Superior" was published. The essay has become, as one blogger put it, the "Andromeda Strain of viral buzz" — the online version has been read by millions and has attracted almost 9,000 comments to date. Facebook posts have surpassed hundreds of thousands and the *New York Times* alone ran five articles on the issue in a single week. As described in her piece, Chua doesn't permit her daughters, Sophia and Louisa, to attend sleepovers, have play-dates, participate in school plays, get any grade less than an A, and not be the No. 1 student in every subject except gym and drama. She even threatened to burn Sophia's stuffed animals if she didn't improve on the piano. Overall, Chua runs her household as a microcosm of an autocratic regime. When Sophia acted disrespectfully toward her mother, Chua called her "garbage" in English. But, it was the "Little White Donkey" incident that pushed most readers to their tipping point. When Louisa was seven years old, her mother forced her to play that piano tune for hours on end, without any breaks for water or the bathroom. She went to the extent of threatening her with no lunch, no dinner, no holiday presents, nor any birthday parties for a period of time.

After pouring over the piece, I arrived at a crossroad. Is this woman sarcastic or mentally insane? To my dismay, it was the latter. If I were Louisa, I would ring up Social Services and report Chua as a child abuser. Journalist Betty Ming Liu writes, "Amy Chua is the reason Asian Americans like me are in therapy." One blogger put it bluntly: "Tiger Mom? More like Bat Shit Crazy Mom!" An observer in the *San Francisco Gate* claimed, "Black folks tell 'yo momma' jokes; Asian folks tell 'my momma' jokes." Tiger Moms know how to crucify the fun out of life.

Now what if the mothers of two of America's most successful entrepreneurs, Karen Zuckerberg and Mary Gates, were tiger moms? Mark and Bill definitely wouldn't have dropped out of school and lived their wildest dreams. Without a doubt, we wouldn't have Facebook or Microsoft. Edward Zuckerberg, when speaking of Mark's upbringing, said in a radio interview that an early exposure to computers inspired his son's love for technology. This is his parenting credo: "Probably the best thing I can say is something that my wife and I have always believed in. Rather than impose upon your kids or try and steer their lives in a certain direction, to recognize what their strengths are and support their strengths and support the development of the things they're passionate about." What if Amy Chua adopted such a parenting style? How different would her daughters be today?

The Tiger Mom stigma is a microcosm of many sentiments in the Asian-American population. To better understand the Tiger Mom hysteria, I reached out to an Asian-American — Wesley Yang, a contributing editor to *New York Magazine* and the author of an upcoming book on the race. On a wet day in New York City, I met Yang for lunch in a cozy Sichuan restaurant on Lexington Avenue and had a riveting conversation with him about the Asian American culture. A year earlier, Yang had penned a trilling commentary on the subject, writing, "Let me summarize my feelings toward Asian values: F**k filial piety. F**k grade-grubbing. F**k Ivy League mania. F**k deference to authority. F**k humility and hard work. F**k harmonious relations. F**k sacrificing for the future. F**k earnest, striving middle-class servility."

After dropping a bucket of f-bombs and admonishing certain Asian values such as obedience, he raised a weighty question: "If it is true that they are collectively dominating in elite high schools and universities, is it also true that Asian-Americans are dominating in the real world?" If you go to any Ivy League campus during the scorching hot Northeast summer, you're bound to spot an Asian tour group frolicking through the campus. No joke. Even with affirmative action in place, a fifth of every Ivy League class is Asian. So naturally you'd expect, many of these graduates to go on and become top business executives and renowned scientists of the nation. The numbers tell a different story. "There are nine Asian-American CEOs in the Fortune 500," writes Yang, "In specific fields where Asian-Americans are heavily represented, there is a similar asymmetry. A third of all software engineers in Silicon Valley are Asian, and yet they make up only 6 percent of board members and about 10 percent of corporate officers of the Bay Area's 25 largest companies. At the National Institutes of Health, where 21.5 percent of tenure-track scientists are Asians, only 4.7 percent of the lab or branch directors are, according to a study conducted in 2005."

Consider the example of Tony Hsieh, the founder of Zappos.com, the online shoe retailer that he sold to Amazon for about a billion dollars in 2009. His humble and unorthodox management style coupled with his ability to create a unified culture in his company has proven him to the unlikeliest of management captains.

Hsieh had strict parents. He was expected to get straight A's in all his classes, and was only allowed to watch one hour of TV every week. During weekends and summer vacation, he was supposed to practice his four different musical instruments: piano, violin, trumpet, and French horn for an hour per instrument per day. Still, he managed to find a way to enjoy his weekends and summer vacations. Hsieh would wake up early in the morning, while his parents were sleeping, and go downstairs to where the piano was. Instead of actually playing the piano, he would use a tape recorder and play an hour-long session that he recorded earlier.

However, his passion wasn't music. It wasn't medicine either, even though his parents had urged to him to eventually go to medical school. Hsieh was much more interested in running his own business and figuring out ways to make money. During his elementary school years, he did a lot of garage sales. In middle school, he had a paper route. Then he quit the route, designed his own newsletter, and sold them at five bucks an issue to his friends.

Comically, he convinced his barber to buy a full-page ad in the next issue for $20. Hsieh credits these experiences along with his tenure in running a pizza business at Harvard as more important than anything he learned in class. He had an instinctive sense of what the real world would require of him, and he knew that nothing his parents were teaching him would get him there.

On the other hand, Amy Chua never found a passion. Born to Chinese parents who were raised in the Philippines and attended M.I.T., Chua graduated from Harvard Law School. In her book, *Battle Hymn of the Tiger Mother*, she confessed that as a student, she wasn't naturally skeptical. Chua just wanted to write down everything the professor said and memorize it. It's no surprise that her conformity-based education had failed to prepare her for life. No wonder Chua says that her parenting style was replicating the way she and her three sisters were raised. It's a wicked cycle. "In other words, *Battle Hymn* provides all the material needed to refute the very cultural polemic for which it was made to stand," asserted Yang in that same *New York Magazine* piece.

College admissions has gone haywire. I like how Deborah Stipek, former dean of Stanford University's School of Education, put it in the film *Race to Nowhere*: "For the most part, high school has become for many of our students not preparation for life or college but preparation for the college application."

At my school, I witness too many students in the rat race. The notion that achieving high grades, studying for hours on end, sacrificing sleep, and taking as many Advanced Placement classes as possible guides their thinking.

It's indoctrination from their parents, colleges, and guidance counselors. I wish kids would start doing what they love. I wish they would start caring about the world they live in and stop only doing things that will pad their college applications.

KILL THE SATS

Gaston Caperton, the former president of the College Board, when recruited, said he didn't want to just run a "testing company." In the late 1990s, when facing plunging earnings, the company transformed into a fruitful, money-making powerhouse. They did this by boosting fees, expanding the Advanced Placement program, and pressing colleges to require the SAT for admission.

Now with soaring profits and shameless executive salaries, the supposedly "nonprofit" organization, College Board, has transformed into a monopoly, unethically manipulating students from around the world to no end. For most students to be admitted to an American college or university, he or she must sit for the ludicrous SAT.

In a captivating piece for *DeadSpin*, Drew Magary, who re- took the SAT when he was thirty-five, writes, "There are many shitty things about being a grownup. You have to make money. You have to do taxes. You have to show up for your bail hearings. It's all really f**king annoying. But one of the few upsides of being an adult is that you NEVER have to take the SAT again."

In 1905, five years after the birth of the College Board, a French psychologist and a eugenist, Alfred Binet, invented the IQ, a test that could measure one's intelligence. Ironically, his intent was to identify slow learners by determining their mental ages so they could receive appropriate forms of schooling. A few decades later, Carl Brigham, also an enthusiastic eugenist, invented the SAT.

Eugenicists believed in the innate superiority and inferiority of races on a scale. In his book *A Study of American Intelligence*, Brigham stated his belief in the biological relationship of race and intelligence, concluding that "race mixture," would pollute the gene bank, making the society dumber and weaker. Then, within a gap of five years, he disowned the book, breaking away from the eugenics movement. Unfortunately, it was too late.

James Conant, the president of Harvard University, started using the SAT for scholarship programs, and shortly thereafter the SAT became a tool of the American meritocracy. Nicholas Lemann argues in his book *The Big Test: The Secret History of the American Meritocracy* that the SAT replaced an aristocracy of wealth and breeding with an equally distorted one purportedly based on academic talent, generating a new elite that undermined equal opportunity.

Today, the SAT is one of education's weapons of mass testing.

The first problem is that the SAT fails to measure any type of intelligences. In 1983, Howard Gardner, professor at the Harvard School of Education, penned his famous book *Frames of Mind: The Theory of Multiple Intelligences*. He began it with some simple, yet very powerful questions: "Are talented chess players, violinists, and athletes 'intelligent' in their respective disciplines? Why are these and other abilities not accounted for on traditional IQ tests? Why is the term intelligence limited to such a narrow range of human endeavors?"

From this emerged the multiple-intelligences theory. That includes eight forms of intelligence. First, spatial intelligence is the ability to see dimensionally in space, to be able to turn a drawing on its head and see it in three directions, to understand the globe or a downtown neighborhood as a map. Second, bodily-kinesthetic intelligence is the intelligence of using the body to experience learning. Third, musical intelligence is the capacity to carry a tune, remember musical melodies. Fourth, interpersonal intelligence is the intelligence of effectively engaging with other people.

Fifth, intra-personal intelligence is the ability to understand oneself. Sixth, naturalistic intelligence is the ability to identify a sensitivity to natural forms. Seventh, linguistic intelligence is the ability to use words effectively. Eighth, logical mathematical intelligence is the ability to work well with numbers and be adept at logic or reasoning.

Even though plenty of people like to argue that the SAT taps the previous two intelligences, the SAT does so in a very narrow way, training kids to learn off of a script. Gardner argues that education should cherish each of the intelligences equally and grant children opportunities to develop their individual abilities and talents.

The SAT is a three-fold disaster split into critical reading, mathematics, and writing. The critical reading section is basically a vocabulary test. Those who have memorized the 5,000 recommended vocabulary words are the winners. In a speech to the American Council on Education in February 2001, Richard Atkinson declared, "I visited an upscale private school and observed a class of 12-year-old students studying verbal analogies in anticipation of the SAT. I learned that they spend hours each month — directly and indirectly — preparing for the SAT, studying long lists of verbal analogies such as 'untruthful is to mendaciousness' as 'circumspect is to caution.' The time involved was not aimed at developing the students' reading and writing abilities but rather their test-taking skills."

The mathematics section is basically an atrociously designed logic test. It sure as hell doesn't have any relevance to the math kids will experience in adult life.

And lastly, the writing section is another calamity. Along with the futile grammar section, students are required to write an essay in 25 minutes based on a given prompt.

At Chyten Educational Service centers, students exhaust five, six, up to 12 hours with a tutor, writing, rewriting, and revising an all-purpose SAT essay. On test day, they repeat the essay, word for word, metaphor for metaphor. At New Oriental, Chinese students learn how to game the essay section. Silu Wang, a Beijing teenager, chose Steve Jobs as her preferred subject of her essay. Ironically, she says, "His experience covers a lot of topics. You can always use Steve Jobs." The last thing Jobs would be doing as a teenager would be preparing for the SAT.

The National Council of Teachers of English has objected to the new SAT writing test, partly on the grounds that it will reduce the time students have to write personal essays about themselves. The rubric for the SAT essay is scored by a formula, with graders searching for specific characteristics: transitions, examples, etc. William Fitzhugh, the founder of *The Concord Review*, the only journal in the world for exemplary history essays by high school students, has said, "Writing for a prompt in 25 minutes tells us basically nothing about students' ability to acquire and understand knowledge or to organize their thoughts in a paper. A lot of work was done on this assessment, but I believe the constraints imposed requiring no knowledge and no time for thought or re-writing, make this assessment sadly uninformative about the real academic reading and writing skills of our students.

"The writing sought is almost inconceivably superficial, formulaic, sentimental, solipsistic, boring, and bland," Fitzhugh adds. What's even more appalling is that the SAT essay graders' speed is around 30-35 essays an hour, meaning they spend one to three minutes per essay. Students are at the mercy of the test graders.

As American political scientist Charles Murray writes in *The American*, "The College Board ran from the concept of aptitude as the Florentines fled the plague."

Often, you will hear the argument that the SAT is a good measure of success in life. It's not. Let's review two spectacular pieces of data.

First, in a longitudinal study of 300 Presidential Scholars, the highest scorers on the SAT and the ACT in the nation, Felice Kaufman found that when "the time came to leave the formal education system, these subjects were at a loss." Their inability to find an identity and be happy with who they were stemmed from the subjects' history of an over-reliance on academic skills. Consider these observations from two of her subjects a decade after their high school graduation:

> [I am] finally making time to catch up with human relationships, having not had time to get properly socialized.

And:

> Much of my difficulty in the job-career area comes from (1) school, school, school— when I was little, what I wanted to be when I grew up was to go to college, and (2) my great diversity of interests. It's a hard thing for those of us who were crammed with so many expectations to even know where we stand after ten years. Now, it's time to try new ways.

Second, researchers Stacy Berg Dale and Alan Krueger, studying data on 23,572 students who entered college in 1976, concluded that the character traits students acquire long before they pay their SAT prep-course fees are what determine success in life. The four-digit scores they get on the SAT don't mean much long term.

Many of the disasters in politics and on Wall Street are caused by people who tested very well. No one can forget the former Governor of New York Eliot Spitzer, graduate of Princeton University and holder of a 1590 out of 1600 on his SATs. Spitzer has had a rough time the past few years. In 2008, he resigned as Governor after a prostitution scandal was reported. Then, his CNN show was canceled. And in August 2011, he got sued for a combined $90 million in twin libel suits. The best schools are obviously missing something.

The only thing the SAT measures is your ability to withstand torture.

As the high stakes of the SAT have grown, I was not surprised to hear that a cheating scandal broke at Great Neck North High School, a school a few miles from where I live. Initial observers of the scandal were reinterpreting Captain Renault's line in *Casablanca*: "I'm shocked, shocked to find that gambling is going on in here."

Cheating happens every single day at my school and other schools in the country. A survey of 43,000 high school students in 2010 revealed that 59 percent admitted to cheating on a test during the past year, with 34 percent doing it more than two times. A graduate of Great Neck South High School, Zak Malamed, stuck it to me, "Cheating is not a practice; it's a culture." With our pressure-packed and hyper-competitive, instead of collaborative, school atmosphere, we are raising a generation of Wall Street tycoons and robber barons: nefarious and villainous.

The SAT is a scam. For one, most people wouldn't think the founder of the Princeton Review would agree with that statement. Well, John Katzman does. Frankly, he told me, "Folks who do well on the SAT are so delighted by their good fortune that they don't want to attack it. And they are the people in charge. Because, of course, the way you get to be in charge is by having high test scores; so it's kind of a rolling scam. Every so often, somebody pokes around and says — well, you know, does it measure intelligence? No. Does it predict college grades? No. Does it tell you how much you learned in high school? No. Does it predict life happiness or life success in any measure? No. It measures nothing. Nothing that a high school kid should be measured by."

Later, Katzman gave me his thoughts on the role of college admissions officers, comparing them to casting directors: "It's about choosing a class that's going to work well together. You want men and women. You want blacks and whites — a diverse class. You want people who are great athletes to be on your teams. People who are great journalists to be on your papers. And people who are great actors to be in your drama program. You're building a team. To say to admissions professionals that they have to turn off their judgment and just use this score, this measure of middle-school math and reading — that's all that's important — is making their job a joke." The SAT is more or less a measurement of the size and value of kids' houses.

Furthermore, the test is really old, 1923 old. Please, I don't want to witness a 100-year anniversary party thrown by the College Board goonies.

Imagine the hell that would break loose if we were still administering the medical exams used decades ago. I'd be frightened if I came down with something other than the common cold. As a society, we should also be alarmed that we are using tests of achievements that are roughly the same as those designed a century ago by a lunatic who believed that a mixture of races would ultimately make society dumber.

Still, the current pattern is uplifting. More and more colleges are moving towards an admissions process where sending SAT scores are optional. Richard Atkinson, former president of the University of California, recommended in 2001 that the school system end the SAT requirement for admissions. Since then, as of Summer 2012, nearly 850 colleges and universities have joined the SAT optional list, touting names from Bard College to Drew University to George Mason University. When an Ivy League university trenches onto the list, only then will College Board feel sheer pressure planted on their shoulders.

Let's protest for more colleges and universities to become SAT optional in the admissions process.

ACADEMIC POLLUTION

The way the College Board describes Advanced Placement courses makes me gag:

> From the moment you enter an AP classroom, you'll notice the difference — in the teacher's approach to the subject, in the attitude of your classmates, in the way you start to think. In AP classrooms, the focus is not on memorizing facts and figures. Instead you'll engage in intense discussions, solve problems collaboratively, and learn to write clearly and persuasively. AP courses can help you acquire the skills and habits you'll need to be successful in college. You'll improve your writing skills, sharpen your problem-solving abilities, and develop time management skills, discipline, and study habits.

Fib after fib after fib. The only skill I have learned from taking AP courses is the knack of memorizing efficiently. It seems that the only exercise most high school kids get is iron-pumping: drilling and killing facts and figures. No sleep? You can sleep when you're dead! My peers' goal is to rack up as many A.P. classes and beat out the competition.

The A.P. curriculum is a mile wide and an inch deep. So, teachers are forced to cover ridiculous amounts of material in less than a school year. The courses are crafted to create multi-taskers: students who can read the textbook as efficiently as possible, while doing normal activities.

"By the end of high school, kids are textbook machines," says Richard Cao, a student at Jericho High School, one of the highest ranking high schools in the nation, to me.

Thus, in the frenzy over college admissions, it's not surprising to hear that the number of A.P. exams taken by high school students has more than doubled, to 3.1 million in 2010 from just 1.2 million in 2000. Plus, record numbers of students are failing the tests. More than 850,000 graduates — about 28 percent of the 2010 class— took at least one A.P. exam, nearly double the number a decade ago. But they failed about 44 percent of all exams, compared with 39 percent in 2001. Sadly, Advanced Placement is a contagion, spreading to communities around the country.

Let's examine the A.P. science, history, and calculus courses.

The Campbell A.P. Biology textbook is 1,393 pages and 55 chapters of hell. In all honesty, I wouldn't be surprised if most kids aren't able to carry the eight pound textbook. I only hear groans and a few sobs when kids are handed these gorillas. In A.P. science courses, memorization is not a dirty word. Powerpoint lectures are the norm. Canned laboratory exercises are frequent. Two, three, or even four-hour homework sessions are a reality. A committee of the National Research Council, a part of the National Academy of the Sciences, called attention to these issues in 2002. Slamming the A.P. science courses as a process of cramming excessive loads of information, the committee noted that the courses failed to allow students to design their own lab experiments. The group recommended that in contrary to students passively learning through lectures, "real learning takes place if students spend more time going into greater depth on fewer topics, allowing them to experience problem solving, controversies, and the subtleties of scholarly investigation." Depth over breadth.

When it comes time to scheduling for the next year, guidance counselors, across the land, scream at kids to take A.P. science courses. They believe the courses will help students perform well in college, and suspect that colleges will give them credit if they do well on the exam.

First off, a survey of 18,000 college students enrolled in introductory biology, chemistry, and physics found little evidence that A.P. courses boost college performance in the sciences. College students in this study who had taken A.P. science courses, scored a 5 on the exam, and then took an introductory college course in the same discipline averaged a college grade of only 90, even after the added study at the college level. Students with an A.P. score of 4 averaged 87 in freshman science courses in the same subject; students who scored a 3 averaged 84; and students who took a non-A.P. high school honors course averaged 82. Not surprisingly, the best predictors of success in college science courses were the high school courses that fostered mathematical fluency, valued depth over breadth, and featured laboratory work.

In addition, more of the top universities have ceased giving credit for A.P. courses, especially A.P. Biology. At M.I.T., professors started noticing that students with 5's on their A.P. exams that placed out of introductory courses ended up having difficulty when taking the next course. So the university stopped giving credit and developed their own placement exams.

Recently, after all the heckling from universities, the College Board gave in and "revamped" their biology and U.S. history exams. The biology test attempts to focus on bigger concepts and help kids, in the College Board's words, "think like scientists" through grueling numbers of labs. If you attempt to read the 61-page course framework, keep your head hovering over an ice bucket to prevent yourself from falling asleep. Even though heralded as a major shakeup in the A.P. Biology exam, there are plenty of multiple choice questions splattered across the tests. And the labs are organized like cookbooks with the ingredients, procedures, and the expected results neatly laid out for students. Déjà vu?

A.P. History courses are a marathon to the May exam. The marathon includes memorizing hundreds of years of worthless facts and dates. Even the College Board agrees, writing on its website, "There is little to be gained by rote memorization of names and dates in an encyclopedic manner." But that's exactly what the test is!

Anna Hagadorn, a student who earned a top score of 5 on the A.P. United States History exam, quipped to the *New York Times*, "A lot of A.P. is memorizing timelines." In my A.P. U. S. History class, we raced through the *American Pageant*, an atrociously written, monotonous, and lackluster textbook — a week on the American Revolution, a day on Abraham Lincoln, and 10 minutes on the Great Depression, with nothing on the Harlem Renaissance, the Statue of Liberty, the Vietnam protests, or the Afghanistan War.

Each night, I was typically assigned to read 20 plus textbook pages and take notes, all of which I did without thinking about what I was scribbling in my notebook. The textbook, as exalted by A.P. history teachers, is the holy grail. It's not. It's full of errors and dreary narratives, only an entranced history teacher would appreciate. Only in the rare occasion did we analyze primary sources and secondary sources through books and research papers by historians. You can go through A.P. U.S. History without being required to read the Declaration of Independence or the U.S. Constitution.

Houston, we have a problem.

Then, the other tragedy of A.P. history courses is having no time to compose research papers. "Instead of having research papers, the A.P. program satisfies itself with responses to 'document-based questions,'" says William Fitzhugh, "so A.P. courses are part of the problem in preventing our students from reading nonfiction books and writing serious research papers before they graduate and head off for Upper Education." However, any steps the College Board is taking to revise the course aren't going to work. They plan on packing more material into future examinations.

Rule of thumb: Remain on high alert of any A.P. test changes and never trust the College Board.

College professors and lecturers have caught onto the loathsome effects of A.P. courses. Paul Von Blum, a senior lecturer at UCLA, picked up on the wreckage wrought by A.P. courses quickly. In my conversation with him, Blum explained that an overwhelming majority of his subject matter, that is the history of American social protest, was foreign to his students. "Early on in one of my classes," he said, "I spent an hour and a half giving names of the events and people associated with labor, civil rights, feminist, anti-war, gay and lesbian, environmental, and other resistance movements. In most cases, out of a class of about 250-300, only two or three people in any given case have heard of these figures. At the end of the activity, I ask the class how many students have taken an A.P. history course and generally it's about 90 percent. So I tell them, 'look what we've done, the majority of you don't know any of these figures, yet the majority of you have taken numerous A.P. History courses.' There's a huge disconnect."

Finally, one of the courses the College Board hasn't attempted to revise is A.P. Calculus. The average textbook for the course tops a thousand pages, chock-full of exercises and miserable attempts to make students enjoy calculus. Sorry Wiley, but I lost interest the second I found out the textbook wasn't going to be about bike riding. Shucks!

Like the A.P. courses I have previously mentioned, the A.P. Calculus course is identical in its format, rushing through an ungodly number of topics at lightning speed. I spoke with Professor of Mathematics at Middlebury College, Priscilla Bremser, who raised some deep concerns about the course. She said, "My students tend to remember the efficient ways of calculus computations and it's unclear to me whether they've deeply thought about the underlying concepts. And if they have, they've certainly forgotten them by the time I get them." This is where the failures of rote learning shine the brightest.

In my experience in A.P. Calculus, I didn't gain a fundamental understanding of calculus nor learn how to apply the techniques to solve difficult problems. Instead, I was forced to complete repeated examples of solving essentially the same problem over and over again. In plainest terms, a typical homework assignment was: solve numbers 1-25 odd on page 1033.

That's not learning. Bremser explains to me, "Having used their A.P. credits to get into Middlebury, a number of our students try to take calculus again, saying, 'I know I got a 5 on the exam, but I didn't really understand it.' I know this genie is out of the bottle, but I would rather teach calculus to a student with solid algebra skills and no A.P. experience than to one who took calculus too soon."

In sum, the Advanced Placement program seems as if it was set up to fail. Bluntly, Paul Von Blum, said, "A.P. participation, for many, is primarily an exercise in memorization and exam passing the antithesis of genuine liberal learning." We don't need a label — A.P. — to challenge students and provide them with a rich 21st century skill-set. Every school that has adopted the A.P. program should abolish it. Scarsdale High School, a well-off public school in New York, known for feeding into top universities, phased out the program, replacing mountains of memorization with creative, unique curriculums. A number of my friends who attend Scarsdale say they enjoy school much more without the program. Other prestigious schools like Dalton, Calhoun, and Fieldston have done the same. Will more schools follow suit?

THE WAR ON COLLEGE BOARD

The SAT and the Advanced Placement program are both under the umbrella of the College Board, a "not-for-profit" organization. They just so happen to post revenues topping half a billion bucks. College Board's president David Coleman, who succeeded Gaston Caperton in May 2012, will earn a base salary of $550,000 with total compensation of nearly $750,000. Why isn't Congress grilling these test company executives for their unethical behaviors?

I don't know a student who supports the College Board. Let's cut off their oxygen supply — the endless flow of SAT and A.P. registration fees. Without a healthy flow of cash inundating their Upper West Side office building, the fat cats will be bankrupt. As John Katzman put it, "It blows me away that we have trusted the College Board for so long."

We will disrupt, dismantle, and defeat the College Board.

PROJECT KALEIDOSCOPE

As a young child in the 1950s, Robert Sternberg scored poorly on IQ tests and was dubbed a loser by his teachers. "As a result of my low scores, my teachers thought I was stupid, and I did too," says Sternberg. "They never came out and told us our IQ scores, but one could tell from the way teachers acted. In first grade, I was a mediocre student, which made my teachers happy because they got what they expected. I in turn was happy that they were happy, and in the end, everyone was quite happy. By second grade, I was slightly worse as a student, and in third grade, still worse."

The man who got a "C" in psychology in college would go on to be elected president of the American Psychological Association (APA) and become a leading cognitive psychologist at Yale, Tufts, and Oklahoma State. Truth is, he wasn't the only president of the association to have received a "C" in the introductory psychology course. His predecessor at APA, Phil Zimbardo, now professor emeritus at Stanford, also received a "C." Zimbardo nevertheless went on to become one of the most famous psychologists in the world, known especially for the "Stanford prison experiment," in which he showed how a simulated prison experiment could turn ordinary college students into people who thought and acted like sadistic prison guards and dehumanized prisoners.

Since then, Sternberg has argued that college admissions have relied too heavily on standardized tests like the SAT and ACT. The system he advocates is called the augmented theory of successful intelligence, which is the ability to succeed in life. This involves three components of intelligence: analytical, creative, and practical.

In terms of college admissions, he raised two penetrating questions in his book *College Admissions for the 21st Century*: "Why is academic skill as important as we make it out to be? If college grades are so important to success, why are top graduates thirty years later often not those who received the highest academic honors?"

The bottom line is that there is no simple formula for success.

As dean of Tufts University, Sternberg put his mojo into practice, instituting Project Kaleidoscope, which aimed to assess applicants on various attributes. For the class of 2017 admissions, students could choose to pen an essay on postulates, laws, and theories, like the Ninth Commandment, $PV=nRT$, Occam's Razor, and others; respond to a Dr. Seuss quote in any medium; or determine your senior superlative. The admissions raters were trained to use specific criteria in assessing responses via rubrics.

Roughly two-thirds of prospective students opted to complete the supplement. As a result, Kaleidoscope has proved most helpful, Sternberg said. In the first year of its implementation, for the Class of 2011, Tufts admitted 30 percent more African Americans and 15 percent more Latinos than the year before. Today, people of color represent about 26 percent of the undergraduate student body of 5,000.

"Our society needs citizens and leaders who are creative, practical, and especially, wise; not just those who are good memorizers and are analytically adept. One way to find and develop such citizens and leaders is to emphasize in college admissions the importance of the broad range of skills that leads to an informed and educated citizenry," says Sternberg to me. "If you look at the fiasco that constituted the debt-ceiling agreement in August 2011, you may see why we need such individuals. Legislators had difficulty formulating a compromise that was creative, practical, and wise. In the end, they formulated a compromise that was none of the three."

While the Kaleidoscope isn't a silver bullet for shaping college admissions, it's an undertaking in the right direction. A remodeled college admissions process is holistic. First, it includes an alternative to the SAT, like the College and Work Readiness Assessment (CWRA), the Collegiate Learning Assessment (CLA), or the iSkills exam. Second, college admissions should require a portfolio of a students' work, whether it be papers, videos, or various projects that documents learning over a period of time. Third, Sternberg's Kaleidoscope Project shouldn't be optional, but a requirement. Fourth, an interview should be mandatory. Interviews reveal much more than any assessment can ever hope to achieve. Those who communicate well will shine. Lastly, throw in extracurricular activities, work experience, community service, and there you go, a remodeled college admissions process.

Overall, these changes will not cost much money, but it will create colleges of organic, rather than standardized, students.

PLASTICS

College was never meant for the masses. In 1940, fewer than five percent of Americans had a college degree. Going to college was "a privilege reserved for the brightest or the most affluent" high-school graduates, wrote Diane Ravitch in her book *The Troubled Crusade* on the history of U.S. education. You went to college to become a professional — a doctor, a lawyer, a teacher. Now, in the eyes of society, college is the only option. Roughly 40 percent of Americans have some kind of college degree with 30 percent of adults 25 and older having at least a bachelor's degree. Still, the country has slipped in global rankings of college completion among young adults to 16th among 36 developed countries. President Obama pledged to retake the lead by 2020. Time and time again, policymakers are missing the mark.

"A diploma wasn't a piece of paper. It was an amulet," writes *New York Times* columnist Frank Bruni. The college degree used to be a one way shot to the top. If you didn't go, you didn't fare too well. Until the early 1970s, less than 11 percent of the adult population graduated from college, and most them could get a decent job. Today, nearly a third have a college degree and the degree no longer has that Midas Touch.

In the classic scene from the famous 1967 film *The Graduate*, Dustin Hoffman's character Benjamin, a hot off the press college graduate, receives some voluntary career advice from a smug Los Angeles businessman at a graduation party around the family pool. "I want to say one word to you. Just one word...Are you listening?" the man asks. Benjamin nods yes. "Plastics."

One of the most dangerous things I was taught in school is that the path to success is simple — get more education under your belt. I find it hilarious to watch the reactions from Tiger mothers and helicopters parents when I say I have doubts whether I want to go college or not. It seems like I attacked their livelihood.

Why are many kids queasy about getting admitted into "their" school? The college admissions process is painted in a very glossy light. On campus tours, I was wowed by newly renovated dormitories, luxurious gyms, and cozy libraries. Days after I visited a college, I was bombarded with countless emails and letters that literally made me feel fuzzy and warm inside. I cannot imagine a student not wanting to go to that school after that experience. No one will discourage your obsession — parents, guidance counselors, teachers, peers. Going to college is a social expectation.

But as Frank Bruni points out to me, "Given that some students approach college principally as a pivot into a dependable job with a good income, we need to ask if we're doing well enough at steering them down the most advantageous paths." Too many kids are going to college. Too many kids are wasting precious time and money for a piece of paper that will not get them a job and burden them for life.

DEBT SLAVES

Kevin Wanek appeared shocked when his latest student loan bill came in the mail. Another $600 this month. Wanek is a computer programmer at iTriage, a mobile healthcare application maker in Denver, Colorado. When he dropped out of Western State College with just a semester to go, he owed more than $65,000 in student loan debt. Wanek came to the realization that he didn't want to spend the rest of his life being an accountant; he loved computers.

"When I matriculated into college, I didn't realize how much debt I was going to be in. I just knew I had to go to college and graduate and that was it," said Wanek to me. He now plans on going back to college to finish his degree in computer science instead.

Wanek is one of thousands of college graduates and dropouts helplessly stuck in the vortex of student loan debt. They cannot escape from it. The cost of public university tuition is about 3.6 times higher than it was 30 years ago, adjusted for inflation. For the first time, outstanding student loans have surpassed $1 trillion, more than credit card debt. About two-thirds of bachelor's degree recipients borrow money to attend college, either from the government or private lenders, according to a survey of 2007-2008 graduates; the total number of borrowers is most likely higher since the survey does not track borrowing from family members. For all borrowers, the average debt in 2011 was $23,300, with 10 percent owing more than $54,000 and 3 percent more than $100,000. Average debt for bachelor degree graduates who took out loans ranges from under $10,000 at elite schools like Princeton University and Williams College, which have plenty of wealthy students and large endowments, to nearly $50,000 at some private colleges with less affluent students and less financial aid.

Zac Bissonnette, a financial journalist and author, tweeted, "Just got an email about someone who is borrowing $80,000 for a degree in, I kid you not, 'Poverty Studies.'" After graduation, this person will definitely have some first-hand experience with this field.

Colleges could care less about rising costs. "I readily admit it," said E. Gordon Gee, the president of Ohio State University, to the *New York Times*. "I didn't think a lot about costs. I do not think we have given significant thought to the impact of college costs on families."

The debt cycle never ends. Guy McPherson, professor at the University of Arizona, asserted in the documentary *The College Conspiracy*, "You get your degree. You get out of school. You bought a house, because culture drives you to. Now, you're in debt. You have to work. You have to be part of the wage slave economy for the next 20 or 30 years until the house is paid off. These days, college is the new house. And you don't even get the house. As soon as you get out of school, you're indentured for life." This is the modern industrial slave complex — graduates are mortgaging their freedom in exchange for a piece of paper. As Jim O'Neill and Michael Gibson of the Thiel Foundation write, "If college is an insurance policy, then maybe it was issued by AIG."

The parallels between the housing bubble and college debt are striking. According to an analysis by *The Atlantic*, "If you add together mortgages and revolving home equity, then from the first quarter of 1999 to when housing-related debt peaked in the third quarter of 2008, the sum increased from $3.28 trillion to $9.98 trillion. Over this period, housing-related debt had increased threefold." Meanwhile, from the first quarter of 1999 to the first quarter of 2011, the balance of student loans grew by more than six times, with no immediate signs of slowing down.

However, there's still a major difference. In the case of a homeowner defaulting on their mortgage, the bank can seize and sell the home. In the case of student loans, the bank can't sell the college degree. If you look at the fine print of student loan law, it says the loans aren't "dischargable." Therefore, even if you file for bankruptcy, the payments continue due. Thus these grim words from Barmak Nassirian of the American Association of College Registrars and Admissions Officers. "You will be hounded for life," he warns. "They will garnish your wages. They will intercept your tax refunds. You become ineligible for federal employment." He adds that any professional license can be revoked and Social Security checks docked when you retire. There's nothing like this. There's no exit.

Peter Thiel, the founder of Paypal, who spearheaded the belief that a college bubble exists, says to *TechCrunch*, "A true bubble is when something is overvalued and intensely believed. Education may be the only thing people still believe in in the United States. To question education is really dangerous. It is the absolute taboo. It's like telling the world there's no Santa Claus."

Thiel adds, "Like the housing bubble, the education bubble is about security and insurance against the future. Both whisper a seductive promise into the ears of worried Americans: Do this and you will be safe. The excesses of both were always excused by a core national belief that no matter what happens in the world, these were the best investments you could make. Housing prices would always go up, and you will always make more money if you are college educated."

No one throws down hundreds of thousands to read Plato and Shakespeare. From diapers to boxers, we've been sold on the premise that if you work hard and got a college degree, you would get a one-way ticket to success. That is how schools brainwash you into getting hundreds of thousands of dollars into debt.

How can we as a society entrust 18-year-olds to decide whether to be a debt slave for the rest of their lives? As College Humor exclaimed in their video, "Student Loan STD's," "Always use protection when you're screwing yourself."

Evaluating the merits of education without considering costs is like saying, "But aside from that, Mrs. Lincoln, how did you like the play?"

4 YEAR PARTY

We are paying too much and learning too little. If the mission of college education is for students to learn, it is certainly not doing its job. In their book, *Academically Adrift: Limited on College Campuses*, sociology professors at the University of Chicago, Richard Arum and Josipa Roksa, paint a gloomy portrait of post-secondary education in the United States. Citing data from student surveys and transcript analysis, tracking academic gains from 2,300 students of traditional college age enrolled at the range of four-year colleges and universities, and combining that with students' results on the Collegiate Learning Assessment (CLA), a depressing conclusion was reached. 45 percent of students "did not demonstrate any significant improvement in learning" during the first two years of college, as well as 36 percent of students over four years of college. And the students who did show improvement tended to show only modest improvement.

Why? They found that large numbers of the students were making their way through college with minimal exposure to rigorous coursework, only a modest investment of effort and little or no meaningful improvement in skills like writing and reasoning. In a typical semester, for instance, 32 percent of the students did not take a single course with more than 40 pages of reading per week, and 50 percent did not take any course requiring more than 20 pages of writing over the semester. The average student spent only about 12 to 13 hours per week studying — about half the time a full-time college student in 1960 spent studying.

"The problem is that for twelve years, we've chained kids to desks and forced them to sit through boring lectures," says James Altucher, hedge fund manager and author of *40 Alternatives to College*. "So it's natural to continue that in college. The real world is uncomfortable and scary."

In 2007, the University of Connecticut conducted a survey of 14,000 college students at 50 colleges nationwide asking them questions about America's history, government, relationship with the world, and the "market economy." Brown, Yale, Williams and M.I.T. are four of 16 colleges where freshmen scored higher than seniors. Students literally lost knowledge.

I'd assume the most popular majors in college include partying, drinking, having sex, and doing drugs — clearly worth hundreds of thousands of dollars of your parents' savings. As a whole, the situation embodies the relationship between students and colleges — students are consumers and clients of colleges. In 1972, the *Journal of Higher Education* published an article in which the author wrote: "It doesn't matter what it's called, who's doing it or where in the institution — it's already happened: universities have entered the marketplace." As a result, grade inflation is rampant. In college, about 43 percent of all letter grades given were A's, an increase of 28 percentage points since 1960, another study found.

College has a consumer-based model, where institutions are pressured to reap massive profits. To keep their balance sheets flowing merrily, many institutions have begun to use hard-sell, Super Bowl-like advertisements to attract students. They sell college like beer (ironically), promoting perks students pine over: tricked-out gyms with indoor waterfalls, gourmet dining, free movie screenings and free skiing. Yet, college remains an uncontested part of the American meritocracy.

YOU'RE SCREWED

Sarah Weinstein is finishing up the last leg of her three-day, 935 mile road trip from Atlanta, Georgia to Austin, Texas. She's on her way to her graduate school at the University of Texas at Austin, where she will be majoring in advertising with a focus on strategy and planning.

Four years earlier, Weinstein had just graduated from Boston University with a degree in creative advertising. From freshmen year of college, she expected that she would have a high-paying job in advertising waiting for her when she got her diploma. There weren't any. So, for the next few years, Weinstein exhausted her time in a number of positions outside her field of expertise.

"In that period, I was part of a graphic design collective with some friends, bartended in a bar in Austin, worked at an email marketing company, and later labored as the PR manager for Austin Pets Alive, an animal rescue shelter, as a volunteer position," says Weinstein. She was constantly shuffling from job to job. After three years of frustration without an advertising job, Weinstein finally decided to apply to graduate school in an effort to "freshen up her résumé."

The idea of college has been oversold. After college graduation, most people didn't expect they would be in low-end occupations. The stories are quite familiar. The math major sweeps the floors at a Fortune 500 company. The literature major waits tables at Friendly's. The philosophy major flips burgers at Wendy's. These students are part of what the *New York Times* calls Generation Limbo: "highly educated 20-somethings, whose careers are stuck in neutral, coping with dead-end jobs and list-less prospects." Like Sarah Weinstein, they did everything they were supposed to — listened to their parents, got in college, and graduated. But now, many are living day-to-day, trying to pay their rent, student loans, and other necessities, sometimes even resorting to government freebies.

More than 5,000 janitors have PhDs. And scores of college graduates are flipping burgers at McDonald's. Over 317,000 waiters and waitresses have college degrees (over 8,000 of them have doctoral or professional degrees), along with over 80,000 bartenders, and over 18,000 parking lot attendants. Something is not right.

With that being said, it was not surprising to hear that the median starting salary for students graduating from four-year colleges in 2009 and 2010 was $27,000, down from $30,000 for those who entered the work force in 2006 to 2008. That is a decline of 10 percent, even before taking inflation into account. Also, the median earnings of people 25 to 34 years old with a bachelor's degree and no graduate degree declined 9.6 percent from 2000 to 2010, adjusted for inflation. When I reveal these numbers to people, most reply, 'Everything will be better when the recovery is over. Don't worry. Trust me.' No, I will not trust you. Companies are doing more with less. Automation, outsourcing, and digitization are screwing up the entire labor market. The middle jobs are being hollowed out, inch by inch until they are all replaced by machines, foreigners, and computers. Even worse, the U.S. Bureau of Labor Statistics was reporting that only 5 of the 20 jobs projected to grow fastest over the coming decade would require a bachelor's degree.

The data is alarming. In April 2012, the *Associated Press* reported that one in two college graduates are jobless or underemployed, the highest share in 11 years. In May 2012, the U.S. Bureau of Labor Statistics found that for the first time ever, a majority of the unemployed have attended college. And a report in the *Chronicle of Higher Education* found that the number of people with graduate degrees who have had to apply for food stamps, unemployment, or other assistance tripled from 2007 to 2010. Yikes to all three!

Thus far, no guidance counselor, teacher, or parent has warned me of these statistics. No one told me the cold hard truth. Either they don't know the reality of the situation or they are denying it. In the past century, college has always been a part of the American Dream. The emerging college bubble is strikingly similar to the Catholic Church selling indulgences, a full or partial remission of temporal punishment due for sins, centuries ago. The public sacrificed themselves over the false promise of the institutions.

Still, I have heard plenty of arguments in support of a college degree. First, since the unemployment rate for college graduates is much lower than those who only completed a high school diploma, you should go. Again, that argument does not account for the underemployed graduates — the 17 million Americans with college degrees working in fields that don't require their degree. The reality is much bleaker.

Second, a common argument I'm presented with is that a person with a bachelor's degree will earn 84 percent more over a lifetime than a person with only a high school diploma. An online salary ranking system called PayScale.com calculates a student's 30-year return on investment at the top 1,300 colleges nationwide based on average alumni salary and tuition costs. Their issued 2012 report suggests that out of the 4,500 colleges and universities in the nation, only the top 800 to 850 give you an annual return on investment greater than four percent. As former U.S. Secretary of Education William Bennett writes, "In pure financial terms, students might be better off investing their tuition money in stocks rather than four years with one of our nation's many colleges."

Why is the value of the degree dropping? The problem is that we have an overflow. Dale Stephens, founder of UnCollege, said to me, "A college degree isn't a ticket to success because so many people are going to college. A bachelor's degree is now the equivalent of a high school diploma."

As James F. Cooper once exclaimed, "All greatness of character is dependent on individuality. The man who has no other existence than that which he partakes in common with all around him, will never have any other than an existence of mediocrity." Putting that into context, if you have a college degree and you can't answer the question: What makes you special?, then you are just one of the millions of carbon-copies like yourself.

Why do people become so defensive when you criticize the value of a college degree? No one wants to be told that they wasted hundreds of thousands of dollars and four years of their youth on crap.

Right now, you're probably getting the vibe that I'm against college. I'm not.

There are some important caveats to mention. If you aspire to be a doctor, a lawyer, or a public school teacher, it is mandatory that you attend college. I would include engineer, Wall Street titan, and politician on that list as well.

Which college should you attend? Look for a college that offers you a high annualized net R.O.I. Over the past decade, research has determined that college graduates earn roughly more than $1 million over their working life than high school graduates. However, new research debunks such claims. From a study conducted by PayScale, there are only 17 schools whose graduates can expect to recoup the cost of their education and out-earn a high school graduate by $1.2 million, including four where they can reach $1.6 million. If you have the opportunity to study at an Ivy League school, M.I.T., Stanford, Caltech, Harvey Mudd, University of Notre Dame, Duke, Lehigh, Union College, Amherst, Worcester Polytechnic, UCLA, or the University of Chicago, go ahead. I would add the top 10 colleges for your major to that list as well. While the likelihood that you will engage with the world is slim, you will graduate with stronger job prospects, phenomenal networking, and access to the best professors in the world.

Virtually no one, however, is asking the question: What if you aren't planning to go into one of those professions and aren't matriculating into a highly prestigious university?

Pick your major wisely. Unemployment rates are generally higher in non-technical majors, such as the Arts, Humanities and Liberal Arts, Social Science, and Law and Public Policy. From the colleges I suggested you attend, there is only one lonely, purely liberal arts college — Amherst.

If your passion is in liberal arts, you will need to do some long, hard thinking. Altucher asserted, "Every book you will need in a liberal arts course is found in the library. Why go $200,000 in debt?" With the Internet, you can access course videos and forums where the material is discussed. If you prefer to engage in person, join Skillshare and General Assembly classes and discussion seminars and find mentors and like-minded people.

There is an old joke that goes something like this:

The engineering graduate asks, "How will it work?"
The physics graduate wants to know, "Why does it work?"
And the liberal arts graduate asks, "Do you want fries with that?"

However, that is not to say that the knowledge from these liberal arts classes is useless. The study of liberal arts is about connecting the dots. A liberal arts education is a fresh prism to look at the world. It is what Albert Einstein called "the training of the mind to think something that cannot be learned from textbooks." Remember, Steve Jobs's experience in his calligraphy class at Reed College (before dropping out) later propelled him to create the Mac typography.

In short, the humanities are a critical wellspring of America's creative capital. These are the building blocks of innovation. But where does this come from? Marc Tucker, the president of the National Center on Education and the Economy, said to the *New York Times*, "One thing we know about creativity is that it typically occurs when people who have mastered two or more quite different fields use the framework in one to think afresh about the other. Intuitively, you know this is true. Leonardo da Vinci was a great artist, scientist and inventor, and each specialty nourished the other. He was a great lateral thinker. But if you spend your whole life in one silo, you will never have either the knowledge or mental agility to do the synthesis, connect the dots, which is usually where the next great breakthrough is found."

David Brooks, *New York Times* columnist, writes, "In an information economy, many people have the ability to produce a technical innovation: a new MP3 player. Very few people have the ability to create a great brand: the iPod. Branding involves the location and arousal of affection, and you can't do it unless you are conversant in the language of romance." I notice so many math and science geeks bottled up in their research, unable to ever make an extraordinary breakthrough, because they have never attempted to look beyond their subject matter. The humanities, alone, do not necessarily lead to national economic advancement, but when married with science and technology, ingenious wonders are produced.

Thus, students who desire to pursue the liberal arts should think twice about going to college. Rather than listening to lectures, reading textbooks and regurgitating on exams, students should learn by doing through apprenticeships, projects, traveling, and volunteering. End this notion of a liberal arts degree. Portfolios should rule. That's how we need to re-imagine liberal arts for the 21st century.

As Sarah Weinstein pulls onto the University of Texas at Austin campus, she tells me that the road trip may very well be a metaphor of her life. "The trip from Atlanta to Austin is a 17 hour drive, which can be completed in two days, but I stretched it over three days, so I could make some interesting stops along the way," says Weinstein.

I ended our conversation with the question, "When you graduate from graduate school, do you expect a high-paying advertising job?" Weinstein replied with a chuckle, "Hopefully."

THE DOERS

If you don't go to college, it isn't the end of the world, folks. The media has presented the success stories of college dropouts or those who didn't go to college in terms of the outliers — Steve Jobs, Bill Gates, and Mark Zuckerberg. There are many more people than just them.

I want to share with you a few stories of four change-makers who have jailbroken their education and are disrupting their respective spaces. They either dropped out of college or never went.

The first is a story of Natalie Warne. Born in an underserved part of Chicago, Warne was raised in a hard-working family. In her teens, her family of five was forced to move from city to city to find work. Attending four high schools in four years, Warne was no stranger to challenge.

In high school, she got good grades and was a typical student.

"When I woke up every morning," says Warne, "I didn't have this sense of purpose to do incredible things, because I needed to get to my math class or finish my A.P. Government homework. That was just my life."

Then her life changed.

"In my senior year of high school, I learned about the plight of child soldiers in East Africa through the film *Invisible Children*," she says. "I asked myself, 'What can I do to help?' That was my 'ah ha' moment. I realized that my life didn't have to be planned out for me — go to high school, go to college, get a career, get married, have kids. My life could have a purpose."

"I was planning on going to a random college. But after seeing the film and talking with my parents, I decided to take some time off between high school and college. I moved to California and started working for *Invisible Children*. *Invisible Children* made me work harder than I had ever worked in my entire life." Warne has never looked back and does not plan to go college anymore.

At age 21, Warne has traveled the planet with *Invisible Children*, has been featured on the Oprah Winfrey show, and has given a TEDx talk that has received hundreds of thousands of views.

"It is the acts that make us extraordinary, not the Oprah moments."

The second case is a story of two entrepreneurs: 17-year-old Paul Henry and 16-year-old Alaxic Smith from Texas. Smith founded Community, which is creating communities of like-minded individuals in order to facilitate interactions with the each other. Henry has worked with Smith on various startups since 2009.

Both Smith and Henry leveraged their curiosity early on. Smith says, "When I was younger, I wanted to be an orthopedic surgeon, because my grandmother has arthritis. Until last year, she was afraid to get her knee replaced. Then in seventh grade, I saved up enough to get an iPod Touch. I went on YouTube and I saw a video of somebody jail-breaking it. I thought it was cool and I wanted to do something like that. I didn't know how, so I used all the freebie websites to do it. Then I realized that there must be something more to this and started to design and later learned HTML."

On the other hand, Henry explained, "I've been home-schooled since third grade. My parents were fairly supportive of me. When I was 12, I took two college computer science courses. I don't have much academic potential, but I have real world experience. For instance, I mentored in a high school robotic team, which went to the national competition."

I must mention, not surprisingly, they both detest school. Smith voices his concerns, saying, "I hate being stuck in this generic, everyone-fits-the-same-mold model. You have to learn this, this, and this, no matter what you enjoy and what you hope your future career will be."

Henry was recently hired as an engineer at Silicon Valley-based startup Wanelo. Both Smith and Henry are affecting their industry at such young ages, yet they haven't even graduated from college.

The third story is of Joichi Ito. Named by *BusinessWeek* as one of the

25 Most Influential People on the Web in 2008, Ito is currently the Director of the M.I.T Media Lab. Note: he's a college drop-out.

I sat down with Ito in his sleek office bathed in sunlight on the second floor of the lab in early April. Indeed, he first attended Tufts University, where he studied computer science, but loathed the drudge work and left. Later he attended the University of Chicago, where he studied physics. Again he didn't like the way he was taught.

Ito explains, "In physics, I liked to understand things intuitively, so I asked my professor to explain the solution to a problem in that manner. He said, 'You can't understand it intuitively. Just learn the formula so you'll get the right answer.' That was it for me."

"I was spoiled. Work should be fun. I had no tolerance of people, activities, and things that didn't interest me. I wasn't motivated to do the work, so I left."

At age 23, he found himself in Chicago and a University of Chicago dropout. Where did he go next? The most unlikely place — the nightclub. He became a disk jockey and an occasional bartender. Describing the nightclub scene, Ito reveals, "Club owners and gangsters came together. I learned a great deal just working and hanging out there. I realized that in comparison with the hyper-competitive club of over-achievers at school, these people were much more socially smart."

Eventually, Ito's mother told him it was time to get a real job and Ito went on to found countless companies and become a venture capitalist years later. Still, the street and social smarts he gained at the nightclub and his other endeavors shaped his life and career. Who would ever predict that a college dropout would become a director in a prestigious university?

All four of these people have done remarkable things all without graduating from college. There are so many like them. Anyone can become a self-directed learner.

Author and entrepreneur Seth Godin argues in Michael Ellsberg's book *The Education of Millionaires*, "Let's say you got into Harvard and didn't go. That's a better story than you got into Harvard and you did go. And a much cheaper story. And it takes four less years! I imagine some kid sending a copy of her acceptance letter to Harvard, along with a copy of her letter declining it, and saying to a potential employer, 'Here's what I did with the four years instead. I have the brains to get into Harvard, and I have the initiative to get a Harvard-quality education on my own, and I think outside the box. Hire me.'"

"Street" credibility is trouncing the college degree. If you told college students that they wouldn't get that lovely piece of paper at graduation, the campus would be a ghost town the next day.

I spoke with Michael Karnjanaprakorn, the co-founder of the New York-based company, Skillshare, on the current changes in higher education. Skillshare is a marketplace of classes to learn anything (e.g. cooking, fashion, programming) from teachers in your community. Eric Mazur, professor of physics at Harvard University, tells me, "Harvard is Harvard not because of the buildings, not because of the professors, but because of the students interacting with one another." Skillshare classes finally fill that social experience gap which online classes lack and create a space for a tribe of individuals that Harvard and other colleges have always provided.

Karnjanaprakorn says, "What we're witnessing is a bottom-up revolution in education: Learners, not institutions, are leading innovation. There's a huge issue that's preventing life-long learners from blossoming into our next generation of highly skilled and employed workers: There's no accreditation process for self-taught learners. The fact is, students are taking responsibility for their own learning and classrooms can be anywhere at anytime these days. From Khan Academy to MIT's OpenCourseWare, educational resources, data, and technology are becoming more accessible than ever. Formal learning environments are crumbling, and learners are finding their own paths to knowledge through independent thinking and experience in the real world."

Make the learning that happens outside of the institution a part of school.

On his popular blog, Godin asks a simple question with razor-sharp insight: "Does a $40,000 a year education that comes with an elite degree deliver ten times the education of a cheaper but no less rigorous self-generated approach assembled from less famous institutions and free or inexpensive resources?"

Karnjanaprakorn adds, "The education paradigm of the future is all about the doers, not the academics or theorists. A paper degree doesn't matter." You have to make yourself stand out.

Imagine if we use the power of the Internet, Skillshare classes, internships, apprenticeships, French salons, libraries, and cities to replace college.

As Eartha Kitt once said, "I am learning all the time. The tombstone will be my diploma." Be immersed in the chaos.

So ask yourself: What if I didn't go?

CHAPTER 5
INNOVATE OR DIE

All children are born artists,
the problem is to remain an artist as we grow up.

PABLO PICASSO

When you innovate, you've got to be prepared
for people telling you that you are nuts.

LARRY ELLISON

Every time I hear a performance at Lincoln Center, attend a TEDx conference, or stroll through Times Square, I get goosebumps along my arms. Feeling the vibrant energy of the people around me, I am constantly reminded of America's greatest asset: the pure creative and entrepreneurial spirit when you mix diverse people with an atmosphere of creativity. Something truly magical happens. Today, all economic value derives from the ability to be creative — shattering the status quo, sparking new ideas, and connecting the dots.

We throw around the words imagination, creativity, and innovation, oftentimes mistaking one for another. First, imagination is thinking of an idea at any given time. Creativity takes it a step further. *Newsweek* defines creativity as: "To be creative requires divergent thinking (generating many unique ideas) and then convergent thinking (combining those ideas into the best result)." One famous definition of creativity is "the process of destroying one's gestalt in favor of a better one." Innovation is applying creativity by turning new ideas into reality.

Creativity and imagination should be nurtured from the moment we take our first breaths. However, for the first time in decades, research shows that American creativity levels are declining. Scores on a historically accurate creativity assessment fell steadily from 1990 to 2008, especially in the kindergarten through sixth-grade age group. Why? One answer lies in the spike of standardized tests in schools, especially at a young age.

The finding was discovered in 2010 by Kyung Hee Kim at the College of William & Mary, after analyzing roughly 300,000 Torrance Tests of Creative Thinking scores of children and adults. The Torrance test, designed by E. Paul Torrance in 1958, measures creativity levels through a series of discrete tasks in 90 minutes. Ted Schwarzrock, an eight-year-old third grader who completed the test in 1958, remembers the moment when a psychologist handed him a fire truck and asked, "How could you improve this toy to make it better and more fun to play with?"

Unlike the SAT for example, there is never one right answer in the Torrance assessment. "They don't feel like tests," says Bonnie Cramond, a University of Georgia professor in the educational psychology department and a research fellow at the Torrance Center, to a reporter. "As opposed to written intelligence exams, the Torrance Tests don't ask questions that inherently exclude some students. For instance, a question about a regatta might make sense to a student from Savannah (Georgia) — and no sense to someone else. The Torrance Tests are blind to culture; they can be given to a kindergartner or a grad student." Kids are encouraged to comprehend the problems, generate a flood of ideas, and invent practical solutions. In fact, Jonathan Plucker of Indiana University recently reanalyzed Torrance's data, finding that the correlation to lifetime creative accomplishment was more than three times stronger for childhood creativity than childhood IQ.

Now, you might be thinking "So what?" Just wait, there's more. In 1992, we were snoozing when the book *Breakpoint and Beyond* by George Land and Beth Jarman revealed a troubling, front-page *New York Times*-worthy study. 1,500 kindergarteners between three and five years old were given a divergent thinking test. The results were mind-blowing. 98 percent of kindergarteners were classified as geniuses at divergent thinking. As noted prior, when we combine divergent thinking with convergent thinking, we can get a sense of creativity. Here comes the calamitous news. After five years of formal education, only 50 percent of children tested at genius level. By age ten, 32 percent remain and at age 15, 10 percent remain. When they tested 200,000 adults, only 2 percent were considered divergent thinkers. George Land concluded that "non-creative behavior is learned." Bingo.

You don't need numbers to prove this. Go to any kindergarten classroom. If you ask them to raise their hand if they think they are creative, every kid's hand will be up in the air. Go to a first grade class. Repeat. Three fourths of the kids will raise their hands. Go to a second grade class. Repeat. About half of the kids in the class this time. Go to a third grade class (typically when standardized testing is in full gear). Repeat. At best, a third of the class will raise a hand. Continue this until you ask a group of adults who have graduated from a post-secondary institution. I would be dumbfounded if more than a few people raised their hands. Here's the bottom line: schools kill creativity. The question of how to teach creativity will be addressed fully in chapter six.

Why is the public oblivious to the crisis? Cody Pomeranz, sophomore at Yale University, tells me, "Too few people recognize the value of imagination compared to test scores, and even fewer act on that recognition."

I typically hear the rebuttal, "Not everyone can be Steve Jobs or Mark Zuckerberg" and "Only a few are creative." People seem to believe that creativity is a magic, only given to the lucky ones born with it. It's not. There's no such thing as a "creative type," because simply, all kids are creative. All kids are creative. If we can maintain a majority of the population at the highest level of creativity, we will be unstoppable. Millions of Jobs and Zuckerbergs will flourish.

FAILURE IS AN OPTION

Joanne Rowling is slowly sipping coffee at a table way in the corner of Nicholson's Cafe off Princes Street in Edinburgh, Scotland. Her daughter is napping beside her in a stroller and her six-year-old manuscript of the first *Harry Potter* was finally finished.

A few years earlier, Rowling was teaching English at a language institute in Portugal, while penning the first draft of the first *Harry Potter* book. Then she hit "rock bottom." Her marriage of 13 months had failed and now she had a baby daughter. However, it was that rock bottom that became the foundation on which she rebuilt her life.

"Failure meant a stripping away of the inessential," says Rowling. "I stopped pretending to myself that I was anything other than I was and began diverting all my energy into finishing the only work that mattered to me." Later, she would leave Portugal for Edinburgh.

In December 1993, when Rowling arrived in Edinburgh, her baby was less than a year old. She began to stay with her sister, Di, that Christmas. While Rowling planned on leaving Edinburgh after the holiday, she never did. Eventually, she read a few chapters of *Harry Potter* to Di, whom responded with a laugh. That re-kindled Rowling's hope.

Rowling was stuck in a mosh pit. She was living in a one bedroom apartment and surviving solely on income support with a daughter. Many years later, she would reveal that she was suffering from depression and did consider suicide.

What did Rowling do next? With a little money from her friend, she decided, with little else to do, to pursue her writing. That was the tipping point — when her life began to get back on track.

Now, it was here in 1995 that the culmination of Rowling's manuscript would set up the next year of her life. She would go on to sign with

Fulham-based Christopher Little Literary Agents to represent her in her search for a publisher. After 12 rejections, yes 12, her book was eventually picked up by Bloomsbury Publishers. The rest is history as Rowling would later become one of the richest people in the world.

When we discuss the stories of very successful people, we often neglect to mention the person's road to get to that point. We leave out their failures and the days when they wanted to quit. Failure is inevitable in life. Unfortunately, in school, children have been brainwashed into believing they aren't supposed to take plunges into uncertainty.

Here's a flashback to a common incident during my days of elementary school. I'm chatting with my fellow classmates when suddenly my teacher hands back last week's spelling test. I get my test back — I aced it, 100 percent — genius status. I turn to the kid next to me and notice that his test is splattered with red marks and a 30 percent is circled at the top. I think to myself — this is the dumb kid, the kid who doesn't care about school. Eventually, I arrive at the conclusion that the only way to succeed in life is to never make mistakes. That dogma was drilled into my skull early on.

In a tune, Bob Dylan, declared, "There's no success like failure." Let's make "F" the new "A." For instance, Thomas Edison performed 9,000 experiments before coming up with a successful version of the light bulb. From cardboard and duct tape to ABS polycarbonate, 15 years and 5,127 prototypes later, Sir James Dyson created his successful bagless vacuum cleaner. It took Dyson fifteen years and nearly his entire savings to develop his creation. From every failed prototype, he learned. Dyson tells *Fast Company*, "I've always thought that schoolchildren should be marked by the number of failures they've had. The child who tries strange things and experiences lots of failures to get there is probably more creative." It was Thomas Edison, the inventor of the light-bulb, who noted, "I have not failed. I've just found 10,000 ways that don't work." Of Shakespeare's 154 sonnets, some "were no better than his contemporaries could have written, and some were simply bad." Compare entrepreneurship to the J-curve of returns: the failures come early and often and the successes take time.

In life, Reid Hoffman, co-founder of LinkedIn and author Ben Casnocha write in their book, *The Startup of You*, that people should adopt ABZ life planning. Author Chuck Frey, in a blog post, writes that we should picture the image of a trapeze artist. Plan A is the bar the artist is holding on to, your current situation. Plan B is a nearby bar the artist can swing to without falling, very similar to your current situation where you can pivot when the time is right. Plan Z is the safety net below, your survivable worst case scenario.

Schools, on the other hand, paint failure in a terrible light. In many of the schools that I have visited, I have observed the poster "Failure is Not An Option" plastered on the walls of the classrooms. I was puzzled, so I turned to an expert to decipher the reasoning behind this. Wrongologist and journalist Kathryn Schulz said to me, "People think that when people fail it is due to some personality or character flaw, because they're irresponsible, ignorant, or stupid. That attitude reinforces the idea that failure is a terrible thing." Yet making mistakes over and over and over again is essentially the way of becoming good at something.

Schulz adds, "In general, kids learn much better when their beliefs are violated, rather than confirmed."

If you're afraid that you might get embarrassed by taking a risk, suck it up! Let's teach kids early on to live by these words: Risk, Survive, Repeat! Smart risks, of course. Go big or go home! The greater the impact you want to have in the world, the more you need to lose sight of the shore.

As Rowling said to the 2008 Harvard University graduating class, "The knowledge that you have emerged wiser and stronger from setbacks means that you are, ever after, secure in your ability to survive. You will never truly know yourself, or the strength of your relationships, until both have been tested by adversity. Such knowledge is a true gift, for all that it is painfully won, and it has been worth more than any qualification I ever earned."

DON'T SHOW, DON'T TELL

In the spring of 2012, I attended the Sandbox Summit at the M.I.T. Media Lab where I was immersed in the playground of designers, gamers, and educators. I touched the latest devices and witnessed the cutting-edge technology from FlickrLabs and Microsoft. At the conference, game designer Eric Zimmerman posed this powerful question: "The 19th century was the industrial age; the 20th century, the age of information. Will the 21st century be the ludic age?"

Play is how kids learn. One report says that play is "the process of weaving together all the elements of life as children experience it." It's an outlet for creativity, exploration, and discovery. Edward Miller, senior researcher at the Alliance for Childhood, said to the *New York Times*, "Play at age five is of great importance not just to intellectual but emotional, psychological, social, and spiritual development." Play is very difficult to define, perhaps it may be frolicking in the sandbox, observing nature's wonders, or building with Legos.

Play creates empathy as kids put on the caps of various roles.

I spoke with Kathy Hirsh-Pasek, professor of psychology at Temple University and a world-renowned expert on play, for some insight. She says kids need to develop the 6 C's skills: collaboration, communication, content, critical thinking, creative innovation and confidence.

Where might you get these skills from? Hirsh-Pasek says you get them, for instance, in the sandbox when you're playing with another kid, "When you're building a tower or a great castle for King Arthur and his knights, what you are doing is collaborating with someone else and communicating your intents and desires as well as listening to their ideas to build the structure. You will need an idea of content — how many pails of sand required to construct your dream. Also, you will need to critically think, because if you don't, the castle will fall down. Then you will need to creatively design and innovate. And lastly, take risks when putting the last pail on top of the tower to be sure that it's sturdy. Finally, the dream castle is a reality."

From an early age, play is hammered out of kids. Play is now a four-letter word in society. A survey of 254 teachers in New York and Los Angeles, the Alliance for Childhood, a nonprofit research and advocacy group, found that kindergarteners spent two to three hours a day being instructed and tested in reading and math. They spent less than 30 minutes playing.

"We took the blocks out of classroom and replaced them with test-prep. We decided that children shouldn't have fun in school while they're learning, because it's more important to know the facts on the exams," says Hirsh-Pasek. Children should be put on the endangered species list. We have taken people out of their playful, natural habitats and put them in a habitat of bubble tests. What gives me even more chills is that research from psychiatrist Stuart Brown claims that most serial killers were deprived of childhood play. That's a road we obviously don't want to go down.

Germany, for instance, realized that play was one of the most important natural resources in this creative economy. In the 1970s, research showed that by fourth-grade, children who attended play-oriented kindergarten classrooms surpassed those from academic-oriented kindergarten classrooms in physical, social, emotional, and mental development. The findings were so compelling that Germany switched all its kindergartens back to being play-oriented. Similarly, the United States needs to transform classrooms that do not foster a cradle of play.

How can we ensure that a child will remain an artist, as Picasso suggests, when he or she becomes older? One possible answer derives from the study, "The Double-Edged Sword of Pedagogy," by M.I.T. professor Laura Schulz, graduate student Elizabeth Bonawitz, and their colleagues. They looked at how four-year-olds learned about a new toy outfitted with four tubes. Each tube could do something interesting: If you pulled on one tube it squeaked, if you looked inside another tube you found a hidden mirror, and so on. For one group of children, the experimenter said: "I just found this toy!" As she brought out the toy, she pulled the first tube, as if by accident, and it squeaked. She acted surprised, exclaiming, "Huh! Did you see that? Let me try to do that!" and pulled the tube again to make it squeak a second time. With the second group of children, the experimenter acted more like a teacher. She said, "I'm going to show you how my toy works. Watch this!" and deliberately made the tube squeak. Then she left both groups of children alone to play with the toy.

All of the children, not surprisingly, pulled the first tube to make it squeak. But then interestingly, the children from the second group, quickly got bored with the toy, while the children from the first group played with it longer and discovered more of its "hidden" features. The bottom line is that children tend to get less curious when given direct instruction.

"If I teach you this one thing and then I stop, then you may say, 'Well that's probably all there is,'" Schulz said to *Science Daily*. Don't show; don't tell. Just observe.

Take the classic tale of Steve Jobs. When he was a young child, his adoptive father passed along his love of mechanics and cars to him, instilling a sense of design that would follow him for the rest of his life. Jobs gained an appreciation for the slightest details, paying close attention to the look of parts the eye couldn't see, later exemplifying them in his future creations, from the iPhone to the iPad.

School for Jobs, however, was quite different. Forced to accept an authority — the teacher — Jobs didn't like it for a second. According to Walter Isaacson's biography of Jobs, he explained, "They came close to really beating the curiosity out of me." Jobs and his parents knew the school was at fault for trying to make him memorize pointless information rather than stimulate his mind. In all, school was rough. It wasn't until he enrolled in the Hewlett-Packard Explorers Club that Jobs' interests were sparked.

The point is that a culture of play and discovery shaped Jobs' childhood. He never stopped playing, be it during his tenure at Apple or his stint at Pixar. That was one of the key ingredients to his success as an innovator. Great innovators never stop playing.

Work hard, play hard. Sometimes the two intermingle.

Most of you reading this book probably aren't familiar with the Australian software company, Atlassian. Founded in 2002 by two college dropouts in a Sydney garage and staffed with 273 employees, the company is worth hundreds of millions of dollars and has won countless numbers of innovation awards. How did they achieve such high levels of success? The answer — once a quarter, they tell their software developers that for the next 24 hours, they can work with whoever, whatever, and however they want. As opposed to the sterile corporate world, this is done in a relaxed environment. Atlassian calls these days "FedEx Days," because you have to deliver something overnight. This engagement built on a passion for something and unyielding autonomy has produced penetrating innovations that might not have existed. The experiment worked so well that Atlassian has extended the "Fedex Days" into 20 percent time. Atlassian's practices are also employed beautifully at a multi-billion dollar, multi-national corporation that has transformed the way the world finds and uses information. Google.

Typically once a week, the brains at Google are asked to devote their time to a type of intellectual R&D, working on special projects that aren't part of the regular workload. Half of Google's products have originated from 20 percent time.

If the 20 percent idea is a new product, writes Bharat Mediratta, it's pretty easy to find a few like-minded people and start coding away. In the *New York Times*, Mediratta, a Google engineer, discloses that when the idea is intended to "make a broad change across the whole organization, you need something new — you need a 'grouplet.'" These grouplets don't have a budget nor a decision-making authority, rather they're a group of people "committed to an idea and willing to work to convince the rest of the company to adopt it." Without this simple, yet elegant time allocation, products like Gmail and Google Talk would have remained pies in the sky.

Why can't every school adopt Google's 20 percent rule? Expanded it to 50 or even 100 percent? Teachers, if you try this in the classroom, you will learn more about your students than ever before.

What happens when a kid has time for unstructured play? Caine's Arcade comes to life. Nine-year-old Caine Monroy from Los Angeles, California with his bubbling and bursting imagination created a makeshift arcade in his father's auto-parts shop over summer vacation. His father, George Monroy, gave him all the cardboard, tape, markers, and scissors the boy could ever need or dream of.

Remember, this was summer vacation. Unlike most kids, Caine didn't have sleep-away camp, music lessons, tutors, or any kind of "acceleration" activities. His father gave him the best gift of all — unstructured free-time. After 280 hours and a professional video documenting his efforts, Caine Monroy has transformed into a viral sensation, with millions of YouTube hits. And he did it without listening to lectures, reading textbooks, or filling in Scantron sheets. Well, would you look at that?

We need to ask ourselves: What can a kid create with 280 hours of free-time? How many 'Caine's Arcades' can blossom? Give kids some power, sit back, and watch the show!

ALL HUMAN BEINGS ARE ENTREPRENEURS

One morning, import-export trader Steve Mariotti was jogging along the East River in Manhattan when suddenly he was mugged and terrorized by a gang of five teens who beat him up and stole his $10. At that moment, no one could have predicted that incident to eventually cause the creation of an organization that would help hundreds of thousands of children, destined to crowd prisons and shelters, transform into small business owners a few decades later.

The mugging changed Mariotti's life. At first, he was emotionally caught off guard. He became paranoid of young people that appeared as though they could hurt him. But after months of contemplating the reasons behind youth violence, Mariotti decided to quit his job in the corporate world and become a teacher in one of New York's most impoverished schools. He was searching for answers and a prescription to combat his fears.

On his first day at Boys and Girls High School in Brooklyn in his class of remedial students, Mariotti's optimism and anxiousness quickly turned sour. His students called him Mr. Manicotti, pelted him with spitballs, and stuck gum to his chair. One student even set another kid's coat on fire. The principal called him the "worst teacher in the school." But it was these troublemakers that gave him the light to see through the tunnel. When Mariotti took a few of them out to dinner and asked why they acted terribly in class, they responded saying that his class was boring and that he had nothing to teach them.

"Then, I asked if anything I taught in class interested them," says Mariotti. One fellow responded that I had caught his attention when I had discussed my import-export business. He rattled off various figures I had mentioned in class, calculated my profit margin, and concluded that my business was doing well. I was dazzled to find such business smarts in a student whom the public schools had labeled 'borderline retarded.'" That was the tipping point in Mariotti's teaching career. In his course, "How to Start, Finance, and Manage a Small Business: A Guide for the Urban Entrepreneur," he started to teach his students how to make money.

During the next seven years, recalls Mariotti, "this course became so successful that even the most challenging and disruptive students settled down and learned a great deal." In his last teaching assignment in the Fort Apache area of the South Bronx, 100 percent of his students started small businesses and reported that they experienced major positive changes in their lives.

Before long, Mariotti came to grips on how successful his classes were. He wanted to help unlock the potential in more children. So, in 1987 he founded the National Foundation for Teaching Entrepreneurship (NFTE). It began as a program to prevent kids from dropping out and teach them how to start their own businesses. More than a quarter century later, the organization has worked with over 450,00 young people.

In early 2012, 33 graduates from 10 countries converged in Manhattan to receive the network's Global Young Entrepreneur of the Year award. The teenagers set up a gallery of their products: from Colombia, plantain-flower veggie burgers; from Israel, a system to text-message homeowners about leaking water pipes; from Connecticut, flame-retardant chef's jackets; and from Germany, a baby sitting service for horses. A crossbow for slinging prizes to bleacher-bound sports fans was invented in Dallas; Chile marketed delicate morel mushrooms; and an aerial photography service based in California, deployed remote-control helicopters. You're looking at the next class of budding entrepreneurs.

Every school in America needs to teach entrepreneurship. In their book, Reid Hoffman and Ben Casnocha write, "You were born an entrepreneur. This doesn't mean you were born to start companies. In fact, most people shouldn't start companies. The long odds of success, combined with the constant emotional whiplash, makes starting a business the right path for only some people. All humans are entrepreneurs not because they should start companies but because the will to create is encoded in human DNA, and creation is the essence of entrepreneurship."

How can we teach entrepreneurship? First, entrepreneurship cannot be taught in the traditional sense — textbooks, lectures, and worksheets. The best way to learn the trick of the trade is to get your feet wet. It's also imperative to learn and extract lessons from successful and failed ventures.

Primarily, the point of the process, over time, is to ripen the entrepreneurial mindset. That mindset is a lifestyle. When you "own" it, you can run with any idea.

How can we cultivate this mindset? For one thing, we must abandon the status quo. In the 1990s, a Kauffman Foundation study found that two-thirds of high school students wanted to become entrepreneurs. Unfortunately, the same study discovered that more than 80 percent felt they had not learned anything about entrepreneurship in school. The results are no surprise to me.

Robin Hanson, professor at George Mason University, said to me, "Our schools are creating less creative people. We're certainly making people fit better into the modern workforce: specialized, routine, more disciplined." Disciplined employees rather than innovators. Indeed, years ago Northwestern Mutual Life Insurance created a research-based entrepreneurship test that deducts a substantial number of points if you were a high achiever in school.

Stop preparing kids to do stuff. Kids shouldn't be creating mock-businesses. Let them get dirty with their own hands and create their own. Stop confining the word "entrepreneur" to its dictionary definition — a person who organizes, operates, and assumes the risk for a business venture. An entrepreneur is someone who wants to bring his or her dream to life. At the end of the day, it all comes down to execution. Anyone can have a good idea; execution separates the winners from the losers.

The message that needs to be loud and clear to all policymakers is: for more new jobs to be created in America, we need entrepreneurship education in every school. Entrepreneurs provide jobs, make our lives healthier, easier, and more entertained with their goods and services that are sold around the globe.

When Steve Mariotti walked into his final class at Boys and Girls High, on his desk, he found a basket of chicken, a record album, and a bottle of cologne. On the blackboard, all of his students had signed their names underneath this salute: "Goodbye, Homeboy. From the Entrepreneurs of Boys and Girls High School."

Rich or poor, white or black, young or old — as Muhammed Younus once said, "All human beings are entrepreneurs."

WE DO BIG THINGS

As exemplified in his 2011 State of the Union address, innovation is President Barack Obama's moon shot. He certainly liked the word "innovation," mentioning it a 11 times in the speech. Encouraging American innovation is the first step in winning the future, the president declared. "None of us can predict with certainty what the next big industry will be or where the new jobs will come from," said Obama.

> Thirty years ago, we couldn't know that something called the Internet would lead to an economic revolution. What we can do — what America does better than anyone else — is spark the creativity and imagination of our people. We're the nation that put cars in driveways and computers in offices; the nation of Edison and the Wright brothers; of Google and Facebook. In America, innovation doesn't just change our lives. It is how we make our living.

I was inspired. As *USA Today* columnist Steve Strauss put it to me, "Entrepreneurship is one of America's best exports."

The United States has captured roughly 40 percent of all the Laureates of the Nobel Prize, miles away from other countries. The World Economic Forum has consistently ranked the U.S. at the upper-end of the list of the most innovative countries on the planet, if not number one. Silicon Valley is the cradle of innovation, hosting companies, like Apple, Google, and Facebook. What strings Americans together is one simple idea: our specialty is inventing game-changing products and services.

However, we are under intense pressure. China or India or Singapore or whomever could eat our breakfast, lunch, and dinner — tomorrow. This isn't globalization voodoo. This is reality. The U.S. doesn't call all the shots anymore.

Fortunately, we have a sense of where we are standing. In September 2010, the National Academies of Science, the country's leading advisory group on science and technology, released a report: "Rising Above the Gathering Storm Revisited: Rapidly Approaching Category 5." Charles M. Vest, the former M.I.T. president and one of the authors of the report gave a pragmatic dose of where we actually rank today:

Sixth in global innovation-based competitiveness, but 40th in rate of change over the last decade; 11th among industrialized nations in the fraction of 25-to-34-year-olds who have graduated from high school; 16th in college completion rate; 22nd in broadband Internet access; 24th in life expectancy at birth; 27th among developed nations in the proportion of college students receiving degrees in science or engineering; 48th in quality of K-12 math and science education; and 29th in the number of mobile phones per 100 people.

This isn't a situation that we can wish to go away. We're getting our asses handed to us by the Chinese and the Indians.

Even with all these unappealing numbers staring at us, we shouldn't hoist the white flag just yet. We have a ripe opportunity to reinvigorate our national formula for success: creating and doing big things.

We will be only as innovative as our best companies. The following is the Top 10 list of *Fast Company*'s "The World's Most Innovative Companies 2012":

Rank	Name
1	APPLE
2	FACEBOOK
3	GOOGLE
4	AMAZON
5	SQUARE
6	TWITTER
7	OCCUPY MOVEMENT
8	TENCENT
9	LIFE TECHNOLOGIES
10	SOLAR CITIES

Make some observations. There's only one company on this list that isn't American — Tencent, the Chinese instant messaging portal company. If you glance at the list of the top 50 most innovative companies, only seven of the companies are non-American.

What explains all of this? The Power Distance Index. It is a concept developed by Geert Hofstede as a result of years of research into management relationships around the globe. Hofstede says that it measures the extent to which the less powerful members of organizations and institutions accept and expect that power is distributed unequally. For example, in the United States, a culture of embodying individual rights, speaking out loud about one's beliefs without any kind of mitigation, and promoting equal hierarchy is cherished. At one extreme, the Scandinavian states, Germany, Austria, the Netherlands, United Kingdom, and the United States score very low on the scale. At the other end, China, India, Iraq, United Arab Emirates, Iran, and Malaysia score at the top of the scale, with Malaysia topping the charts. Roger Neill, director at the Center for Creativity in Professional Practice in the United Kingdom, told me, "For example, if a senior manager in a country with a high score pours cold water over a new idea, it's far more likely to be fatally damaged." Challenging your boss or rocking the boat isn't just frowned upon, it is essentially non-existent.

Let's scrutinize innovation in China a little bit closer. In retrospect, ancient China was highly inventive, home to the Four Great Inventions: the compass, gunpowder, paper-making, and printing. Yet over time, the country paved the way for the powerful Western cannons by the 19th century.

Today, which country is home to the greatest number of Nobel Prize winners? The answer is the United States. There are only 12 Chinese Nobel Laureates, compared with 323 American Nobel Laureates. It's imperative to wonder the following: When will we see a Nobel-Prize winner who was educated and conducted their research in China? Probably not for a long time.

More scientific papers come out of China than out of any other country in the world, but plagiarism has crippled their scientific ambitions. *The Journal of Zheijiang University-Science* found that 31 percent of papers had excessive copying. The figure jumped to 40 percent for papers in computer science and life science.

"Only 20 percent of people are doing innovative work, while the other 80 percent are merely copying others," says Zhang Yaqin (Zhang), corporate vice president of Microsoft and chairman of Microsoft Asia-Pacific Revelopment and Development Group, to the *GlobalTimes*. Many ambitious, prospective Chinese entrepreneurs find the copycat culture to be antithetical to creating a novel invention. Or, as the Council on Foreign Relations senior fellow Adam Segal puts it in his book *Advantage*, "With quick profits available to companies that successfully reverse engineer already proven technologies, it makes little sense to risk failure by putting money and effort into further technological innovation."

What's more, *Thomson Reuters'* Science Watch website asserts that China isn't even in the top 20 when measuring the number of times a paper is cited on a national basis. Quality trumps quantity.

To create the "next big thing," the Chinese government understands that China cannot copy its way to fame (Eight of China's top nine government officials are scientists). A few years ago, trying to stave off the copycat stigma, the government published "The National Medium and Long Term Plan for the Development of Science and Technology (2006-2020)." Look at all the creativity oozing out of the title. The government starkly recognizes China's challenges declaring, "...despite the size of our economy, our country is not an economic power, primarily because of our weak innovative capacity." Calling for a "great renaissance of the Chinese nation," it intends to fulfill China's innovative capacities. Perhaps pointing to the fact that China is the world's low-cost workshop, one trend the report recognizes is moving from "Made in China" to "Created in China."

Are we going to stop this? America's new motto: Innovate or die. Only then will America will remain the greatest country in the world.

CHAPTER 6

IT'S THE CURRICULUM, STUPID!

I hate school. Why? At its bare bones, I detest what and how I am taught. I don't want my brain to be stuffed with pointless content. I want to be taught how to create and do things.

In conversations on changing the curriculum, the word "rigor" is often brought up. In education, rigor is a buzz word. Very few people know what it means. To some, rigor means more homework and stronger standards. That's flawed. Rigor is about doing work that matters and has relevance to the world and focusing on depth over breadth. The late education reformer Ted Sizer once offered a three-word slogan for a revolution in teaching: "Less is more."

Decades ago, Ralph Tyler, the Director of Research for the Eight-Year-Study, a major investigation uncovering the effects of progressive education, explained the flaws of the traditional curriculum: "It is clear that a statement of objectives in terms of content headings...is not a satisfactory basis for guiding the further development of the curriculum." The purpose of a curriculum should be rather to empower creative and motivated human beings.

The question, "How can we light the fire of learning in kids?," should be guiding the curriculum.

COMMUNICATION

When I was really young, I adored reading. I loved going to the library. I would check out books of literally every genre. I have continued this love of reading to this date.

However, I have never enjoyed any of the books I have read in school. None. The dullness of some of the books I have been assigned by my teachers has drained the life out of me and my peers.

Kids love to read. They love to read great books, rich in captivating text and plot. Plenty of children will pick up a *Harry Potter* book and read for hours on end without being forced to, yet, you can't get a kid to stay awake for five minutes to read a novel like *The Scarlet Letter* or the epic poem *Beowulf*. They are both boring as hell works of fiction.

I turned to Kelly Gallagher, author of *Readicide: How Schools Are Killing Reading and What You Can Do About It*, for some insight. He told me that American schools are actively (though unwittingly) fostering the decline of reading. There are three major problems. First, he notes that schools are valuing the development of test-takers over the development of life-long readers.

Second, teachers often over-teach books. "I tell teachers that if you are taking nine weeks to teach a novel, that's not a novel anymore, it's a nine-week worksheet," Gallagher says. "Many teachers try to teach all things in one book rather than one thing in a really great book. They cut it up so much that the actual book gets lost."

Third, teachers also under-teach books. They just assign books without actually dissecting and explaining the material.

After all this, kids start to abhor reading. Don't believe me? A majority of the U.S. adult population never reads another book after high school. We fail to value reading in our society.

At school, teachers must expose kids to a cadre of books. Let kids read books like *The Kite Runner, The Life of Pi,* or *The Da Vinci Code.* Nonfiction as well as fiction. Add in non-American and non-British works. I will guarantee you that students will not Sparknote, CliffNote, or even, yes, Schmoop these works. It seems to me that a new book summary site is published on the web every day.

Imagine how many kids we can get hooked onto reading.

After reading books in schools, it's paramount to draw connections to the kids' lives. Make it personal. I still vividly remember the day I met Lemony Snicket, the author of *The Series of Unfortunate Events*, in person at a Barnes & Noble bookstore in New York City. It further kindled my love for reading. As a teacher, if you don't schedule a Skype call with the author, if he or she is alive, of the books you and your students are reading, you are doing a disservice to them. Along with books, from elementary school onward, students should read newspaper and magazine articles.

We also need to move past the jargon of "English class." Teaching literature in terms of the pieces written by Shakespeare, Homer, or Dante is not necessary for a majority of students. Harold Bloom, a professor of English at Yale University and an academic book reviewer in the *New York Times* claimed that no one disagrees that everyone should read, "Homer, Plato, the Bible, Virgil, Dante, Chaucer, Cervantes, Shakespeare, Montaigne, Milton." Well, guess what? I disagree.

Yes, great fiction can help some people propel into worlds and experiences they could have never imagined, but there is not enough evidence demonstrating that is what requiring the reading of Homer or Shakespeare does. Literature should be an optional, never a mandatory part of school.

To raise a reader, parents also have an instrumental role. Early on, get your child a library card, ask the librarian to show your child how to navigate through the children's section, and then let them explore the shelves. Help them pick books that advance their reading level. At home, parents need to read to their kids every day. Make it a routine, and sooner or later it will become a natural habit. My mother did this with me when I was younger and my love for reading has never subdued.

The second "R" is wRiting. Even on this highly technological planet, the importance of writing is not discounted. It is often overlooked as a tenet to transforming learning. Michelangelo, a sculptor and artist, understood a writer's challenge clearly. The man thought of his art as little more than the task of releasing the figure that was already present from the block of marble in which it had always been embedded.

As I mentioned in the first chapter, a third of all workers fall short of employers' expectations in written communication skills. As George Orwell said, "If people cannot write well, they cannot think well, and if they cannot think well, others will do their thinking for them." Writing is an indispensable skill for everyone.

In most schools, writing is neglected. Thus, only about a quarter of all high school seniors were able to meet or exceed the proficiency level on the National Writing Achievement exam. When writing is taught in school, it is mainly overshadowed by frivolous grammar drills. The irony is that in school, I believe I have spent more time learning grammar tricks than actually writing something. Writing goes beyond simply mastering grammar, punctuation, spelling, and usage. I know students who are able to identify every part of speech and perfectly diagram sentences, but write absolutely terribly. Experiments over the past five decades have shown negligible improvements in the quality of student writing as a result of grammar instruction. Why? First, the information doesn't stick, since students are just trying to find the "trick." Second, these grammar drills fail to connect the dots to students' authentic writing across the curriculum.

Furthermore, by the end of high school, students have been trained like chimpanzees to manufacture five-paragraph essays that are formulaic and bland. Then they are reared to produce a response to a prompt in 25 minutes on the SAT writing section. This is contrary to everything in the teaching of writing: students should be encouraged to take more time to divergently think, collaborate, and communicate.

What happened to the old fashioned term papers? They were once prominent features of secondary education, where students were required to research intensely and write in large volumes. William Fitzhugh, publisher of *The Concord Review* which showcases high school research papers (from 39 countries since 1987), revealed to me that most U.S. public school teachers have stopped assigning such papers — a shift attributed to the time it takes to grade them and an increasing number of students in the class. Most of the Advanced Placement teachers say they don't have time to ask students to write research papers, because they "have to get students ready for the A.P. Exam in May." Still, in a nationwide survey of public school history teachers in 2002, about 95 percent of them said assigning long research papers was important.

In this day and age, the Internet can supply us with all the information we need, but by means of a research paper, we can digest, synthesize, and comprehend that information. The process cannot be automated, like a typical five paragraph essay, rather it must be organic and creative. Fitzhugh explained, "A research paper can show the student whether he or she has really understood as much as he or she supposed about a subject. The exercise of writing helps a student to organize and examine the information gathered in a careful way."

In school, more time should be devoted to writing. Skip all the time on grammar drill chanting and just let kids write. Teachers, if you take anything out of this section, it should be that in teaching writing, an authentic audience is everything. For example, Nichole Pinkard, professor at DePaul University, said at the *New York Times*: Schools for Tomorrow 2011 event, that in her journalism class, she published her students' work on her blog. That action had a profound motivational effect for her students.

I have never been driven to take extra time and write something extraordinary for a school assignment. Why? First, the assignment is usually pointless. Second, I know the only person that will read it will be my teacher. Do I write for my teachers or do I publish for the world? The latter sounds much more attractive.

What if there was no gap? What if the best work we produced was showcased to the world? Teachers need to extend the mediums of writing into blogs, letters to the editor, opinion pieces, and yes even tweets. If a student's letter or article is selected for publication in a paper, he or she will embrace writing for a long time to come. Mark my words. And that passion will continue into adult life. As Sir Francis Bacon wrote in 1625, "reading maketh a full man, conference a ready man, and writing an exact man."

As we will see later, we must end the notion of "writing class" or "English class." With public speaking added into the mix, "English class" becomes "communication class," a medium for students to engage with the world.

SITCOM-SIZED PROBLEMS

When I was younger, I used to love math. I dreamed of becoming an engineer. Then they fed me textbooks and worksheets and that was the end of that dream. When I recollect math class in elementary school, frightening images of chanting the times tables and racing to finish up the hundreds of exercises in the textbook often crop out. What happened? My hunger for knowledge was squashed.

Paul Lockhart, a math teacher in New York, writes that if he had to design a system for the express purpose of destroying a child's natural curiosity and love of pattern-making, he couldn't possible do a better job than the one currently being done. He explains that he simply wouldn't have the "imagination to come up with the kind of senseless, soul-crushing ideas that constitute contemporary mathematics education."

The debate over math education is like a noisy and loud dinner table on Thanksgiving. The school administrators are yelling, "Smart-boards will solve everything." The teachers are screaming, "Better textbooks." The politicians are barking, "Raise the standards." Where are the kids? The kids are ignored. At school, I hear students complaining about the subject every single day. All of their concerns draw from one simple and justified question: When will any of this help me in life? Math education in school has failed to answer that question.

Math is taught as computation, instead of a means of exploration and discovery. Lockhart writes:

> It is not doing society any good by having people walk around with vague memories of algebraic formulas and geometric representations, and clear, consistent memories of dreading them. Math should be taught as art for art's sake. Beethoven could easily compose hundreds, if not thousands of advertising jingles, but his underlying motivation for learning music was to create something beautiful.

The crunch is that in school, kids are exposed to aspects of math that are recipe-like, cut-and-dry, and so boring that they often don't see the purpose of it. I sure didn't see the purpose of it. A good rule of thumb is that the future mathematics field loses half of its mass each year. In kindergarten, many students eventually want to go into a profession related to mathematics. In second grade, half of them do. And so on, until you're left with just a few at the end. We are losing so many potential mathematicians who are rejecting the subject very early on.

School has become a practice of learning tricks for the test one week and forgetting the next. The bottom line is that formula sheets aren't really math. "You expect sitcom-sized problems that wrap up in 22 minutes, three commercial breaks and a laugh track," explains Dan Meyer, a math teacher, in a TED talk. "No problem worth solving is that simple." He says the way our textbooks — particularly mass-adopted textbooks — teach math reasoning and patient problem-solving, is functionally equivalent to turning on "Two and a Half Men" and calling it a day. Teachers have attempted to prescribe this "textbook medicine," to their students, but as Lockhart writes, "Operate all you want, doctors: your patient is already dead."

Today, American schools have a very rigid hierarchy in the subject of math. In elementary schools, kids come to understand that you are expected to follow directions, fill out worksheets, and master a set of concepts. I came to comprehend that math isn't supposed to be fun. When I asked questions about how I was learning, teachers didn't have answers, just judgments.

By the time I reached middle school, I was fed up. I was bombarded with cute notations, all in preparation for Algebra I.

Algebra I is another train-wreck. I memorized an unheard of number of random formulas and notations for some apparent reason. I can compare my experience of learning algebra with Bertrand Russell's recollection: "I was made to learn by heart: 'The square of the sum of two numbers is equal to the sum of their squares increased by twice their product.' I had not the vaguest idea what this meant and when I could not remember the words, my tutor threw the book at my head, which did not stimulate my intellect in any way." Right back atcha.

Next in the sequence is Geometry, another disaster of epic proportions. For example, elegant proofs have been substituted by fixed step-by-step formal deductions. Geometry textbooks lay out the postulates, definitions, and proofs students must know. Trained to "can" arguments, I spent a large portion of the time unaware what my teacher was saying. I wish students were using geometry to create proofs and construct geometrical models and applying it to fix the country's lagging infrastructure, perhaps. Instead, we have a monstrosity. Euclid, if alive today, would shutter at the sight of the way geometry is taught in classrooms.

After Geometry, I flowed into Algebra II and Trigonometry. My fellow classmates and I were doused with tedious calculations, from logarithms to rational expressions. All we were learning were stupid mnemonic devices like "SohCahToa" and "All Students Take Calculus."

Then comes Pre-Calculus. A mumbo jumbo of disconnected topics. The course was intended to prepare me for calculus by stretching out topics that could be taught in less than 3 months into a full-year affair. Everything revolves around the function $f(x)$, a concept most students will never come across in their adult lives.

After Pre-Calculus is Calculus. Many schools offer Advanced Placement Calculus AB and BC. I briefly explained the way they are taught in chapter four. The objective of such a course is to gain a fundamental understanding of single-variable calculus. The problem is that you don't. I was taught how to memorize hundreds of formulas to regurgitate on exams. What's favored is repeated examples of solving essentially the same problem over and over again. The course is crap. To be repeated in college, verbatim.

The mathematics curriculum pyramid is founded on arithmetic and algebra, all building up to one subject. At the top of the pyramid is calculus. That is the wrong summit.

Richard Rusczyk, founder of the Art of Problem Solving, "a revolution in mathematics training for high school students," told me a fun story about this. He says, "One of my friends was at the graduate school at U.C. San Diego and he was telling me that he and his colleagues were arguing over what math was the most important for high school students to learn. Is it really calculus? Another group wanted to argue it was linear algebra. They argued back and forth: Calculus or linear algebra?" Eventually, he said, they all agreed the answer was statistics and probability.

While mathematicians, engineers, physicists, and particular scientists use calculus in a meaningful way, in their day to day lives, most people are not. Ironically, M.I.T. graduates, a very technically trained group in science and mathematics, were surveyed regarding the math that they most frequently in their work. Behind the survey was the assumption that if any adults used higher-level math, M.I.T. graduates would be among the majority. The results: while a few did, the overwhelming majority reported using nothing more than arithmetic, statistics, and probability. We have a clear mismatch. There is no evidence that demonstrates that learning calculus in high school correlates to success in college and life. None whatsoever.

We need a mathematics curriculum that is grounded in real-life problems. We need room for the study of statistics and probability. In a data analysis course, students can gather data sets, applying it to a wide range of fields from biology to Major League Baseball. Students need a firm grounding in that subject. Most people cannot read and understand the *New York Times, Time,* or even *USA Today* without being able to deconstruct statistical information and identify errors. Clifford Konold, a professor at the University of Massachusetts, counted data displays in *The New York Times.* He found that in 1972 there were four graphs or tables in 10 consecutive weekday editions, excluding the sports and business sections. There were eight in 1982 and 44 in 1992. Next year, he could find more than 100.

Statistical reasoning bolsters decision-making while navigating through treacherous waters. Moreover, statistics and probability is not enough. We need to show kids mathematics that is fun and beautiful. You can do this with discrete math: topics such as combinatorics, probability, number theory, set theory, logic, algorithms, and graph theory. Because discrete math isn't found in standardized tests, it is often overlooked. Some very bright kids who are turned off by algebra and calculus, often get rescued by discrete math. Kids are not zombies; they respond to beauty.

Let me pose this question: How should mathematics be taught?

Richard Rusczyk says that we need to start with the problems — learning to solve problems you have never seen before. He launched Art of Problem Solving (AOPS), an online community for students who love math. In discussion forums, free online learning opportunities, online competitions, and fee-based classes, students receive both challenge and support as they hone their mathematical problem-solving skills. AOPS' teaching is quite unique.

Rusczyk asserts, "We want students to discover through working with hard problems. We won't tell them how to do it and we won't have preceded that problem by saying 'here's a trick that will go to work on the next problem, do the same thing and you'll get the right answer. Instead of doing that, we expect them to try to figure out what the tricks are, what the techniques are, and what the strategies are as they work through the problem."

Then, he notes, "after they work through the problem, we'll highlight what the key steps are. The mathematics becomes their mathematics, rather than information that was told to them."

At the core of his program is the skill of problem solving, overcoming obstacles you've never encountered before. The key to becoming an excellent problem solver, Rusczyk says, is learning how to learn. As Albert Einstein infamously declared, "The formulation of a problem is often more essential than its solution."

According to Conrad Wolfram, founder of Wolfram Research Europe, there are four steps to doing math. Step 1 is posing the right question. Step 2 is taking that real world and moving it into a kind of math formulation. Step 3 is computation, taking that formulation and turning it into an answer. Step 4 is transforming it back from the mathematical form to the real world and verifying it. Wolfram says, "We insist that the entire population learns how to do Step 3 by hand. Perhaps 80 percent of doing math education at school is step 3 by hand and largely not doing Steps 1, 2, and 4. Yet Step 3 is the step that computers can do vastly better than any human being." His motto is: Stop Teaching Calculating; Start Teaching Math!

I spoke with Wolfram on the prospect of a revitalized mathematics curriculum. He argues for the open-ended use of computers, to solve much harder problems. Wolfram explained, "Problems in the real world look knotty and horrible. They've got hair all over them. They're not just simple, dumbed-down things that we see in school math."

I asked him, "Can't hand-calculations help teach understanding?" Wolfram replied, "The answer is possibly yes. But there's a much better way to learn about procedures. It's called programming."

Duke University Professor Cathy Davidson, argues that we should add the 4th R: "algoRithm" to the typical 3 R's of reading, 'riting, and 'rithmetic. It's an easy to way to check your understanding and nail down the procedure without tedious hand calculations. Programming language environments like Scratch created by the M.I.T. Media Lab and spearheaded by Professor Mitchell Resnick, turn kids from media consumers into media producers. Kids can program interactive creations by simply snapping together graphical blocks, much like LEGO bricks, without any of the rough lingo of traditional programming language.

For example, Thomas Suarez, a middle school student, gave a fabulous talk on his two published apps: "Earth Fortune," which is a fortune teller that colors the earth different colors depending on the fortune and his most successful "Bustin Jieber," a whac-a-mole game app that replaces the mole with a photo of Justin Bieber. With Mark Zuckerberg as my generation's role model, imagine how many kids can get inspired by app development and computer programming.

For assessments in math class, Conrad Wolfram says, "let kids use computers." Mathematical models can be toyed with easily. Real-world applications, like determining the best insurance policy, can be put into the curriculum. Math should be an integral part of experiencing the world.

What's impeding our kids' love for mathematics more than anything else is an excitement deficit. Currently, there are no math museums in the United States. But fortunately, that will no longer be true with the opening of the Museum of Mathematics in New York. Glen Whitney, the museum's founder and a former hedge-fund quantitative analyst, is betting that MoMath can provide the element of surprise and excitement that textbooks cannot, with a formula that looks like this: math = discovery = beauty = fun. He asserts, "We want to be a place where that spark can ignite."

The problem is that there are all sorts of myths about mathematics out there. Whitney says, "Math is hard, math is boring, math is for boys, math doesn't matter in real life. All these are cultural myths that we want to blow apart." At its core, the museum will offer a place where kids actually get to explore math, rather than be told about it.

In sum, the mathematics curriculum pyramid needs to be scrapped. I have learned so much more about math by playing games, doing puzzles, and unraveling mathematical patterns than by hearing lectures and doing textbook problems. Notation and technique do not really matter, because it is very easy to learn it later on. Teachers, the odds are all against you. Your goal is to create a mathematical thinker. Don't do anything that doesn't bring you a step closer to that objective.

The only required mathematical areas of study in school should be statistics and probability coupled with discrete math. When you love mathematics, you can see magic in numbers. When I was younger, my face literally lit up when I observed something new about a number. Something similar and very interesting happened with a great Indian mathematician. Srinivasa Ramanujan, a humble clerk in Madras, India, had a unique flair for numbers. In a letter to an eccentric English mathematician G.H. Hardy, Ramanujan claimed, among other things, to have devised a formula that calculated the number of primes up to a hundred million with no error. Note: This was a man who failed his school examinations, had little formal schooling, and self-taught himself almost everything. As a seven-year-old, he was very inquisitive with questions like, "Is zero divided by zero is also one? If no fruits are divided among no one, will each still get one?" Perhaps, we should be inspiring our kids with stories like this to first, show that anyone, regardless of their amount of schooling, can create great things and second, bring a lasting love for the beauty of numbers. I want to re-live my childhood excitement.

Let's remind them that a mathematical expression is just a brush stroke used to paint one of the great wonders in the world. When kids are exposed to the power and beauty of mathematics, the possibilities are endless.

THE KNOW-NOTHINGS

In which of the following subjects do American high school seniors fare the worst? English? History? Math? Science?

It's history. The National Assessment of Educational Progress determined that only 12 percent of high school seniors demonstrated proficiency. And just 2 percent of seniors correctly answered a question concerning the case Brown v. Board of Education, one of the most important decisions of the United States Supreme Court in the past century. As historian David McCullough tells the *Wall Street Journal*, "We're raising young people who are, by and large, historically illiterate."

Citing a 1998 survey, more young Americans could name the 'Three Stooges' than the three branches of government.

One of the dilemmas is that history is one of the least-liked subjects, if not the least in high school. It is the only field in which the more courses a student takes, the more stupid they become. The conventional wisdom is that an educated person has the ability to make wise decisions, think critically, and understand what is going on in the world. Wrong.

Sociologist James W. Loewen disclosed to me, "Americans incorrectly believe that more schooling is a good thing and equate *educated* with *informed* and *knowledgeable*." Look to the Vietnam and Iraq War. Educated people were against the withdrawal of troops in Vietnam and a majority of American college graduates favored keeping troops in Iraq. Americans blatantly ignored the lessons from Vietnam and history repeated itself with thousands of American servicemen and women dead.

Still, I don't blame them 100 percent for their ignorance. First, history is de-emphasized in school, especially in elementary school due to a stress on mathematics and reading for No Child Left Behind. Second, the way we teach it makes students loathe the subject. History in school is a process of memorizing hundreds of dates, people, and events. That's no fun! It's no coincidence that in the *Harry Potter* series the most boring subject at Hogwarts is history. Mr. Binns, the teacher, is so tedious that he has bored himself to death — without noticing.

At the heart and soul of this cataclysm are the filthy textbooks. No one is going to get excited by a 5.2 pound, 1,000 page gorilla textbook. Not even historians. Thus, comparative historian Marc Ferro has observed, "The United States has wound up with the largest gap of any country in the world between what historians know and what the rest of us are taught."

Why do textbooks suck? James W. Loewen said to me, "First, publishers do not want to offend anyone. Take President Franklin W. Pierce. He is my candidate for the second worst president in American history. He was an alcoholic and suffered a terrible blow just after he took office — the death of his son in a railroad accident. He was also pro-slavery and a terrible leader. Pierce wasn't even re-nominated by his party — the only president in history to have won his first term and not renominated for a second. When he left office, it was said that no one met his train when he arrived home in New Hampshire. Since he's the only president to come from New Hampshire, however, the state now has a positive historical marker of him and named a college after Pierce. As a result of this changed climate of opinion, I do not know a single textbook that will give you the same description I gave. Why not? They do not want to lose sales in New Hampshire."

Loewen continues, "The second reason is incompetence. The textbooks are generally written by clerks or nameless graduate students that publishers hire, not by the names placed on their outside covers and title pages. The combination of publisher caution and incompetence is a recipe for failure."

In his provocative book *Lies My Teacher Told Me: Everything Your American History Textbook Got Wrong*, Loewen explained how he found similarities in high school textbooks while updating his book about inaccuracies in history texts.

Language in both the 2005 edition of *A History of the United States*, a high school history textbook by the Pulitzer Prize-winning historian Daniel J. Boorstin and Brooks Mather Kelley and the 2005 edition of another textbook, *America: Pathways to the Present*, by a different author were substantially identical. How did these books get approved in the first place?

For teachers, teaching to the textbook makes life very easy. Everything is laid out neatly — the list of key terms, main ideas, dates, timelines, fill in worksheets, and Powerpoint lessons for class. Overall, my fellow students are tricked, under the impression that the class is rigorous and they are learning something.

Teachers also do not like controversy; they like to keep things plain vanilla. Ninety-two percent of teachers did not initiate discussion of controversial issues, 89 percent did not discuss controversial issues when their students brought them up, and 79 percent said they should not. In class, I am usually the one to provoke a debate. Immediately, teachers give me a death-like stare and I am pressured to stop talking. It is difficult for teachers to teach open-endedly. They are afraid to not be in control of the answer and are afraid of losing their authority over the class. John Goodlad, education researcher and theorist, concluded after his researchers visited more than 1,000 classrooms, "Not even one percent of instructional time was devoted to discussions that required some kind of open response involving reasoning or perhaps an opinion from students...The extraordinary degree of student passivity stands out." This isn't a small problem in select classrooms; this is a nationwide crisis.

One of the founding fathers of this nation, Thomas Jefferson, urged the teaching of political history so that Americans might learn "how to judge for themselves what will secure or endanger their freedom." We are not grooming citizens — people who are able to comprehend our nation's story, distinguish between fact and fraud, and elect qualified people for office. I cannot trust my generation to do that.

History is not about remembering facts or dates; it's about learning from it and assuring that the same blunders are not repeated. No one will ever need to regurgitate the date of Custer's Last Stand or the name of the British general who fought at the Battle of Yorktown in the American Revolutionary War. However, you will need to understand how events in history shape the way America functions in the present-day.

Loewen adds, "Most kids never take a history course ever again, because it bored them to tears in high school." It's time for a drastic overhaul in the way we teach history.

First, let's throw out the textbooks! Rip 'em part and recycle them. We should really have a 'National Recycling Textbooks Day.' Let's replace textbooks with primary and secondary sources.

I want Howard Zinn's *A People's History of the United States* in the hands of every single history teacher in America. I want books by Pulitzer Prize-winning historian, David McCollough, on students' Kindles and laptops.

I want films in the classroom. A study concludes that showing popular history movies in a classroom setting can be a double-edge sword when it comes to helping students learn and retain factual information. This is perfect opportunity to sharpen navigation skills. Students can dissect errors in the film and learn from them. For example, to reel students into the Revolutionary War, show clips from *The Patriot* or *1776*. Every now and then, Hollywood gets historical.

I want games in the classroom. When I was younger, I was addicted to the online game, "Where in the World Is Carmen Sandiego?" I was glued to the computer screen; my mother couldn't take me off. In that experience, I gained an appreciation for history and geography. Games are much more than simply entertainment.

As the Native American poet, Simon Ortiz, says, "there are no truths, only stories," Students should understand that history has been written down by countless numbers of people, not just those in power. In terms of sources used, the important thing to remember is to offer all sides of the debate. Question everything! Make sure students are on the tips of their toes at all times. Let them form, debate, and rebut opinions and points.

Second, let's teach controversy. Loewen conveyed a fascinating story, "A teacher in rural southwestern Virginia emailed me a few years ago saying, 'Loewen, the picture you use of a lynching is pretty tame.' It is tame. I show a blurred image of an African-American man being burned to death and in the background there are twenty well dressed white men and women who want to be photographed in the act for this terrible crime. You don't see body parts. There are much more horrible photos available."

"The teacher, who teaches mostly white fifth graders and uses very harsh images of lynching, said, 'Kids arrive into my class expecting history to be boring. By October, my students don't find my class to be boring. By Christmas, you notice that my class is influencing them. For example, they no longer want violent video games. Their values are changing.'"

Interestingly, Loewen says the only problem the teacher has is when the students graduate from his class and go onto sixth grade social studies. The kids do find that class is really boring by comparison. So that teacher doesn't like him very much.

Third, favor depth over breadth. Let's introduce fewer topics and examine them more thoroughly. Instead of employing 10 minutes on the French and Indian War, allocate a few days to actually analyzing the events and people through projects, plays, primary sources, and films. The point is to focus on the big picture and connect the dots along the way.

Fourth, bring competitions like National History Day into the classroom. Every year, more than 600,000 students create presentations "that bring primary-source research to life through table-top exhibits, documentaries, live performances, websites, and research papers." A few years ago, I participated in the live performance category. For the preparation, I conducted a hoard of research and did a few interviews. In the performance, I mimicked Steve Jobs and Thomas Friedman in attire and language and offered a sharp dialogue on globalization and technology. I have been infatuated with technology ever since.

Fifth, let students write research papers. Let them select a topic in the area of study and then let them be free. Teachers should give students months to work on the paper, set deadlines, create discussion groups, and offer time to work one-on-one and communicate with the teacher. The best papers can then be sent to *The Concord Review*, in hope for publication. That is the real world verification.

Sixth, take kids to historical places — the White House, the Statue of Liberty, Mount Rushmore. When I was very young, my trip to the Natural History Museum made me fond of history. I have never forgotten that experience to date.

It is crucial to commence this process in elementary school and continue it in middle and high school. In an interview with the *Wall Street*

Journal, David McCullough advises, "They can learn anything in a flash. The brain at that stage in life is like a sponge. And one of the ways they get it is through art: drawing, making things out of clay, constructing models, and dramatic productions. If you play the part of Abigail Adams or Johnny Appleseed in a fourth-grade play, you're never going to forget it as long as you live."

"We're too concentrated on having our children learn the answers," McCullough summarizes. "I would teach them how to ask questions — because that's how you learn."

If kids start to love history from the start, there is nothing stopping them from continuing.

One day, they will be the ones writing history.

DEMOCRACY IS NOT A SPECTATOR SPORT

While I watch the man-on-the-street interviews on the *Tonight Show with Jay Leno*, I am flabbergasted at the amount of civic ignorance in this country.

I also came across this exact predicament on multiple occasions in one of my English classes. One day, a student asked, "What is the Tea Party?" Another day, a different student queried, "Who is the Vice President of the United States?" Third, another student wondered, "Who is Herman Cain?" while we briefly discussed his campaign suspension before the period began. I couldn't catch a breath. I was literally dying. I was embarrassed. My fellow peers are supposed to be voters in the 2016 presidential election.

Similarly, most students who took the National Assessment of Educational Progress (NAEP) 2010 Civics Assessment, bombed it. According to data released in May 2011, a disturbing 24 percent of high school seniors scored at a proficient level or above on the assessment, which probed questions like understanding the major aspects of the Constitution and interpreting a graph about voter participation. The problem is not just the kids. When *Newsweek* gave 1,000 adults in the U.S. a random sample of the questions on the test that immigrants must pass in order to become citizens, 38 percent failed and 29 percent did not even know who the current Vice President is. Thus, this lack of civics knowledge seeps into adult life. What's even more depressing is that this deficiency was present in a February 2011 poll, which found that 22 percent of Americans incorrectly believed the 2010 Affordable Care Act was repealed, with another 26 percent unsure or unwilling to say.

While it's easy to dismiss these finding as irrelevant, a research study analyzed by Michael X. Delli Carpini and Scott Keeter in *What Americans Know About Politics and Why It Matters* documents important links between basic civic information and civic attributes that we have good reason to care about, noting, "Other things being equal, civic knowledge enhances support for democratic values, promotes political participation, helps citizens to understand better the impact of public policy on their interests, gives citizens the framework they need to learn more about civic affairs, and reduces generalized mistrust and fear of public life."

As Vice President Joe Biden might say, "This is a big f**king deal."

Even though the average amount of schooling Americans have has escalated in the past century, the civic knowledge of my generation is no more than past ones. In response, critics may point to the tremendous resurgence in political activism on part of high school and college students during the 2008 presidential election. While I agree this is true, there is no evidence that these students understood the political process and the issues at hand.

When I ask students the question, "Why don't you pay attention to the news?" I get a range of excuses: "It doesn't affect me...I hate the government, so why should I care?...The government is so far away...I can't change anything."

The problem is two-fold. First, most schools don't require a civics course. Second, when a civics course is offered, like Advanced Placement Government and Politics, the class is defined by rote memorization of terms and names that will never excite students about politics. O.K., you scored a 5 on the A.P. exam, but do you know anything about the government, how to examine candidates, and decide whom to vote for? In many cases, you don't.

As one Minnesota student said in a study, "You sit in a classroom and you read your dusty books with your dusty professors about dusty things, and then you don't learn anything about what you can do with it." First, civics or political science should be assimilated into every year of schooling, from elementary school all the way to high school. We could convert our supply of shrewd newspapers, magazines, and scholarly journals into school curriculums. One possible subject could consist of learning about the mass media. You would learn about the political arena from the left and right and independents, from *Fox News* to *MSNBC* and everything in between. This could be applied to issues like the impact of electronic media on American culture and our nation's politics. Perhaps, one day, teachers would allow students to watch clips of *The Daily Show, The Colbert Report, Fox and Friends,* or *Charlie Rose,* break the segments down into pieces, and debate about it. Let kids act like statesmen and stateswomen where they weigh the evidence at hand, choose a position, and formulate solutions. That's when the juices will start flowing.

This issue is personal. I love politics. I got interested in the subject after reading President Obama's book *The Audacity of Hope* and being injected into the fabric of the 2008 presidential election. It all began when I asked a few questions about the political process and the snowball started rolling.

It is not simply enough to learn about politics in school. To really understand how politics works, you have to experience it yourself. Go to your local representative town-hall. Call up your Senator's office to make an appointment to chat. Volunteer at a candidate's campaign headquarters. Make phone calls. Join or form a Model United Nations, Model Congress, or Junior State of America club at your school.

Do not fear political activism. Once at an event, a student asked former President Jimmy Carter how he felt years earlier when his freshman daughter was arrested at a protest against apartheid. He answered: "I cannot tell you how proud I was. If you young people cannot express your conscience now, when will you? Later you will have duties, jobs, families that make that harder. You will never be freer than now."

We are at critical point in this country. We have a dangerously large populace of ignorant Americans. Benjamin Rush, a signer of the Declaration of Independence and one of the first advocates for public education in America, argued forcefully that schools play a crucial role in preparing the citizens of a democracy. "There is but one method of rendering a republican form of government durable," he stated, "and that is by disseminating the seeds of virtue and knowledge through education."

But we have allowed our politics to decay into a spectator sport that breeds partisanship and congressional back-room deals. We have presided over the erosion of schools that are failing to cultivate generations of citizens that understand what is occurring in this nation, what is ahead for us, and what path we must embark on.

Citizenship is not a privilege; it is a duty. It is so much more than having papers and being a voter, a leader, and a fellow neighbor. Citizenship drives the way we live.

THE ARTS

"Art does not solve problems, but makes us aware of their existence," sculptor Magdalena Abakanowicz has noted. Arts education, on the other hand, does solve problems. Kids need a reason to come to school. One of them is the arts — music, dance, visual arts. They are fundamental to fostering a child's creativity and a facet of honing right brain skills: empathy, emotion, and drive.

Business leaders and school administrators agree. A 2008 study, "Ready to Innovate," touts the importance of arts education in building the 21st-century work force. The report revealed that 99 percent of the surveyed school superintendents and 97 percent of the surveyed employers believe that arts training is crucial to developing creativity.

In school, the arts can capture a student's imagination. Art class could very well be the best part of a kid's day. Perhaps, it may even prevent a kid from dropping out.

Creative thought is one thing that separates humans from machines. By being introduced to the world of visual arts, dance, and music, over time, students will gain the persistence in tackling problems and the ability to observe carefully, express clearly, and be skeptical. It especially teaches observation skills. Linda Friedlaender, curator of education at the Yale Center for British Art, tells me, "Students need to be reminded that looking at something requires time and effort. Observation in an art museum is a process, and a slow one at that, unlike other looking experiences, such as video games."

While there is a growing consensus and plenty of research that demonstrates that the arts are a catalyst for positive change in a child's life, our nation's public schools are offering lesser and lesser access to the subject. Some statistics suggest that fewer than half of adults report having participated in arts lessons or classes in school — a decline from about 65 percent in the 1980s. The decline follows years of steady increases in reported participation between the 1930s and the 1980s. Moreover, it has become even more apparent in the last decade with the full wrath of No Child Left Behind's policies, narrowing out the arts in lieu of more instruction in mathematics and English.

In his 2011 State of the Union address, President Obama repeatedly spoke about the merits of STEM education: Science, Technology, Engineering, and Mathematics. If teachers add an "A" — the arts — to STEM, "learning will pick up STEAM."

Art, when connected with science, for example, can result in wonders. At the Yale School of Medicine, all first-year students are required to take a unique art class. Linda Friedlaender designed a course that hones student's observation skills, something that could help save a patient's life. She said to me, "When you facilitate visitors unpacking a painting, they have to be reminded how to look carefully before trying to figure out what is going on. With select groups, such as medical students, we spend a lot of time describing the picture in as much detail as possible, before moving on to interpretation or drawing conclusions about the painting's narrative. This process has helped medical students in the clinical setting when observing patients for a diagnosis, that is, slowing down the careful observation of a patient."

The Enhancing Observational Skills' collaboration with the Yale Medical School and the Yale Center for British Art began in 2001, and has become a model for over twenty other medical schools in the country.

We must end this hierarchy, where math and science are at the top and the arts are a "frill." The ancient Greeks, for example, made no concrete distinction between the arts and other subjects. Why shouldn't we do the same? By connecting subjects, both society and students will hold them in equal esteem.

PETER PANS OF HUMANITY

Every kid is a natural scientist. They ask plenty of "why" questions, explore uncertainty, and like to touch everything in their sight. The problem is making sure they remain scientists, figuratively or literally, into adulthood.

We have a number of problems to hammer at. First, the level of science literacy in this country is abominable. While scientific literacy has doubled over the past few decades, only a sliver of Americans are scientifically aware. Every day you will find someone who still believes the moon goes around Jupiter, evolution is not real, and climate change is a hoax. We've come so far, but we still have ignoramuses lacking comprehension of basic scientific ideas. Second, many students get weeded and funneled out of the science field in higher education. Studies have confirmed that 40 percent of students planning engineering and science majors end up switching to other subjects or failing to get any degree.

Why? I spoke with high school physics teacher Frank Noschese who argued, "Students perform the exact opposite of scientists in school. Instead of creating, exploring, discovering, and reasoning like scientists, students consume, watch, verify, and recall." Science is dulled down to an extent that it discourages children at very young ages. There's this age-old belief that teaching equals explaining. We don't "do" science, we intake it, by force. Like in most courses, rote learning and the fact-driven curriculum turns kids off. The current science standards movement impedes learning and teaching. In addition, Shirley Malcom of the American Association for the Advancement of Science, tells me, "My colleague Mary Budd Rowe once estimated that there were more terms introduced in the first year of biology than in the first year of foreign language." Parents and teachers, if your child or student isn't drained out by this learning style, there is something seriously wrong with them.

Not only is science taught in a mundane fashion, but society tunes out the profession as a whole.

"The public gets what it celebrates," says Lawrence Bock, executive director of the USA Science and Engineering Festival, in a conversation with me. "We currently celebrate Britney Spears and Lindsay Lohan and we generate 'a lot of them,' but we fail to celebrate science and engineering."

He continues, "First, if you ask kids to draw a scientist, they will probably draw someone that looks mad and has crazy hair. Second, if you ask kids to name a science model, most can't name a living person. They'll say someone like Albert Einstein, but as great as he was, he isn't the standard model of a scientist." Where's the "Sam the Scientist" figure for kids?

Science falters under what I call the "geek effect" where kids think you need to be insanely intelligent to think of becoming a scientist.

When I was younger, I was enthralled by science when I did experiments. I grew tadpoles and caterpillars and watched them grow. I built models with my bare hands. I loved it. All my love for science evaporated when I needed to do worksheets and read textbooks. I no longer wanted to be an engineer. I cannot watch another child experience what I went through.

We need to wage a war on the way we teach and honor science in schools and society, respectively. There are two pieces left in this puzzle to devote our focus to — the curriculum and informal learning.

First, let's reinvent the wheel — the curriculum.

Generally, science is taught in a pattern of a year of biology, then a year of chemistry, and finally a year of physics, beginning in elementary school and repeating in that pattern until the end of high school. Let's scratch subjects. Instead, we should, as Jack Hassard, Emeritus Professor of Science Education at Georgia State University, argued to me, "begin science learning in a context (a polluted stream, a smoggy atmosphere, a disease), and involve students by examining the context or problem, and then bring to the table the science, social science, history, math, geography, needed for students to investigate, discuss, make proposals, etc." Even forensics science involves the chemistry of vomit analysis, the biology of DNA profiling, and the physics of ballistics and blood spatter analysis. We are now starting with the application, rather than the theory. Some call this the science-technology-society movement or the alternative education movement. As I'll explain in detail later, these methodologies are parts of an anti-disciplinary curriculum.

In practice, learning is done best by engaging in experiments. To Nobel Laureate physicist Dudley Herschbach, the best model for teaching science is the way children learn to speak their native language. "They learn with very little help from adults, because they're not worried whether they're getting it right," he points out in an interview. "They just play and they experiment. In scientific research you have to play in a way and you have to guess. Really good science is opening up your eyes to more things you don't know."

From all the scientists I've interviewed or spoken with, an early childhood experiment made them want to be a scientist. By contrast, what you'll often see kids do in laboratory exercises at school is literally follow a cookbook. There is little thinking or reasoning involved. The expected answer is already stamped on the sheet. There's no thrill or excitement.

Something more extravagant is desired. Robert C. Richardson, Nobel Laureate in Physics and professor at Cornell University, said to the *New York Times*, "When I teach undergraduates, one of the most popular things I do is take a $5 watch apart and show how it works. There's a billion dollars' worth of research in that watch, and the kids are fascinated."

As American theoretical physicist Richard Feynman once said, "What I cannot create, I cannot understand."

High school teacher Frank Noschese has implemented model-based instruction through experiments in his physics class. He says the three steps include:

Model Development: Groups of kids start off with the lab by constructing models, getting data, and sharing results.

Model Deployment: Problem-solving by using multiple representations — looking at a problem in many different ways.

Model Failure: Understand when models work and fail. Tweak if the model fails.

I understand lab materials and equipment cost a lot of money and school districts are strapped for cash, but do you feel the same way about your school dances and sports programs?

Second, let's push informal learning in science.

Decades before the American school system was erected, Lyceums, modeled after the early Greek halls of learning, brought the public together with experts in science and philosophy for lectures, debates, and scientific experiments. Years later, science got stuck in brick and mortar classrooms.

Today, most science is learned outside of the classroom. Luckily, America is host to a lineup of museums, aquariums, national parks, zoos, and landmarks, all of which hold a center of trust and honor within communities. A majority of Americans said they had visited an informal science institution. Experts write these institutions off as part of "free choice science learning." Research from John H. Falk and Lynn D. Dierking shows that free-choice learning experiences represent the single greatest contributors to adult science knowledge; childhood free-choice learning experiences also significantly contributed to adult science knowledge. Schooling ranks at the bottom of significant sources of adult science knowledge. No kidding. Since informal learning settings disregard tests and grades, it is often hinged on non-cognitive measures, like motivation.

We aren't harnessing the power of these institutions to the fullest extent. Urban schools, especially, should pay attention. Through exhibits, hands-on activities, games, and lectures, they can bring abstract, theoretical concepts to life. For example, the American Museum of Natural History in New York City is building partnerships to offer inquiry-driven science in its programs. Understand, these "high protein" experiences as Ellen V. Futter, president of the museum puts it, are far more valuable than the old "day off from school" field trips. Why hasn't this transition happened? One of the most dangerous things we are taught in school is that learning only happens in a classroom.

Seeing is believing.

Nobel Laureate physicist Isidor Isaac Rabi once exclaimed, "I think physicists are the Peter Pans of the human race. They never grow up, and they keep their curiosity." If kids don't grow up and stay "forever young" in mind and soul, they will be scientists. For a Sputnik moment to come to fruition as the President hammered on in his 2011 State of the Union address, we must let kids be kids.

It's also time to shift the mantra of "science literacy" into "science is for all Americans."

As Brian Greene, author and professor of physics at Columbia University, writes in a beautiful *New York Times* piece:

> Science is a perspective. Science is the process that takes us from confusion to understanding in a manner that's precise, predictive and reliable — a transformation, for those lucky enough to experience it, that is empowering and emotional. To be able to think through and grasp explanations — for everything from why the sky is blue to how life formed on earth — not because they are declared dogma but rather because they reveal patterns confirmed by experiment and observation, is one of the most precious of human experiences.
>
> Science is the greatest of all adventure stories, one that's been unfolding for thousands of years as we have sought to understand ourselves and our surroundings. Science needs to be taught to the young and communicated to the mature in a manner that captures this drama. We must embark on a cultural shift that places science in its rightful place alongside music, art and literature as an indispensable part of what makes life worth living.
>
> It's the birthright of every child, it's a necessity for every adult, to look out on the world, as the soldier in Iraq did, and see that the wonder of the cosmos transcends everything that divides us.

*

Thomas Jefferson once said, "The purpose of public education is not to serve a public, it is to create a public." What we teach in school must help our children become dynamic and robust citizens in our democracy. If a subject area does not add to that process or is simply irrelevant to the era, we cannot make it mandatory. Aside from reading, writing, arithmetic, and programming, citizens should have:

1) Understanding of statistics, probability, and basic arithmetic computation
2) Basic scientific and health literacy
3) Civic and financial and economics literacy
4) Comprehension of United States history
5) Understanding of at least one foreign language

It's time to redefine the essentials. That means we should not require the teaching of chemistry, physics, biology, algebra, geometry, trigonometry, calculus, and literature. It would be ludicrous on many measures to force kids to learn those subjects.

Lastly, the question we have not answered yet is: How should we learn?

KILL THE LECTURE

The norm of the teaching styles in most classrooms is didactic — lecture-based. I cannot stand them. It is absolutely the worst way to learn something. Research conducted over the past few decades demonstrates that it's impossible for students to take in and process all the information presented during a typical lecture. Lecturing dates back to the 14th century, with the word "lecture" literally meaning "action of reading." In medieval universities, before the Gutenberg printing press was invented, teachers would read from the original text to a group of students who would then regurgitate the information. Then, in the late 20th century, something magical happened. The Internet was born. Almost everything found in books could be accessed seamlessly on the web. Yet in schools, we are still teaching the same way as our 14th century predecessors.

It took Eric Mazur, professor of physics at Harvard University, a few years to catch onto the problem of lecturing. Like most professors, he delivered polished lectures. He loved it. Mazur justifies, "It's a lot more fun being on stage delivering a lecture than it is sitting in the audience watching it." He saw nothing wrong with it as he continued to get high student evaluations for his courses. Then after reading about research completed by Arizona State professor David Hestenes and one of Hestenes' graduate students, Ibrahim Halloum, he had an epiphany. After devising a test to check students' conceptual understanding of physics and administering it to about 1,000 students in introductory physics courses taught by seven different instructors at two different schools, Hestenes and Halloun deter-mined that the courses had taught the students almost nothing. Mazur was puzzled. So, he used the test to experiment on his own students and they didn't do much better. After deep rumination, Mazur says, he eventually scrapped lecturing in class and introduced a "peer-instruction" approach, where rather than teaching by telling, he teaches by questioning.

In the data, he says, "If you objectively measure the learning gains by assessing the students by a test at the beginning and repeating it at the end of each semester, the learning gain doubles easily and sometimes triples. There is much bigger retention of material, because the material makes sense."

Furthermore, a recent study compared the outcomes of two classes, a control class that received a lecture from a Nobel Prize-winning physicist and an experimental section where students worked with graduate assis-tants to solve physics problems. Test scores for the experimental group (non-lecture) was nearly double that of the control group (74 percent to 41 percent).

In Harvard classes, student Hemi H. Gandhi writes that Facebook use "has become so ubiquitous that no one even questions it" — not even professors. And as author Albert Camus once said, "Some people talk in their sleep. Lecturers talk while other people sleep."

Yet, schools are still buying into lecture driven ideas like Khan Academy and the "flipped" classroom. From absent-minded policymak-ers to nonsensical journalists, Khan Academy is deemed "a revolution in education." That's the last thing it should be called. Khan Academy, started by Salman Khan, a former hedge-fund trader, is a disguise of rote learning through technology.

Karim Ani, the founder of Mathalicious, a site that teaches math through real-world topics, had a remarkable piece deconstructing the Khan Academy empire, noting, "Khan Academy is great for what it is — a sup-plemental resource; homework help — but we've turned it into something it's not. Indeed, something it was never intended to be." We are unable to look past the Scantron and delivery system of learning.

Of the roughly thirty people who work at Khan Academy, none have ever taught in a public K-12 school classroom in the United States. Now, Khan and his fellow "revolutionaries" are touting the "flipped class-room" model of teaching, where students watch videos at home and get assistance at school. However, as Frank Noschese, a physics teacher at John Jay High School, argues, "It's Lecture 2.0. The way people with power and money view education is simply 'sit-and-get.'"

I don't find a video lecture to be very engaging. Instead of getting our hands dirty, we are acting like kids who are distracted in a candy store. "There's a saying that goes, 'Don't hate the player, hate the game.'" No-schese adds, "Khan Academy is merely a player. We need to change the game."

Lecturing does not equal learning. Drum that into people's heads. Think of the most enjoyable experience you have ever had in a class in school (If you can't, I absolutely understand). Was it sitting in a desk and hearing a lecture? Or was it doing a project or an experiment? I bet it was the latter.

Let's finally kill the lecture in schools.

ANTI-DISCIPLINARY

We live in a cocoon. Jeff Hoffman, CEO of ColorJar and serial entrepreneur agrees. I met Hoffman when he spoke at TEDxWallStreet in March 2012. He has spent the last few decades, immersed in the fields of the Internet, e-commerce, and entertainment. In business, Hoffman says, "We tend to be in the same surroundings every single day until it becomes a blur. We never step back and pretend we were never there before."

He continues, "Say I'm from the health care industry and a person asks me to come to a banking conference, you would ask, 'Why would I go to a banking conference? I'm in health care.' In fact, every once in a while, it's important to break out."

When people of all different fields and backgrounds inter-mingle and intersect, spectacular breakthroughs are a result. Author Frans Johansson described this phenomenon as "the Medici effect," referring to the creative explosion in Florence, Italy when the Medici family brought together creators from a wide range of disciplines — sculptors, scientists, poets, philosophers, painters, and architects. As connections were forged and ideas were contested, what spawned was the Renaissance, one of the most innovative eras in history. It's all about connecting the dots.

So what does Jeff Hoffman do? Every morning, he checks the Top 10 searches on Yahoo just to see what the world tuned into. "Is that the absolute answer?" he asks. "No, they're trends. After a while, you notice the ebbs and flows of what's going on in people's minds." Hoffman calls this technique info-sponging or, in other words, taking a big gulp of the universe. One of the reasons he is so successful is because along with checking the Top 10 searches on Yahoo, he takes 20 minutes to pretend that he wasn't in his industry and didn't have customers. Hoffman observes drifts occurring in other sectors, writing down anything that strikes him.

He asks, "What can I do today that I couldn't do yesterday?"

Look at InnoCentive, a company that links organizations with problems to people around the world that want to get money to solve them. It was pioneered by pharmaceutical giant Eli Lilly in 2000 when the company had a difficult time managing the R&D process. Shortly after, the site took off at huge paces, racking up solutions from people around the globe. In 2007, Karim Lakhani, a professor at the Harvard Business School, began analyzing hundreds of scientific problems posted on the site. According to Lakhani's data, nearly 30 percent of the difficult problems posted on InnoCentive were solved within six months. Why was it so successful? The secret was outsiders. The more diverse the interests of the base of solvers, the more likely the problems were to be solved. Interestingly, Lakhani found that the more expertise a person had in the field of the problem, the less likely they were able to solve it. Often, an expert may undergo "tunnel vision," which stunts singularity in solving problems. However, if the problem fell completely outside a solver's expertise, that raised his or her chance of success by 10 percent. Having an unbiased perspective changes the game. In education, I am an outsider and an insider. While I am not an expert in education policy, my student perspective offers a unique angle to the conversation.

What if we take the lessons from InnoCentive and Jeff Hoffman and apply it to education?

Can creativity be taught? Absolutely. The real question is: How do we teach it? In school, instead of crossing subjects and classes, we teach in a very rigid manner. Very rarely do you witness math and science teachers or English and history teachers collaborating with each other. Sticking in your silo, shell, and expertise is comfortable. Well, it's time to crack that shell. It's time to abolish silos and subjects. Joichi Ito, director of the M.I.T. Media Lab, told me that rather than interdisciplinary education, which merges two or more disciplines, we need anti-disciplinary education, a term coined by Sandy Pentland, head of the lab's Human Dynamics group.

"Today's problems — from global poverty to climate change to the obesity epidemic — are more interconnected and intertwined than ever before and they can't possibly be solved in the academic or research 'silos' of the twentieth century," writes Frank Moss, the former head of the M.I.T. Media Lab.

Schools cannot just simply add a "creativity hour" and call it a day.

Principal at High Tech High, an innovative, project-based learning school in San Diego, California, Larry Rosenstock, points out to me, "If you were to hike the Appalachian trail, which would take you months and months, and you reflect upon it, you do not divide the experience into the historic, scientific, mathematic, and English aspects of it. You would look at it holistically."

After indicating the problem at hand, scoop out the tools, research, networks, and people required to get it solved. Get out of your comfort zone.

In practice, this means the elimination of English, mathematics, history, and science class. Instead, we need to arrange the curriculum around big ideas, questions, and conundrums. What does learning look like in this model? Letting kids learn by doing and creating — the essence of the philosophy of educator John Dewey. He wrote: "The school must represent present life — life as real and vital to the child as that which he carries on in the home, in the neighborhood, or on the playground." Let kids travel to places, work with mentors, and inquire about the world around them.

Diana Laufenberg, former teacher at the Science Leadership Academy, described to me, "The role of inquiry is the starting point of learning. School-based education has always been about telling and getting of information, rather than exploring or investigating." Let kids create for themselves. We can start by employing project-based learning, where students probe real world problems collaboratively. Back in 1918, William Heard Kilpatrick wrote a famous article laying out what he called the "project method": a curriculum based on "wholehearted purposeful activity proceeding in a social environment...the essential factor [being] the presence of a dominating purpose." In project-based classrooms, learning literally comes alive.

Let's examine three institutions: The Brightworks School, a K-12 private school; Stanford d.school, an institute of design; and the M.I.T. Media Lab, a graduate program.

The Brightworks School in San Francisco, California, which opened its doors in September 2011, epitomizes a new style of learning. Founder Gever Tulley told me, "If the pedagogical unit of traditional public education is a day divided into a series of 45 minute periods, then the pedagogical unit of Brightworks is the arc, which is divided into three phrases." Each arc, he says, has a central theme.

The first phase of the arc is called exploration. "Within this phase," Tulley says, "we create a landscape of experiences populated by passionate people who have devoted some portion of their lives to an aspect of the topic." The children begin a journey looking through a kaleidscope of perspectives and eventually mold a clear statement of what they intend to accomplish in the next phase. The second phase is expression. Tulley notes, "During this phrase, the mixed age teams work together, sharing skills, to take the ideas to completion — within the deadline." The final phase is called exposition, where the public gets to view what the kids have done.

The first topic of the previous school year was cities. For three weeks, the students looked at the history of cities, how cities work, and the future of cities. Eighteen field trips were built into their schedule. Almost every day, Tulley explains, "we went into the city to see something or work with someone who has dedicated their life to some aspect of the city. Be they in waste water management, city planners, or architects."

"The point is to see the topic in as many ways as you possibly can," says Tulley. "Part of that is to expand the notion of cities in the students' minds."

Note: project-based learning is not necessarily expensive. He reveals, "If you look at the net aggregate cost of putting a child through a nearby public school in terms of public expenditure, at Brightworks, we do not spend anymore on kids in our private school in terms of net aggregate cost."

At the Stanford d.school, an institute of design, projects drive the curriculum. Bringing majors from engineering, business, medicine, science, and design to come together to solve real or abstract problems is the underpinning of the institution's philosophy. The goal is to have students become what are called "T-shaped" students, who have depth in a particular field of study but also breadth across multiple disciplines. Its founder and director is David Kelley, whose mission is to transmit "empathy" into his students to encourage them to see the human side of the challenges posed in class. He wants to help students regain their creative confidence which is often lost in the early years of schooling.

Based on the axioms of what Kelley has called "design thinking," instead of being spoon-fed problems to solve, students must first define problems themselves through observation, research, and dialogue. Afterwards, students visualize and brainstorm potential solutions with one another in the stage of "ideation." Next, by means of prototypes, students make sketches and three-dimensional models of potential ideas to iterate continuously. Lastly, students add the final touches on a finished prototype.

The school concentrates on four areas: the developing world, sustainability, health and wellness, and K-12 education. From extracting water for irrigation in Burma to supplying solar lanterns for the poor in rural India and Africa to building infant warmers in Nepal, these students are certainly making their mark on the world.

Similarly, the M.I.T. Media Lab has an anti-disciplinary approach to learning. Their research program is "focused on inventing a better future through creative applications of innovative digital technologies." Instead of lectures, grading, and tests, roughly 25 groups of graduate student researchers and a few undergraduate researchers work with faculty members and scientists on a research topic. Due to its non-linear and collaborative process, fascinating innovations are born: from Aida, a dashboard-mounted robot for cars and trucks, to a trillion-frame-per-second video, to Huggable, a robot teddy bear companion for pediatric hospital patients.

How can we evaluate projects? We can't grade them the same way as tests. Gever Tulley offered me a very relevant hypothetical situation:

> Suppose you and I decided to build a boat. Our hypothesis might be: we can build a boat under $30 using recycled materials and sail it across the Hudson River. Our teacher or mentor can help us shape that to ensure that the challenge meets our cognitive and intellectual development. If the teacher thought the task was too easy for us, he or she might add a twist — the boat needs to have two masts or sail power. Half a day, a few times a week, you and I would work on this project and we have a deadline.
>
> Suppose then we build the boat, drop it in the Hud-

son River, and it sinks. No one has to tell us that our boat is not working. We don't need the 'F.' Its unnecessary and inappropriate. That first version of the boat could have been a hypothesis. We learned from the experience and the next version will be more well thought out. So after going back to drawing board and making tweaks, we test the final version. We find that the boat sails well downwind, but cannot sail upwind.

What grade should a teacher give? Is that a 'C' because it only went in one direction? Or is that an 'A' because we tried a bold idea but we neglected 3,000 years of sailing history and would have been able to sail it in both directions if we had done our research? You can't decide. The feedback from the boat is its own incentive to improve our thinking for the next project.

The point is that evaluation is no longer about giving a single number, but rather a documented process from start to finish. At the Brightworks School, students will leave with an iPad, filled with all the projects they completed in their term. Plus, publishing your work online is one of the biggest motivators for kids. When she was teaching at the Science Leadership Academy, Diana Laufenberg said that if you Googled her students' names, you would find an entire web history linked to them. Couple that with the fact that in project-based learning, kids are working on something they have a passion for, thus they have a stake in the outcome and will keep trying even when something isn't working. That's true in life as well.

Why hasn't project-based learning picked up yet? There are a few reasons. First, the model of education says principal Chris Lehmann where kids sit in rows, read textbooks, and hear lectures has lasted so long, because it never goes that wrong. "It's boring as hell, but most principals don't yell at their teachers if they walk by their classroom and all they see is a quiet classroom with kids reading the textbook. No one gets in trouble."

"If you go into a classroom," says Lehmann, "where there isn't that structure, kids aren't exactly on pace, projects look messy, and it's loud, teachers have gotten in trouble for that."

Second, the way students attempt to learn via projects does not work. Tulley says, "It amounts to kit-based experiences in 45 minute periods. 'We're going to do a biology kit.' We already know that those recipe like exercises do not stimulate creativity."

I also spoke with Harvard Professor Eric Mazur on this issue. He says, "You can have students do laboratories and hands-on activities and learn nothing, because they are following the cookbook and going through the motions without having their brains on. The word 'hands-on' is overused and abused."

The role of the teacher in project-based learning as Laufenberg likes to say is an "architect of opportunity. Through a scaffolding strategy, they help students make sense of what they have learned. Still, teachers must understand that learning is uncomfortable, messy, and complicated." Get over compliance and control!

In a summary published on *Edutopia*, Brigid Barron and Linda Darling-Hammond reviewed numerous studies and found that:

1. Students learn more deeply when they can apply classroom-gathered knowledge to real-world problems, and when they take part in projects that require sustained engagement and collaboration.

2. Active-learning practices have a more significant impact on student performance than any other variable, including student background and prior achievement.

3. Students are most successful when they are taught how to learn as well as what to learn.

As the old adage goes, "Tell me and I forget, show me and I remember, involve me and I understand." Harvard Professor Howard Gardner told me that schools should incorporate the best of two models of learning: a children's museum, which encourages open-ended exploration, and an apprenticeship, which provides a more structured environment for practicing meaningful skills in an authentic, real-life context.

The bottom line is that you don't have to learn the boring stuff before you start applying it. Start rolling around in the dirt from the get go.

TECHNOLOGY

The two questions that everyone is asking, but very few seem to have the answer to is: How do you scale education? How do you appropriately use technology in school?

Let's begin with the first. You might hear that the best way to personalize and scale education is via technology. In some ways, that is true. Sites like Khan Academy, Udemy, Udacity, edX, and Coursera are permitting anyone with a broadband connection to free videos on almost any topic of their choice. However, once again, watching videos aren't engaging nor are they the best ways to learn something new. First, plenty of education companies have tried to create personalized education, using data-driven platforms that track and assess students, ultimately promising better test results. The phrase "Any time, any place, any pace" comes to mind.

But we have got it all wrong. Educator and author Will Richardson argues that the answer is not personalization. He writes, "'Personalized' learning is something that we do to kids; 'personal' learning is something they do for themselves." We need the latter. Second, scaling also lives by this similar terrible misconception. Can you imagine if every child in America stayed at home, learned by hearing online lectures from teachers, and were tracked by online multiple choice quizzes and tests? Perhaps that would be Horace Mann's 21st century prescription for training for obedience. Nevertheless, scaling is really defined by students tapping into networks, establishing their personal brands, building bridges into the real word, and sharing wisdom with others.

To address the second question, technology has been around for so long, but most schools haven't adopted its tools on a mass scale. Why? They're scared. I proposed to one of my teachers to allow students to use laptops in class to engage with social media and online videos. He replied in a disturbed tone along the lines of, "Absolutely not. Technology does not have a place in school. I am not letting myself be replaced by a screen." I tried to conceal my squirms of laughter.

When technology has been used in schools, it hasn't been used to do anything differently. For example, Apple announced a program to change education through the iPad. Schools have jumped on, some doling out iPads to their entire student population believing they are doing a favor to this tech savvy generation. The iPads are loaded with a thousand page plus textbooks filled with pages of monotonous, vanilla exercises. If a kid doesn't like reading the regular paper textbook, what makes you think he or she will like the digital? You can't trick kids. We should instead be making full use of the rich resources of the iPad — the applications and the easy-to-use interface.

Technology is a double-edged sword. It can streamline processes, but it can also be extremely isolating and useless. Take SMART Boards: they aren't going to change learning in classrooms. Period. It's one of the biggest wastes of money in school budgets. We'd do well to heed the words of Henry David Thoreau: "We are in great haste to construct a magnetic telegraph from Maine to Texas; but Maine and Texas, it may be, have nothing important to communicate." Overall, schools need to stop being blinded by the latest trends. Instead of clunking down thousands on frivolous technologies, what if you asked teachers and students to spend the money based on their specific needs?

Principal Chris Lehmann argues, "Technology needs to be like oxygen — ubiquitous, necessary, and invisible. It's got to be everywhere. It's got to be part and parcel of everything we do. And then we've got to stop talking about it quite so much. It's just got to be part of the day-to-day work that we all do." Every child should have access to a laptop or a tablet. Integrating these devices is a piece of cake. Plus, rather than blocking social media, let's embrace it. Teaching social media to my generation is like teaching human beings to breathe. Let kids blog, post videos and pictures, and engage with networks. Without social media, I would not have had some incredible opportunities and met some extraordinary people.

It doesn't make sense that teachers do not let their students use Facebook, Twitter, and other social networks during class. Nobody will stop them from using these tools in the world. Children are being impaired when they aren't taught digital citizenship. Teachers, if you don't know how to use technology and social media, don't rob your students of the ability to use it. Start by working with your students to understand how they use these tools outside of school and communicate with educators on Twitter by participating in the weekly #edchat, #soschat, or #stuvoice chat.

The purpose of school is to create life-long learners. Period. Let's jump from the Alcatraz prison-like school system to a community and apprenticeship-based system. Every school, John Dewey wrote in *The School and Society*, must become "an embryonic community life, active with types of occupations that reflect the life of the larger society and permeated throughout with the spirit of art, history, and science. When the school introduces and trains each child of society into membership within such a little community, saturating him with the spirit of service, and providing him with instruments of effective self-direction, we shall have the deepest and best guarantee of a larger society which is worthy, lovely and harmonious." A learning revolution will only transpire when students become captains of their learning.

CHAPTER 7

NATION BUILDERS

Stephen Ritz is closely observing groups of people. A few are adjusting the seed incubators. Others are watering a wall of plants. Some are transporting trays of newly grown vegetables. No matter where you look there is activity.

Except this isn't a farm; it's a classroom. And Ritz isn't a farmer; he's a teacher. A teacher in a South Bronx high school in one of the poorest congressional districts in America where almost every student lives below the poverty line. However, that doesn't stop Ritz.

Ritz, along with his class and fellow community members, have grown 25,000 pounds of vegetables. His students were growing enough food in one classroom to feed 450 students a vegetarian meal every 90 days. It's down right spectacular. Ritz credits his students with all the success — "my students are the orchestra, I am just the conductor." His students are certainly playing harmonious notes.

Years ago, a much younger Stephen Ritz was just graduating from SUNY Purchase. He had hoped to play basketball overseas in Europe. Though that didn't quite work out, Ritz says in a joking tone to me.

After traveling in Europe, he became a teacher in the South Bronx, the birthplace of hip-hop, in the 1980s. In his first year of teaching, his paycheck was less than $10,000. "I was struggling to make ends meet," recalls Ritz. "I then opted into the private sector — construction and remodeling — anything that paid better. But I always planned on going back to public education."

After his stint in the private sector, he wound up scoring a scholarship to Arizona State University. There, says Ritz, "I met a wonderful professor, Stanley Zucker, who specialized in working with at risk youth and adults. He took a chance on me, and I eventually got a master's degree in special education. Stan changed my life."

From Arizona, Ritz trekked to New York City to open a series of restaurants, learning about "creating entrepreneurial and economic opportunities in areas of high need." But he was stuck with the bug and finally after many years went back to teaching full time and has "never looked back."

*

The problem is that teachers around America are under attack. We are discouraging 'Stephen Ritzs' from becoming and remaining teachers. The blame game is more severe than the partisan climate in the halls of Congress. It is appropriate to deem the conflict as the 'War on Teachers.' The attack crusade, led by corporate reformers, many of whom have never stepped into a public school, is peculiar. First, why has this crusade attracted such strong bipartisan support? Second, why has the public failed to recognize their threat? Call it ignorance, but I believe it is a reluctance to act.

In a *New York Times* piece, Dave Eggers and Nínive Clements Calegari, founders of the 826 National tutoring centers and producers of the documentary *American Teacher*, write, "When we don't get the results we want in our military endeavors, we don't blame the soldiers. We don't say, 'It's these lazy soldiers and their bloated benefits plans! That's why we haven't done better in Afghanistan!' No, if the results aren't there, we blame the planners. We blame the generals, the secretary of defense, the Joint Chiefs of Staff. No one contemplates blaming the men and women fighting every day in the trenches for little pay and scant recognition."

Eggers and Calegari go on to assert, "Yet in education we do just that. When we don't like the way particular schools perform, we blame the teachers and restrict their resources."

We treat teachers atrociously. Our rationale revolves around the saying, "Those who can't do, teach." We pay them pathetic salaries, offer little to no feedback or autonomy, and shame them with pitiless accountability measures. What kind of sane person would want to become a teacher in the conditions we put them in? Teaching is the only white collar profession with a blue collar mentality.

The always brilliant former *New York Times* education writer, Michael Winerip, puts it, "Can an education reform movement that demeans and trivializes teachers succeed? It's hard to imagine, but that is what is going on in parts of America today."

In South Korea, teachers are respected and lauded as "nation builders." "Don't even step on the shadow of a teacher," says one Korean proverb. The same is true in Finland where the best and brightest go into teaching. Teachers deserve to be given more than simply respect. We have to honor them.

There was a great cartoon that showed a sports fantasy camp with a group of athletes waiting to get an autograph from a short, balding man. One player points to him and says, "I wish I had that kind of money and respect." Another athlete points to the man and says, "Wow! A teacher!" Overall, the message says a lot about America today. We *kowtow* to our steroid-pumped athletes and plastic pop stars. Rather it should be the great teacher that triggers the 'Wow!' Simply put, behind every great person is a great teacher.

Look at the teacher power struggle in our bureaucracy. There are little to no sane teachers crafting education policies. I dare you to show me a teacher that loves No Child Left Behind or Race to the Top. I triple-dog dare you (If you happen to find one, I ask you to email me because I'd love to have a conversation with him or her). The pyramid in education goes something like this: At the top is the President and Congress, then the Secretary of Education and his or her gang, the states with their legislatures are next in line, then the school boards, then the administrators, and finally the teachers. The hierarchy is top-down. Teachers are shunned out of the decision making process.

Meanwhile, the United States is at a cusp of a pressing teacher shortage. Of the roughly 3.3 million teachers nationwide, roughly half are baby-boomers approaching retirement in the coming decade. Warren Buffet once said, "Only when the tide goes out do you find out who is not wearing a bathing suit." Absolutely. The American teaching force has been "swimming buck naked" for far too long. Without an army of qualified teachers, our country will wane. Our nakedness will be in full sight.

I wish it were as easy as telling kids "your country needs you," but it's not that simple. In my conversations with thousands of students in my high school and others, I have came across only a handful of students who said they wanted to be a teacher when they get older. This disturbing sentiment may be due to the students' concern of being labeled a failure, not making enough money to sustain life, or becoming a person who didn't fulfill his or her potential. It's ridiculous.

As many pundits and reports have declared, "The quality of an education system cannot exceed the quality of its teachers." We need to revolutionize the teaching profession. How? Let's find out.

THE TOP THIRD MYTH

In Finland, if I applied to a graduate education program, it would be more difficult to be admitted than medical school. Only eight universities are permitted to prepare teachers. In 2008, the latest year for which figures are available, 1,258 undergrads applied for training to become elementary school teachers. Only 123, or 9.8 percent, were accepted into the five-year teaching program. Since the entry into a teaching program is very selective, teachers are well respected in Finnish society.

A 2010 McKinsey study found that nearly 100 percent of new teachers in Finland, Singapore, and South Korea come from the top third of their graduating class, while the figure is 23 percent for the United States. In fact, according to Martin Gross, author of *Conspiracy of Ignorance*, the majority of U.S. education majors do not come from the top 10 percent of their class but from the bottom third. He further states that they also tend to have the lowest SAT scores of any college major. Want to know the easiest major at any college? According to author Lynn O'Shaughnessy, it's education.

Wait, don't draw any conclusions just yet! Read the disclaimer in the McKinsey report: "We recognize that 'top third' students can be defined in a number of ways. For the purposes of clarity for our market research, top third is defined in this report by a combination of SAT, ACT, and GPA scores." Ah ha! SAT, ACT, nor GPA scores cannot determine one's ability to teach. A spotless 100 percent of teachers coming from the top third of their class, by that definition, should not be our goal. It makes no sense.

The fabulous film *American Teacher* follows a handful of talented teachers. One is a gifted young African-American teacher, with a bachelor's degree from Harvard University and a master's degree from Columbia University, who has to explain to family and friends why she chose teaching. "You could do anything! Why teaching?" In a family of doctors and lawyers, that kid is often dubbed the "failure." The tragedies of American society.

SALARY

Money isn't usually the reason why a person enters the teaching profession, but it may be the reason why some people do not enter. It's this simple: We get what we pay for. The average teaching starting salary is $39,000; the average ending salary — after 25 years in the profession — is $67,000. In real terms, teachers' salaries have declined for 30 years. The difference in starting salaries between teaching and other professions wasn't always as large. In 1970 in New York City, for example, a starting lawyer going into a prestigious firm and a starting teacher going into public education had a differential in their starting salary of about $2,000. Today, including salary and bonus, that starting lawyer makes $160,000, while a starting teacher makes $39,000. At the very least, teachers deserve to live comfortably and not worry about putting food on the table or raising a family.

The average income of the top 25 hedge fund managers in 2009 was $1 billion. So, on average, one top hedge fund manager makes as much as 14,900 veteran teachers.

As one commentator writes, "In Michigan, where I live, the average starting salary for a teacher is about $35,000 for nine months. That works out to about $20 an hour. A bartender can make double that. Which job do you think is more important?" No wise cracks, please.

Look to how other countries pay teachers. Recently, the Organization for Economic Cooperation and Development (OECD) released a report,

"Building a High Quality Teaching Profession: Lessons from Around the World," which analyzes how high-performing countries have created highly professional and effective teaching forces. For each participating nation, OECD calculated the ratio of the average salaries of teachers with 15 years of experience to the average earnings of full-time workers with a college degree. The U.S. ranked 22nd out of 27 countries on this measure. In Finland, salaries are modest, starting at around 81 percent of GDP per capita, slightly above the U.S. at 79 percent. At the high end of the OECD scale, in South Korea, the average teacher at this level makes a full 221 percent of the country's GDP per capita. Talk about respect.

Ultimately, these countries not only reward their teachers with healthy salaries, they ensure their pay is in line with starting salaries for graduates in other professions. We will not remain the greatest country on Earth if we only recruit run-of-the-mill teachers.

Additionally, we have teachers on top of their regular duties forced to take second jobs to pay their bills and support their families. I came across the piece, "Years of Despair Add to Uncertainty in Florida Race" in the *New York Times* one day:

> Only four years ago, life certainly seemed on the upswing for Kate and Marcus Freeman, young professionals who had recently moved from Worcester, Mass., into a new house here in sun-splashed central Florida, where they hoped to enjoy the warmer weather and new jobs. He was an accountant. She would be teaching preschool.
>
> The future was not supposed to look like this: On Saturday, Mr. and Ms. Freeman were sweating at an intersection off Interstate 4, selling chili for $5 a jar to help save their home, which is in foreclosure. Mr. Freeman, 38, was laid off last year. The couple, who have two sons, fell behind on mortgage payments. Now, hope is in a jar of chili with a label that reads "Freeman's Home." On a good weekend, they can clear $130 after expenses.

A teacher selling chili for $5 a jar on the weekends to feed her family. What is going on? Why are teachers being forced to take on second jobs? Why are teachers paid the lowest of the low when they have our children's minds in their hands? The deputy superintendent of South Carolina nails it when he says: "When you have teachers who have to have second jobs...teachers that are living at the poverty level. Then I think there is something wrong...And as a society we need to really change that culture. We need to flip it around to say that being a teacher is the most important job in our society."

In 1981, about 11 percent of teachers were moonlighting. Sixty-two percent of American teachers have jobs outside of the classroom. On many occasions, I see teachers outside of school — coaching local basketball teams, running day-cares, and tutoring students for the SAT.

What happens when teachers are burnt out? They leave. Fourteen percent of American teachers leave after only one year, and 46 percent quit before their fifth year. Estimates put the costs of teacher attrition at $7.3 billion a year. The amount of turnover in Finland? 2 percent.

Fortunately, a majority of the public agrees that teachers are underpaid. Recently, a study by Raj Chetty and John N. Friedman of Harvard and Jonah E. Rockoff of Columbia, all economists, concluded that elementary and middle school teachers who help raise their students' standardized-test scores seem to have a wide-ranging, lasting positive effect on those students' lives beyond academics. From my own experiences, I concur that a great teacher can have a powerful, even lifelong effect on students. However, proving that scientifically through flawed measures of standardized tests makes me shake my head. And why are the economists sticking their noses in the education debate? Shouldn't they be involved in, I don't know, fixing our ongoing economic Armageddon?

My school has a fairly good pool of talented teachers, because we pay them high salaries. What should the country, as a whole, do? Pay teachers more. McKinsey polled 900 top-tier American college students and found that 68 percent would consider teaching if salaries started at $65,000 and rose to a minimum of $150,000. Is this even possible? If we're committed to radically reinventing the profession, we must.

The teaching profession is very similar to the free agent market in Major League Baseball. The teams with the biggest budgets get the best players, leaving the smallest budget teams with crap. In schools, the best teachers often go to the wealthiest communities, while the less off teachers are dumped in low-income schools, where the pay is low and the conditions are subpar. What's the first step to reducing the achievement gap? Offer higher teacher salaries in high risk schools. Simple.

One more important point on teacher pay: It's an ancient argument. Richard Nixon said more than five decades ago in a 1960 presidential debate: "We want higher teachers' salaries. We need higher teachers' salaries...I favor higher salaries for teachers...Teachers' salaries very fortunately have gone up fifty percent in the last eight years as against only a thirty-four percent rise for other salaries. This is not enough; it should be more."

The pundits who say that teachers are overpaid are living in a parallel universe. Many of my teachers pay for classroom supplies out of their own pocket. And they work damn hard. Please show them some respect.

Don't lecture me on how we can't pay for this. We paid for two wars, the Bush tax cuts, a Medicare prescription drug plan, and a Wall Street bailout. We can pay teachers a little bit more, alright. How many times do I need to say it?

GRADUATE EDUCATION SCHOOLS

During the 19th century, normal schools emerged, predecessors to today's graduate schools of education, intended to train high school graduates to be teachers. By the 1920s, normal schools lost ground to the term "teachers colleges," and eventually revamped into four-year programs that granted degrees. From the beginning, teacher-training programs faced what Stanford University historian David Labaree calls a "devil's bargain" between quantity and quality either producing enough teachers to meet demand, or preparing fewer teachers to high standards. Under pressure, he says, they chose quantity. Today, these institutions have become a monopoly in awarding education degrees, preparing more than 90 percent of the nation's teachers and school administrators.

One Harvard lecturer said to a blogger, "The dirty little secret about schools of education is that they have been the cash cows of universities for many, many years."

Traditionally, education schools divide their curriculums into three parts: regular academic subjects, to make sure teachers know the basics of what they are assigned to teach; "foundations" courses to give them a sense of the history and philosophy of education; and finally "methods" courses that are supposed to offer ideas for how to teach particular subjects.

Most graduate education courses are useless. Perhaps it is because education school professors often have little contact with actual schools. A 2006 report found that 12 percent of education-school faculty members have never taught in elementary or secondary schools themselves. Some professors have never set foot in a classroom or have not done so recently. In my research, I stumbled upon reports from Arthur Levine, President of the Woodrow Wilson Foundation and former president of Columbia Teachers College. In my conversation with him, Levine said, "The teacher-education curriculum in universities is a confusing patchwork. When universities began adopting teacher education programs, the programs became increasingly theoretical. In general, education schools do better at preparing students for doctorates and academic life rather than teaching careers. The nation is shifting from a national, analog, and industrial economy to a global, digital information economy. The teacher education curriculum remains a product of the former. In this sense, we have a teacher force that has been prepared for a different world."

Only a semester of student teaching is included in a typical standard teacher-certification program. However, to become a licensed master plumber in NYC, for example, includes "at least seven years total experience...under the direct and continuing supervision of a licensed master plumber." Even if you're a registered architect or an engineer, you still need to have at least three years of apprenticeship under your belt. What's more, a license to practice medicine requires an undergraduate degree, two years of graduate level courses, and six to 12 years of apprenticeships through internships, rotations, and a residency.

What makes the training to be a teacher any different? Teachers hold the future of our country in their hands, the future of the pool of citizens in our democracy. We coddle teachers until they are thrown into the classroom. Most of them drown. Like doctors and plumbers, teachers need to get their feet wet before they are fully integrated into the practice.

Thus, this segregation of theory and practice must be terminated. Once again, we must look to Finland as our paragon. Pasi Sahlberg, Director General of the Center for International Mobility (CIMO) in Finland, told me that all teachers complete a five-years master's degree. At university, he says, "students have a lot of guided teacher training, gaining feedback from a trained supervisor." Here's what graduate education schools need to emphasize: a combination of theory, classroom observation, intense coaching and mentorship, and side by side teaching with experienced, senior level teachers. Courses need to spotlight learning how to create and teach hands on, social media, technology, project-based, and anti-disciplinary classes. The goal is that eventually education school alumni will not attest that their graduate programs didn't prepare them to teach.

We should also follow Harvard Innovation Fellow Tony Wagner's suggestion. He said to me that we should create a West Point for teachers: "We need a new National Education Academy, modeled after our military academies, to raise the status of the profession and to support the R&D that is essential for reinventing teaching, learning and assessment in the 21st century."

Malcolm Gladwell, in his book *Outliers*, explains the "10,000-hour rule," claiming that the key to success in any field is a matter of practicing a specific task for a total of around 10,000 hours. While the number of hours isn't exactly on the dot, teachers don't reach their peak until several years on the job. That means they need constant professional development when they become assimilated into the profession — not the absurd conferences where you just hear people market their products. Schools should allot a few days a month, fully compensated, for teachers to experiment, tinker, and learn how to apply new concepts in the classroom.

Levine writes in the *Washington Post*, "The Willie Sutton principle says graduate education school is the wisest area for states to focus upon if they are serious about improving teacher education. When asked why he robbed banks, Sutton replied, 'Because that's where the money is.' Higher education is where the teachers are." Let's begin right there.

TEACH FOR AWHILE

In her senior thesis at Princeton University, Wendy Kopp suggested the creation of a program that would place high performing college graduates in very disadvantaged, poverty-stricken schools to teach for at least two years. However, she didn't expect her adviser to tell her that she was "quite evidently deranged." Kopp, unfortunately, chose not to listen and started what is now known as Teach for America. While she ultimately earned an A on her thesis, TFA deserves a big, fat F.

TFA is literally one of the dumbest concepts I have heard in the education reform debate. Putting "top" college graduates, based on superb test scores, in the classrooms of low-income students sounds like a Saturday Night Live skit or a poorly sketched Hollywood film plot.

The program relies on the assumption that recent undergraduates are somehow better than traditional teachers. In a 2002 study in the *Education Policy Analysis Archives* comparing TFA members to veteran teachers, students taught by TFA students did not perform significantly different from students taught by other under-certified teachers. And students of certified teachers out-performed students of teachers who were under-certified. Three years later the same journal published an article once again concluding that certified teachers consistently produce stronger student achievement gains than do uncertified teachers. Again, while I despise using standardized test scores as a yardstick, they are the sole quantitative measure in this case.

Another TFA assumption is that anyone can teach if they understand the subject matter. Not true. In *Democracy and Education*, John Dewey is clear that method is not separable from subject matter. He surmises:

> Subject matter knowledge alone does not make a good teacher. Teachers teach subject matter to students. It is a triangle enclosing a pedagogical space. Just teaching the subject matter does not mean one is teaching well. To teach well, the teacher must connect the subject matter to the needs, desires, interests, stage of cognitive development, etc. of the student, within the physical, social, and political context that the students and teachers find themselves. Good teaching requires moral as well as cognitive perception of the needs and abilities of the student. It also requires a complete and confident command of the subject matter to reconfigure it to meet the needs of every individual student.

Most importantly, teachers need many years of serious training in and out of the classroom. The application process to be accepted by TFA is a joke. It includes an online application, a phone interview, a presentation of a lesson plan, a personal interview, a written test, and a monitored group discussion with several other applicants. If accepted, after a five-week training session, the applicants are officially qualified to teach in impoverished schools with students who often lack financial security, deal with the incarceration of friends and family members, reside in violence stricken neighborhoods, and live with no health insurance.

Answer the following questions: Would you feel safe allowing a college graduate with five weeks of training perform brain surgery on you? To give you a kidney transplant? I certainly wouldn't. Teachers are no different. If you screw up a kid's life early, it can cause a ripple effect for the rest of his or her life.

In the *Wall Street Journal*, William V. Healey, a practicing clinician, declared that medicine needed something similar to TFA, which he touted as "Heal for America." After a "short, but rigorous training program," where the recent graduates would "learn to take and understand vital signs (pulse, respirations, temperature, and blood pressure)," a member of HFA could "fill in the chinks in the log cabins of some patients' care." But, most importantly, Healey foreboded that HFA members would never be able to take the place of "amateur physicians, physician's assistants, or substitute registered nurses." Experience is just one attribute that TFA seems to pass over.

Kopp should change the name of Teach for America to "Teach for Awhile." More than 50 percent of TFA teachers leave after two years and more than 80 percent leave after three years. Only 11.34 percent of TFA teachers reported that they had intended to make teaching a lifelong career when they matriculated into the program. Teaching is not a career for this organization; it is an "experience." You can include it on your résumé for that plum opportunity at Goldman Sachs or Morgan Stanley. Two years teaching poor, disadvantaged kids. Isn't that cute?

Still not convinced? Read how much two years of teaching changed this TFA alumnus:

> Looking back, I'm so glad I chose to teach before embarking on this next phase of my career. I developed skills that empowered me to excel beyond my peers in business school: organization, effective time management, dexterity in communication and public speaking, and the ability to think on my feet. The responsibilities I shouldered in the classroom prepared me like nothing else could for the challenges of management, communication, and intense focus that characterize my current position, where I conduct industry re-

search, create financial models, identify industry trends, and explain their implications.

—Scott, an analyst at Lehman Brothers

I'm touched. Kudos to you, Scott. You are an even better financial analyst. Isn't that what the teaching experience is all about?

At the very least, our country's most disadvantaged children deserve a highly trained teacher rather than a quack padding his or her résumé for a corporate career. A piece by Brandon Mendez, an elementary school student, in the satirical newspaper *The Onion* sported the headline: "Can We Please, Just Once, Have a Real Teacher?" The student continues with a priceless narrative, writing, Do "we have to be stuck with some privileged college grad who completed a five-week training program and now wants to document every single moment of her life-changing year on a Tumblr? For crying out loud, we're not adopted puppies you can show off to your friends." I couldn't stop laughing after reading that.

The underlying dilemma is that the media, corporate donors, and politicians have been easily swayed by this "feel good" program, so they have showered TFA with millions. Its iron fist on the beat of the national conversation is slowly halting efforts to change the teaching profession.

Occupy Teach for America, anyone?

MERIT PAY: THE SEQUEL

Merit pay. Diane Ravitch calls it the idea that never dies and never works. In fact, the pay-for-performance movement arrived in the United States in 1969. Under pressure to close the achievement gap between black and white students, public schools in Texarkana, Arkansas adopted performance contracting. The district made the federal government an offer it would be dumb to refuse; it would return funds for students who failed to pass tests at a stipulated level. The results were striking, but they were too good to be true, as an investigation later discovered widespread cheating.

More than four decades later, *Merit Pay: The Sequel* is coming back to haunt us. This blockbuster stars the corporate reformers, who have adopted merit pay as part of their panacea for changing American schools. The very, very rich got together somewhere and collectively decided that they know exactly how to reform education better than anyone else in the country, including the students, the parents, the educators, and the administrators. Somebody gave them the right to barge into education with their big fat wallets.

For the past few decades, the "pay for performance" system has been the cup of tea among management experts. These corporate hijackers believe in competition and monetary incentives. They want principals to act like CEOs and squeeze teachers to boost test scores by dangling carrots in front of them. From the beginning, Republicans engaged in this delirious behavior, but Democrats have tagged along for the ride. What's unfortunate is that the Obama administration has proposed nearly a billion dollars in merit pay programs as part of the Race to the Top funding. Why is the administration clinging onto this silly ideology as a means for change? Beats me.

Empirical studies in Tennessee and New York City show that a merit pay system has no overall impact on student achievement. In 2010, the National Center on Performance Incentives at Vanderbilt University published what it termed the first scientifically rigorous study of merit pay for teachers. Many people expected that this trial would show positive results because the bonus for students getting higher scores was so large: Teachers in the treatment group could get up to $15,000 for higher scores. After a three-year trial, the researchers concluded that the teachers in the treatment group did not get better results than those in the control group, who were not in line to get a bonus. The bottom line: Merit pay is an empty promise, an idea that looks great in a lab, but doesn't survive when placed in the real world.

The very next day after the release of the Nashville study, the U.S. Department of Education handed out millions of dollars for merit pay programs across the country and announced its intention to spend $1.2 billion on merit pay. Shocker.

Still not convinced?

Last year, an even bigger study was released from Roland Fryer, a prominent Harvard economist and an architect of some of these programs. In the paper, he examines the effects of pay-for-performance in a school-based randomized trial in over 200 New York City public schools. Fryer writes that he found "no evidence that teacher incentives increase student performance, attendance, or graduation, nor do I find any evidence that the incentives change student or teacher behavior. If anything, teacher incentives may decrease student achievement, especially in larger schools."

At the cost of $75 million to New York City taxpayers, we were endowed with information we already had.

If you aren't dazzled by the numbers, let's put the ball in the billionaire's court. Let's take a gander at the pay for performance model in the business world.

Decades ago, Frederick Herzberg, whose 1968 treatise against incentive pay, "One More Time: How Do You Motivate Employees?," explained why money doesn't motivate in the long term. Money, he argued, is a "hygiene factor": Not enough of it causes distress, but money alone has little to do with job satisfaction or performance. Many companies are started to get accustomed to Herzberg's mantra. Likewise, W. Edwards Deming, a leading proponent of systems thinking, has argued that merit pay "nourishes short-term performance, annihilates long-term planning, builds fear, demolishes teamwork, and nourishes rivalry and politics."

How's that for a taste of your medicine? Merit pay doesn't work in companies, so how the hell is it going to work in schools? This isn't Wall Street. Yes, I'm looking at you, Mayor Bloomberg. Teachers don't go for the bucks, like your fellow Wall Street fat cats.

Why doesn't merit pay work? Daniel Pink has an answer. In his book *Drive: The Surprising Truth About What Motivates Us*, Pink reinforces the idea that incentives increase output only for workers engaged in simple, straightforward, mechanical tasks. However, in occupations that involve even "rudimentary cognitive skills," monetary rewards actually lower performance. Pink points out that we are "purpose maximizers." We care about mastery and we want self-direction. Money and the focus on pay and incentives "unmoors us from purpose."

Extrinsic rewards kill intrinsic motivation. The science is there. The math is there. Yet, Michelle Rhee, Michael Bloomberg, and the Obama administration consistently decide to brush it off.

Merit pay keeps coming back to haunt us. Now is our opportunity to kill the beast.

How should we reward the best teachers? Alfie Kohn says, "We shouldn't. They are not pets. Rather, teachers should be paid well, freed from misguided mandates, treated with respect, and provided with the support they need to help their students become increasingly proficient and enthusiastic learners." I don't want my teachers motivated by money. I want them motivated by the fact that they have the duty in creating life-long learners.

THE TEACHER WITCH-HUNT

In the Obama administration's Race to the Top competition, New York was one of the states to receive grants. To be eligible, states needed to adopt a basic teacher evaluation system. In January 2012, the Department of Education foreboded New York that it could sacrifice its share of the money if it did not comply. So New York Governor Andrew Cuomo threatened education officers and the state teachers' union that if they couldn't come to terms, he would impose his own "solution." Eventually, a deal was struck at the 11th hour, allowing student test scores to be used in evaluating teachers. One word to describe the deal: Crap.

The new system known as the Annual Professional Performance Review system, or A.P.P.R., is sold as "balanced." It's not. On a scale of 1-100, teachers will be ranked. Then they will be sorted into one of the four bins: ineffective, developing, effective, or highly effective. Up to 40 percent of their "grade" will be determined by test scores, while the remaining 60 percent will be determined by subjective measurements, primarily classroom observations by principals. You might be thinking: 'It's not all bad. Even if the teacher has a class of poor scores, if the observations go well, the teacher could still be rated highly.' Wrong! The devil is in the details. In the agreement, it discreetly notes: "Teachers rated ineffective on student performance based on objective assessments must be rated ineffective overall." The 40 percent based on test scores is technically inflated — 100 percent. After two years of ineffective ratings, a teacher is fired.

Cuomo has ignored the more than 1,400 principals across New York who expressed grave concerns about the evaluation system. He has ignored the worries of New York State's Teacher of the Year. He has ignored cries from students. And most importantly, he has shamelessly ignored the teachers. He has failed us all. Instead, he chose to *kowtow* to the advice of the corporate reformers, many of whom have never stepped into a public school.

The performance review will be based on a value added model — students will be given the same test at the beginning and at end of the year to assess what they have learned. States will then fire teachers, whose students do not improve their scores. However, experts continually cite these methods as "inaccurate, unstable, and unreliable."

Teachers can't choose their students. When you choose blueberries or apples, you often pick the most plump and juiciest looking fruit. Teachers are forced to live by the maxim: you get what you get and you don't get upset. Thus, the batch of kids varies each year.

In February 2012, the New York State Court of Appeals ordered New York City to release the ratings of 12,700 teachers, which were based entirely on test scores and issued over the last three years. Weeks later, the reports were published in various newspapers on a Friday morning. I heard a pundit remarking that teachers' names and some teachers' pictures were smeared all over as if they had gotten D.U.I.s rather than T.D.R.s (Teacher Data Reports).

On Friday evening, *New York Post* reporters arrived at the doorstep of the father of Pascale Mauclair, a sixth grade teacher at P.S.11, the Kathyrn Phelan School in Queens. They broke the news to him that his daughter was one of the worst teachers in New York, based solely on the released reports. After, the reporters made their way on over to Mauclair's home. Even though she said she didn't want to comment on the matter, the reporters bombarded Mauclair with questions about her inability to teach students.

The next day, Saturday, Jeane Macintosh, Kevin Sheehan, and Daniel Prendergast, published the story in the *New York Post* with the headline: "They're doing zero, zilch, zippo for students." The article assured "that DOE brass were confident she was ranked where she was supposed to be" albeit no officials were actually quoted. Damn. What's more, these reporters asked the public to send them emails of the names of these low-ranking teachers.

On Sunday, another reporter, Georgett Roberts, published a story claiming that Mauclair was the city's worst teacher. The piece quoted a parent calling for the firing of Mauclair and her salary to be given back to the school.

Here are the facts: Mauclair is an experienced and well-admired English-as-a-second-language teacher. She works at one of the city's elementary schools with new immigrant students who do not yet speak English. The school has an experienced and accomplished staff, with a minimal turnover rate, and a strong educator and leader as its principal. When Mauclair returned to school that Monday morning, her colleagues met her with a standing ovation. Still, nothing cannot make up for the emotional damage Mauclair was forced to undergo for days on end.

After digging through the mayhem, we can draw two conclusions. First, the ratings are bogus. Second, the release of ratings is a new low for the public schools. How can you compare a teacher with a class of kids living in poverty, violent neighborhoods, and single parent households and a teacher with a class of kids living in a wealthy lifestyle, having access to food and water regularly, and staying in a two parent household?

Judging solely from the media coverage of the ratings tragedy, one could quickly confirm that teacher bashing is now a trend in society. Education crusader Diane Ravitch, in a piece for The *New York Review of Books*, writes, "The current frenzy of blaming teachers for low scores smacks of a witch-hunt, the search for a scapegoat, someone to blame for a faltering economy, for the growing levels of poverty, for widening income inequality."

Enter William Johnson. He's been humiliated, beaten down, and labeled a "bad" teacher. Johnson, when he was special education teacher at a high school in Brooklyn, New York, was rated "unsatisfactory" by his principal two years ago. Between then and today, he's fortunately transferred to another school in Brooklyn where there is a "great administration."

Most teachers, it seems, have learned simply to "shut up and teach" (as one conservative blogger has advocated). Not Johnson.

As the criticism over teacher evaluation system was mounting, Johnson, in March 2012, penned a snappy Op-Ed for the *New York Times*, documenting his struggles and concerns. I then reached out to him for an interview.

In his class at the previous school he was teaching at, Johnson's students had learning disabilities ranging from autism to emotional disturbances. His job was very difficult. He explains that because of stinging budget cuts and various changes in special education policy, many students with very severe learning disabilities were being pushed in "inclusion classes like mine" where they must follow the curriculum mandated by the state and sit for all standardized tests.

"Then, on top of that, I was humiliated when I was given a bad rating," says Johnson. Why? When Johnson was observed by his assistant principal at that time in his writing class of students aged 14 to 17 at reading levels ranging from third grade to seventh grade, a freshmen girl classified with an emotional disturbance began cursing and throwing pencils.

"I told her to stop, tried to distract her, but ultimately sent her out of the room to the dean's office in an effort to protect the other students," recalls Johnson. "Days later, I was notified that my lesson was rated unsatisfactory, because I had sent that student to the dean instead of following our school's 'guided discipline' procedure."

But there was something else. Why was the rating so peculiar?

"The feedback the same assistant principal was giving me was contradictory," says Johnson. "In a previous observation, she told me to improve my 'assertive voice.' A month later, she said my classroom management was fine, but my focus needed to be entirely on lesson-planning. Then, another time, she said I needed to emphasize group work. I was receiving mixed messages. Yet, this same individual had written on my behalf for a citywide award for 'classroom excellence.'" Was he really a "bad" teacher?

In his time at that school, Johnson believed he was certain that his administration was not supporting him at all. He said, "If the people you work for don't want you to succeed, it's frightening."

Teacher morale has stumbled as a result of the inhumane pressures put on teachers by administrators and the government. More than half of teachers expressed at least some reservation about their jobs, their highest level of dissatisfaction since 1989, the survey found. The results, released in the annual MetLife Survey of the American Teacher, expose some of the insecurities fostered by the high-stakes pressure to evaluate teachers at a time of shrinking resources. About 40 percent of the teachers and parents surveyed said they were pessimistic that levels of student achievement would increase in the coming years, despite the focus on test scores as a primary measure of quality of a teacher's work.

Later, I asked Johnson about how to improve the teacher evaluation system. He replied saying, "Administrators need to be more welcoming to teachers. Right now, most teachers are very distrustful of their superiors and aren't comfortable with them being in class. Second, administrators need to use the evaluation processes to support and help teachers, not throw out teachers that have students that don't produce good test results. When we focus solely on quantifiable outcomes, we are truly missing the forest for the trees."

I have yet to meet a teacher who says: "Give my students more tests to better evaluate me." Or a parent who says: "Give my child more tests so I can tell whether my child's teacher is teaching well."

None of this madness seems to bother Mayor Michael Bloomberg. The bean counters he has rounded up to run NYC schools function by a flawed dogma which is that the art of the teaching can be condensed to an absurd mathematical contraption. Bloomberg's cronies do not want to admit that 10 years of his mayoral control of schools has been a failure. Still, a poll in February 2012 found 57 percent of voters believed it was; only 24 percent thought Bloomberg's policies have been a success.

We aren't stupid, Mr. Bloomberg. You will not get away with this. It's time to end this inappropriate teacher witch-hunt.

EVALUATION

In June 2012, over a hundred students from Staples High School in Connecticut decided to protest Connecticut's education reform law, Public Act 12-116. The law called for teacher evaluations to linked largely to standardized test results. At the protest, students actually wore name stickers, scribbled with numbers, which connoted hypothetical scores. Why aren't we listening to students? Teachers, you can always count students to have your back.

Look, teachers obviously need to be evaluated. However, when you hear the words "accountability" or "evaluation," it is usually nothing more than a code word for punishment. What's the purpose of accountability? Simply to assure that the best teachers are in the classroom and those that are incompetent and unwilling to teach are kicked out. Pasi Sahlberg disclosed, "Finnish educators speak not of accountability, but of responsibility. Our teachers are very responsible; they are professionals."

Policymakers push to link standardized test scores to a teacher's evaluation. Until every class is balanced in terms of socio-economic status, special education, behavior, and English-as-a-second-language, there is absolutely no way to judge a teacher based on test scores. If a prospective teacher knows that their job security is going to be boiled down to how their students perform on a standardized test, why would someone want to become a teacher? We are dispelling a population of young people who want to become teachers.

Thus, it's time to finally acknowledge that test scores are not a correct indicator in determining quality teachers. Teachers would subscribe to Bob Seger's tune, "I feel like a number. I'm not a number. I'm not a number. Dammit I'm a man. I said I'm a man."

Evaluation is not a spreadsheet; it is a conversation. The point is not to stamp a teacher with a number. You can never bully a teacher into caring for children. Why are Americans blind to the fact that collaboration among teachers, not competition, is the key to success? Real winners do not compete. Finnish teachers, for instance, thrive on collaboration. When I asked Sahlberg how Finnish teachers would react if they were told they would be judged by their students' test scores, he replied, "They would walk out and they wouldn't return until the authorities stopped this crazy idea."

As one motto goes, "The purpose of teacher evaluation is to improve, not to prove." What does a revamped evaluation system look like? All the fruitless quantitative data is non-existent. No more spreadsheets.

You can tell great teachers by looking into their students' eyes. Are they awake? Are they interested? Above all, do they love learning?

There are three facets to effective evaluation. First, we can evaluate teachers by the quality of their students' work — whether it is worth the time and effort and has lasting value to their lives. As I noted in previous chapters, digital portfolios are a great start.

Second, there should be multiple observations by principals and fellow teachers. By observations, I do not mean annual hour-long check-ins, but conversations and feedback on a regular basis. Practice makes perfect.

Third, encourage teacher to self-evaluate themselves. Well known education researcher Robert Marzano emphasizes the importance of self-reflection in any kind of effective teacher assessment. Educator Marvin Mitchell recommends that teachers ask: If I were a student, would I want me as a teacher? If yes, list the reasons. If no, list the reasons. Continue to ask your students for opinions and tips. They always know best.

Fourth, let students evaluate teachers. Teachers, I know, you are getting frightened, but it can be successful if implemented appropriately. Always remember, this is just one part of the process. Perhaps we should take a good, hard look at how the Sudbury model of schooling does evaluation. Research professor of psychology Peter Gray explains in *Psychology Today*:

> No staff members at the school have tenure. All are on one-year contracts, which must be renewed each year through a secret-ballot election. As the student voters outnumber the staff by a factor of 20 to 1, the staff who survive this process and are re-elected year after year are those who are admired by the students. They are people who are kind, ethical, and competent, and who contribute significantly and positively to the school's environment. They are adults that the students may wish in some ways to emulate.

While I don't argue that evaluation should be as radical as the Sudbury model, we, the students must be a part of the evaluation process. I know my best and worst teachers. I deserve to have a stake and a voice.

YOU BELIEVED

Traditionally, the role of the teacher has been the gatekeeper of knowledge, the all-knowing fountain of wisdom students, or the "sponges," are expected to soak up. The interests of the students are given no regard. There were no iPhones, laptops, Internet, nor the 24 hour news cycle to freely access all the information at our fingertips. Information was a sparse commodity.

Now everything has changed. All information we desire is a click away. The teacher is not the "know-it-all" anymore. Thus, the role of the teacher must change from a gatekeeper to a guide, a facilitator, a mentor, and a broker of learning opportunities. Teachers, you never know who your students are, what they love, and where they have come from, if you just lecture. It's time for you to fade into the background.

Sometimes called the "guide on the side," this model defines the roles for the teacher and student quite differently. Of this model, progressive educator John Dewey wrote, "The teacher is not in the school to impose certain ideas or to form certain habits in the child, but is there as a member of the community to select the influences which shall affect the child and to assist him in properly responding to these influences."

As the role of teachers change, they become even more paramount in the classroom. Students and teachers are partners. It is up to the teacher to create an inquiry driven classroom and compete for the student's attention. These are the teachers who pursue their love through the art of teaching. They will never burn out of the profession if given respect, an adequate salary, and autonomy.

Remember teachers: It's not about you. It's about them. The second teachers forget that, they become figures of authority, not mentors or friends, but Machiavellian figures. I, myself, can immediately determine a teacher's swagger. When a teacher walks into my classroom, I am observing their body language, composure, and speaking style. If it is different than if the teacher were talking with a colleague or a friend, I can sense it.

Teachers are vitally important to the education of our youth, but they must understand their shift in roles. They will change, because they love learning, love children, and love that they are creating the future of this planet.

As William Arthur Ward conveyed, "The mediocre teacher tells. The good teacher explains. The superior teacher demonstrates. The great teacher inspires."

My favorite teacher is Thomas Barrella. We have regular conversations about literally everything, which are usually the highlight of my day. I want every kid to be inspired by a great teacher — a teacher who will give up their afternoon to chat about life and give you hope and a boost when you are down. I want them to have a teacher like Mr. Barrella, who always puts his students above anything else.

Czech educator John Amos Comenius said, "Teaching is the most splendid profession under the Sun." Parents are putting their greatest treasure in the hands of teachers for 180 days a year. Let's start treating teachers as "nation builders."

At the Save Our Schools March in August 2011, actor Matt Damon gave a genuine, straightforward speech:

I flew overnight from Vancouver to be with you today. I landed in New York a few hours ago and caught a flight down here because I needed to tell you all in person that I think you're awesome.

I was raised by a teacher. My mother is a professor of early childhood education. And from the time I went to kindergarten through my senior year in high school, I went to public schools. I wouldn't trade that education and experience for anything.

I had incredible teachers. As I look at my life today, the things I value most about myself — my imagination, my love of acting, my passion for writing, my love of learning, my curiosity — all come from how I was parented and taught.

And none of these qualities that I've just mentioned — none of these qualities that I prize so deeply, that have brought me so much joy, that have brought me so much professional success — none of these qualities that make me who I am... can be tested.

I said before that I had incredible teachers. And that's true. But it's more than that. My teachers were empowered to teach me. Their time wasn't taken up with a bunch of test prep — this silly drill and kill nonsense that any serious person knows doesn't promote real learning. No, my teachers were free to approach me and every other kid in that classroom like an individual puzzle. They took so much care in figuring out who we were and how to best make the lessons resonate with each of us. They were empowered to unlock our potential. They were allowed to be teachers.

Now don't get me wrong. I did have a brush with standardized tests at one point. I remember because my mom went to the principal's office and said, 'My kid ain't taking that. It's stupid, it won't tell you anything and it'll just make him nervous.' That was in the '70s when you could talk like that.

I shudder to think that these tests are being used today to control where funding goes.

I don't know where I would be today if my teachers' job security was based on how I performed on some standardized test. If their very survival as teachers was based on whether I actually fell in love with the process of learning but rather if I could fill in the right bubble on a test. If they had to spend most of their time desperately drilling us and less time encouraging creativity and original ideas; less time knowing who we were, seeing our strengths and helping us realize our talents.

I honestly don't know where I'd be today if that was the type of education I had. I sure as hell wouldn't be here. I do know that.

This has been a horrible decade for teachers. I can't imagine how demoralized you must feel. But I came here today to deliver an important message to you: As I get older, I appreciate more and more the teachers that I had growing up. And I'm not alone. There are millions of people just like me.

So the next time you're feeling down, or exhausted, or unappreciated, or at the end of your rope; the next time you turn on the TV and see yourself called "overpaid;" the next time you encounter some simple-minded, punitive policy that's been driven into your life by some corporate reformer who has literally never taught anyone anything... Please know that there are millions of us behind you. You have an army of regular people standing right behind you, and our appreciation for what you do is so deeply felt. We love you, we thank you and we will always have your back.

At the end of his book, *Teacher Man*, Francis McCourt, who is preparing to leave teaching, is giving advice to a young substitute. "You'll never know what you've done to, or for, the hundreds coming and going," he says. "Yeah, but the hundreds know, the hundreds who are millions who are us. They made us. We owe them." Teachers are heroes.

*

Stephen Ritz would go on to teach a decade in middle school. Then, the sudden tragedy of the death of his son, altered his working situation. To be closer to his wife, he went to work in various high schools in the Bronx and finally ended up at his current teaching position at Discovery High School.

The special education teacher sincerely loves his job and his students. He says, "I am the oldest sixth grader in the world. I want to be doing something meaningful on a day to day basis or then it's a big waste of everyone's time. I treat my students like I treat my own daughter."

So how did the South Bronx phenomenon all start? How did these green angels of the South Bronx grow 25,000 pounds of vegetables? How did attendance in Ritz's class mushroom from 40 percent to 93 percent?

It began when kids who just got out of prison caught Ritz's eye. "These kids were ones that everyone gave up on," says the teacher. "It turned out that I knew many of them." And these kids were now in his class.

Thereafter, Ritz started a garden in his classroom. It grew. Big time. His bubbling classroom is like no other. There are gardens, seed incubators, fish tanks, mini ecosystems, and Lego sets — a far cry from the traditional desks in rows with a teacher at the head of the class. Shortly after the first garden, the classroom sported the first indoor edible wall in the city. And the kids started to change. Attendance doubled. These disadvantaged, underserved, and ignored students finally loved going to school. They came early and stayed late. The moral of the story is: To end the dropout crisis, we need to make kids love going to school.

With an inundating tank of student enthusiasm to fuel the ride, there was nothing stopping their efforts. By the spring of 2010, Ritz and the students founded the Green Bronx Machine, a non-profit organization that expanded their reach far beyond their small Bronx classroom. Ritz tells me that they've installed green roofs and green walls at Rockefeller Center in New York City, the John Hancock Tower in Boston, and houses in the rich's playground of the Hamptons on Long Island. In particular in the Hamptons, Green Bronx Machine students were paid $3,500 a week and even learned how to surf.

Through the means of project-based learning, Ritz has trusted his students and has treated them like adults. *Trust* is the key word. When teachers and students both understand the balance of trust, the classroom transforms from top-down to bottom-up. Also, by literally pushing the walls into the community, learning is disrupted. Ritz said, "How else can you teach asexual reproduction than by using plants? Nothing thrills me more seeing kids pollinating plants instead of each other."

Spending five minutes with Stephen Ritz is a better energy booster than a shot of Red Bull.

While Ritz's program at Discovery High School was discontinued, the Green Bronx Machine, in his words, is "bigger, stronger, more inclusive, and expansive than ever before." It is now taking its show on the road, expanding to cities across America. When you can give kids healthy food, it changes the equation. He says, "I have never seen more parents and uncles and aunts before. I had 500 people at my farmers market."

In my life, I'm tired and sick of hearing excuses and whining and carping. Don't tell me you can't do something. To be successful, sometimes you will need to step on some shoes, push over some people, and shun the non-believers.

Ritz has accomplished extraordinary feats. He made his students' thinking and learning visible. He turned future inmates into future innovators. As Ritz quipped to me, "We aren't planting plants; we are harvesting hope and cultivating minds in the South Bronx."

   If a classroom in a school in one of the most impoverished communities of this nation can close prison doors and instill a love for learning in children, why don't we follow their lead?

   "Si, se puede," declares Ritz. Yes, we can, indeed.

EPILOGUE

When I started this journey in the Summer of 2011, I was not able to predict how my life would change in just a year. In my endeavors, I have given talks to thousands of people around the world from Doha, Qatar to Madrid, Spain. I was able to check off the item: "Making a television appearance" off of my bucket list when I was interviewed on the *Fox Business: Varney & Co.* show. I have had the opportunity to interview the forefront thought leaders in education, business, entrepreneurship, and media. I have met the most brilliant minds on this planet and forged friendships that I will cherish for a lifetime. I have learned more about myself in the past year compared with the other sixteen years of my life. And I am proud of every day of school that I have skipped to attend conferences and travel.

None of this would have been possible unless I took a risk to write a book. Do you know what the number one regret of the dying is? The answer is: I wish I'd had the courage to live a life true to myself, not the life others expected of me.

I didn't want to fall into such a trap. I didn't want to be just another high school student. I didn't want to be just another 17-year-old. I didn't want to wait to disrupt the world. Society pressures you to do what others tell you to do and not screw with the status quo. Most people don't realize that the world isn't out to get you; it's here to help you. To succeed, you need to give it a chance.

This book is not the end. It is not even the beginning of the end. But it is, perhaps, the end of the beginning. This book is an inauguration for revolutionizing the American education system. It is call to action for all the stakeholders — whether you are a student, a parent, an educator, an administrator, or a concerned citizen. Now is our prime opportunity to transform schools.

Jonathan Ive, Senior Vice President of Industrial Design at Apple, once remarked, "To start something that is genuinely new, you have to start again. With great intent, you disconnect from the past." To revolutionize education, we need to start from scratch.

In the previous chapters, we jawed a number of practical proposals. In chapter one, we said we must: Group kids by ability, not age. Reinvent the classroom. Make the public aware of the larger education problems.

Teach 21st century skills. Shift from pedagogy to andragogy. Let kids be in control of their learning.

In chapter two, we said we must: Ignore the PISA rankings. Reduce the amount of standardized testing. Stop trying to replicate other school systems in the world.

In chapter three, we said we must: Repeal No Child Left Behind. Abolish Race to the Top. Establish a national curriculum based on lean guidelines. Create a national council of teachers, parents, students, policy-makers, and administrators to create such guidelines. Abolish grades. Use portfolios, authentic, and performance assessments. In lieu of standardized tests, offer new assessments, like the College and Work Readiness Assessment. For accountability, sample, rather than test the entire school population.

In chapter four, we said we must: Abolish preschool entrance exams, the SAT, and the Advanced Placement program. Transform the college admissions process. Tell students to think twice before automatically going to college.

In chapter five, we said we must: Bring play into the classroom. Never stop failing and taking risks. Implement the 20 or greater percent rule in school.

In chapter six, we said we must: Reinvent the English, math, history, civics, science, and the arts curriculum. Stop lecturing in school. Adopt an anti-disciplinary curriculum. Let project-based learning rule. Engage students with social media and particular types of technology. Make school a community and apprenticeship-based system.

In chapter seven, we said we must: Pay teachers more. Give teachers more autonomy. Terminate the segregation of theory and practice in graduate education schools. Create a West Point for teachers. Stop the spread of Teach for America. Stop promoting merit pay. Stop tying teacher evaluation to standardized test scores. Transform the teacher evaluation system. Change the role of the teacher from the fountain of knowledge to an "architect of opportunity." Treat teachers like "nation builders."

Now that I have put my solutions on the table, you can decide whether to listen or ignore them. Give me your best shot. If we delay efforts to implement a 21st century model of education, it will already be the 22nd century. I cannot watch another child be suppressed by our schools. We cannot afford to wait.

Don't let anyone tell you that public education cannot work. If we give students dominion of their education, honor teachers, fund schools adequately, and treat students like human beings, it can. Never anymore will kids ask, Will we ever need to know this for real life? One of my favorite interviews was with M.I.T. linguist Noam Chomsky. I asked him what the purpose of public education is. Chomsky replied, "I know of no better formulation than that of Bertrand Russell, who held that the goal of education should be 'to give a sense of the value of things other than domination,' to help create 'wise citizens of a free community' in which both liberty and 'individual creativeness' will flourish, and working people will be the masters of their fate, not tools of production. The educational process should nurture and support the natural curiosity and inventiveness of children, help them discover and develop their own abilities, aspirations and potentialities, the joy of free creation, and of working cooperatively with others to achieve common ends." Exactly.

Instead of saying: 'Let's prepare kids for real life.' Make school real life. Entrepreneur and author Seth Godin said to me, "Education is like medicine. It's not open to lot of new change." We must push the rock that starts the avalanche. When students love going to school, we will finally know the system is working.

One of my interviewees, Joichi Ito, director at the M.I.T. Media Lab, writes some dynamic words in the book *What Matters Now*, "We live in an age where people are starving in the midst of abundance and our greatest enemy is our own testosterone driven urge to control our territory and our environments. It's time we listen to children and allow neoteny to guide us beyond the rigid frameworks and dogma created by adults." A generation is a terrible thing to go to waste. More than half of the world is under the age of 30. In other words, start listening to young people! Give students a seat at the table.

For all the students, teachers, parents, and administrators that are forced to shut up, do not get discouraged. Don't settle for good enough. Stand up and sing your song from the rooftops so the whole world can hear you. Don't stop until your demands are met.

As author Stephen Covey once said, "Leave this world better than it was when you got here." Americans have always been the masters of change. No other nation on this planet is even close to the pool of manpower that we harness. In every decade of American history, you will come across many of the identical dilemmas ailing us today — lagging economic growth, poor infrastructure, high energy prices, too many military conflicts, and a putrid education system. But every time, this country surprised the world. We were the Tim Tebows of the Fourth Quarter. We can and we will do it again.

Founder of Grameen Bank and Nobel Laureate Muhammed Yunus once famously said, "It's not necessary to wait to see the impact on millions of people. 'Millions is a big number. But if your work has a positive impact on five or 10 people, you have invented a seed. Now you can plant it a million times."

I want to plant a seed and watch it grow. Education is what makes my heart sing and dance. What matters most are the people you've met, the lives you've touched, and the seeds you've sowed. Never wait for permission to do something remarkable.

ACKNOWLEDGMENTS

I could not have written this book if it wasn't for the love, encouragement, and help from my friends, mentors, and family. I owe you all a debt of gratitude.

First and foremost, I'd like to thank Don Tapscott for writing the foreword.

Second, I owe a tremendous amount to my interviewees for sharing their time and insight with me. Without them, this book would be incomplete: Nick Perez, Tony Wagner, Bernie Trilling, Charles Fadel, James Kaufman, Mark Runco, Daniel Pink, Warren Berger, Larry Rosenstock, Sugata Mitra, Didi Kirsten Tatlow, Frederick Tatlow-Coonan, Yong Zhao, Yichao Cen, Randy Pollock, Arnold Dodge, James Fallows, Vivek Wadhwa, Pasi Sahlberg, Diane Ravitch, Milton Chen, Alfie Kohn, Deborah Meier, Joe Bower, Vicki Abeles, Wesley Yang, William Fitzhugh, Zak Malamed, John Katzman, Richard Cao, Paul Von Blum, Priscilla Bremser, Robert Sternberg, Frank Bruni, Kevin Wanek, James Altucher, Sarah Weinstein, Dale Stephens, Natalie Warne, Alaxic Smith, Paul Henry, Joichi Ito, Michael Karnjanaprakorn, Cody Pomeranz, Kathryn Schulz, Kathy Hirsh-Pasek, Robin Hanson, Steve Strauss, Roger Neill, Kelly Gallagher, Conrad Wolfram, Richard Rusczyk, Frank Noschese, Larry Bock, Shirley Malcom, Jack Hassard, Chris Lehmann, Eric Mazur, Jeff Hoffman, Gever Tulley, Diana Laufenberg, Howard Gardner, Stephen Ritz, Arthur Levine, William Johnson, Noam Chomsky, and Seth Godin.

I am fortunate to be surrounded by truly exceptional people in my life. I'm indebted to a number of people who read portions of the manuscript and offered feedback, including Joe Antenucci, Matthew Appel, Adam Bellow, Blake Boles, Rachelle Bradt, Bob Brown, Dean Curran, Tony Chen, Ravi Gill, Lucia Grigoli, Alex Horowitz, Trevor Joyce, Alex Krichmar, Ryan Klobus, Gary Lei, David Loitz, Michelle Long, Deepak Malani, Blake Marggraff, Cliff Michaels, Amber Miley, Carlo Monsanto, Lisa Nielsen, Holly Ojalvo, Charles Peralo, Priya Prabhakar, Stephanie Rivera, Isabelle Rizo, Olivia Rosenzweig, Jake Schlessinger, Kelly Schmidt, Curtis SerVaas, Simran Sethi, Aron Solomon, Jason Steinberg, Justin Strudler, Adora Svitak, Daniel Weiner, Nathan Wong, Allison Wu, Irvin Zhan, and Dexter Zhuang.

I'd like to give a special thanks to Priscilla Sanstead, Nikkol Bauer, and Monika Hardy, who worked with me on the the manuscript for months on end. I hope I didn't trouble you too much!

While I cannot name all of you, I'd like to offer my sincere appreciation to my mentors, who have guided me in the past year on literally everything. You know who you are.

Jim Rohn has this great saying, "You are the average of the five people you spend the most time with." Without the following people in my life, I would not be who I am today. Thank you Zak Malamed, Charles Peralo, Alex Oshinsky, Zach Hammer, and Joshua Lafazan for being the greatest companions I could ever have. And thank you Thomas Barrella, my absolute favorite teacher.

Collaborating with my editor Josh Cook and my publisher Jerry Mintz has been an absolute pleasure and an honor. I'm fortunate to have worked with both of you on this endeavor.

My deepest debts are to my family. My grandmother and grandfather, Vina Agarwal and Sri Krishna Agarwal, have instilled wisdom and courage in me from when I was young to today. The bond with my sister, Nikita, will never be breakable. And then there's my parents, Vimal and Divya. You may think I'm the crazy kid in the family, but I cannot live without your constant love and affection. This book would not exist without both of you.

Finally, to the millions of children whose voices are not heard, "the times they are a-changin.'"

Nikhil Goyal
Woodbury, New York
August 2012

NOTES

PROLOGUE

Interview: Daniel Pink

19 "A global platform": Thomas L. Friedman, *The World Is Flat: A Brief History of the Twenty-First Century* (New York: Farrar, Straus and Giroux, 2005).

19 "The connected world": Thomas L. Friedman, "How Did the Robot End Up With My Job?," *New York Times*, October 2, 2011.

21 Between 90 and: Richard Dobbs, "The world at work," McKinsey Global Institute (2012).

21 "Black-collar workers": Philip Auerswald, "Bliss is on the Way," *GOOD Magazine*, March 12, 2012.

22 "Saying they would": "Nation's Students to Give American Education System Yet Another Chance," *The Onion*," August 17, 2011.

1: STOP SUPPRESSING CHILDREN

Interviews: Nick Perez, Tony Wagner, Bernie Trilling, Charles Fadel, James Kaufman, Mark Runco, Warren Berger, Larry Rosenstock, Sugata Mitra

24 When Nick Perez: Thanks to Lisa Nielsen for allowing Nick Perez to share his story publicly on her blog: *The Innovative Educator*; http://theinnovativeeducator.blogspot.in/2012/05/dropping-out-was-great-idea.html.

25 Contrary to popular: JM Bridgeland, "The silent epidemic: Perspectives of high school dropouts," Civic Enterprises in association with Peter D. Hart Research Associates for the Bill & Melinda Gates Foundation (2006).

27 Mann returned home: Matt Miller, "First: Kill All the School Boards," *Atlantic Magazine*, January/February 2008.

27 Education crusader John: John Gatto, *Dumbing Us Down: The Hidden Curriculum of Compulsory Schooling* (Canada: New Society Publishers, 1991).

28 "The aim of": H. L. Mencken, "The Library," *The American Mercury*, April 1924.

28 "Grouping kids by": Deborah Ruf, "The Other Achievement Gap," Center of the American Experiment, August 2010.

28 Finally, it is: Phillip D. Long and Richard Holeton, "Singposts of the Revolution? What We Talk about When We Talk about Learning Spaces," *EDUCAUSE Review*, March/April 2009.

28 "Has the Fordist": Walter Russell Mead, "The Once and Future Liberalism," *The American Interest*, March/April 2012.

29 John Gatto, in: *The Ultimate History Lesson: A Weekend with John Taylor Gatto*. Tragedy and Hope Communications, 2012. DVD.

29 "My whole life": Alex Williams, "New York's Literary Cubs," *New York Times*, December 1, 2011.

29 According to Cathy: Virginia Heffernan, "Education Needs a Digital-Age Upgrade," *New York Times*, August 7, 2011; http://opinionator.blogs.nytimes.com/2011/08/07/education-needs-a-digital-age-upgrade/.

30 Since the amount: *Shift Happens 2010*. Dirs Karl Fisch and Scott McLeod, 2010.

31 "Discovery skills," described: Jeff Dyer, Hal Gregersen, and Clayton M. Christensen, *The Innovator's DNA: Mastering the Five Skills of Disruptive Innovators* (Cambridge: Harvard Business Review Press, 2011).

31 A virtually unanimous: "Beyond the Three Rs: Voter Attitudes toward 21st Century Skills," Partnership for 21st Century Skills (2007).

31 Some estimate that: Bernie Trilling and Charles Fadel, 21st Century Skills: Learning in Our Times (San Francisco: John Wiley & Sons, 2009).

31 In a study: Richard Paul, Linda Elder, and Ted Bartell, "Study of 38 Public Universities and 28 Private Universities To Determine Faculty Emphasis on Critical Thinking In Instruction," Center for Critical Thinking (1995).

32 Progressive education theorist: John Dewey, *How We Think* (Lexington: D.C. Heath & Co., 1910).

32 A survey revealed: "AMA 2010 Critical Skills Survey," American Management Association (2010).

33 "people who can": Daniel Pink, "Revenge of the Right Brain," *Wired*, February 2005

33 A survey conducted: "2008 U.S. Workplace Survey," Gensler (2008).

33 "One leading investment bank": Lawrence Summers, "What You (Really) Need to Know," *New York Times*, January 22, 2012.

34 The College Board: "Writing: A Ticket to Work...Or a Ticket Out: A Survey of Business Leaders," College Board (2004).

34 The Commission estimates: Madlen Read, "Employers say one-third of workers' writing skills fall below job standards," *The Asheville Citizen-Times*, September 19, 2004.

34 No wonder 70: James C. McCroskey, "Communication Approaches: What We Have Learned in the Last Four Decades," University of Alabama Birmingham.

35 Studies have confirmed: Ibid, See 31: Jeff Dyer.

35 A University of Michigan: Warren Berger, "Big Innovations Question the Status Quo. How Do You Ask the Right Questions?," FastCo.Design, March 17, 2011.

36 "My mother made": "Great Minds Start With Questions," *Parents Magazine*, September 1993

36 "Work matters, but": Doc Searls, "Getting Flat, Part 2," Linux Journal, April 29, 2005; http://www.linuxjournal.com/article/8280.

36 A study uncovered: Ronald A. Beghetto, "Correlates of intellectual risk taking in elementary school science, *Journal of Research in Science Teaching*, February 2009.

37 Malcolm Gladwell in: Malcolm Gladwell, *Outliers: The Story of Success* (New York: Little, Brown and Company, 2008).

37 Thomas D. Kuczmarski: Jena McGregor, "How Failure Breeds Success," *Bloomberg Businessweek*, July 2, 2006; http://www.businessweek.com/stories/2006-07-09/how-failure-breeds-success.

37 Author Malcolm Gladwell: Ibid, See 37: Malcolm Gladwell.

38 "You have to": *The College Conspiracy*. National Inflation Association, 2011; http://www.youtube.com/watch?v=A75KERKwEQM.

38 In the book: Thomas J. Stanley, *The Millionaire Mind* (Kansas City: Andrews McMeel Publishing, 2000).

38 "When you grow": Jake Halpern, "Fame Survey;" http://www.jakehalpern.com/famesurvey.php.

39 "Most of the brilliant": Sir Ken Robinson, *The Element: How Finding Your Passion Changes Everything* (New York: Penguin Books, 2009).

40 "The days of": Thomas L. Friedman, "Help Wanted," *New York Times*, December 18, 2011.

41 Experience including error: Malcolm Knowles, *The Adult Learner: A Neglected Species* (Houston: Gulf Publishing, 1984).

2: LET MY COUNTRY AWAKE

Interviews: Didi Kirsten Tatlow, Frederick Tatlow-Coonan, Yong Zhao, Yichao Cen, Randy Pollock, Arnold Dodge, James Fallows, Vivek Wadhwa, Pasi Sahlberg

43 The scores, which: "PISA 2009 Results," Organisation for Economic Co-operation and Development (2009).

44 There is a: Christopher Tienke, "Rankings of International Achievement Test Performance and Economic Strength: Correlation or Conjecture?," *International Journal of Education Policy and Leadership*, April 3, 2008).

45 "Our education system": Didi Kirsten Tatlow, "Education as a Path to Conformity," *New York Times*, January 26, 2010.

46 "In one experiment": David Brooks, *The Social Animal: The Hidden Sources of Love, Character, and Achievement* (New York: Random House, 2011).

46 "I...got an": James Fallows, "While I'm at it, a Chinese and an American view on Chinese education," *The Atlantic*, May 10, 2009.

46 A survey by: "Chinese students lack imagination, creativity," *People's Daily Online*, August 4, 2010.

47 Thus, the meritocratic: See: Confucianism and the Chinese Scholastic System; http://www.csupomona.edu/~plin/ls201/confucian3.html.

47 When Deng Xiaoping: Ann Hulbert, "Re-education," *New York Times*, April 1, 2007

48 In Sichuan Province: "College entrance students within the hyperbaric chamber oxygen decompression," *New of China (Beijing)*, June 5, 2009.

48 At Xiaogang High: "Chinese pupils 'hooked up to drip' to prepare for dreaded June exam," *The Telegraph*, May 10, 2012.

48 Chinese teenagers have: Rob Schmitz, "The Damaged Generation," *Marketplace*, June 6, 2011.

48 In 2011, one: Erica Ho, "Middle-Aged Man Takes China's College Entrance Exam for 16th Time," *Time*, June 9, 2011.

48 When the results: "Gaokao No Predictor of Success?" *Wall Street Journal*, June 30, 2010.

48 Keeping track of: Yan Weijue, "Top gaokao scorers fail to live up to expectations," *China Daily*, June 28, 2010.

49 What's more, a: Chen Jiangping, "University Network: One Hundred Richest," *Sdaxue.com*, July 2012.

49 More than 30: Didi Kirsten Tatlow, "Gingerly, Chinese Parents Embrace the Value of Fun," *New York Times*, January 26, 2010.

49 There were three: Guo Qiang, "Three die amid Gaokao test," *China Global Times*, June 9, 2010.

49 "Liu Yang, a": Andrew Jacobs, "China's Army of Graduates Struggle for Jobs," *New York Times*, December 11, 2010.

50 "They share every": Ibid.

50 "It is if": Gordon G. Chang, "Few Promising Opportunities," *New York Times*, September 1, 2011; http://www.nytimes.com/roomfordebate/2010/12/02/what-is-a-college-degree-worth-in-china/few-promising-opportunities-for-chinas-college-graduates.

50 China's college graduates: "The data show that college students and mi-

grant workers starting salary gap narrowed for the first time," *Beijing News*, November 22, 2010.

50 In fact, it: "China to Cancel College Majors that Don't Pay," *Wall Street Journal*, November 23, 2011.

50 "The Chinese hand": Bill Frezza, "The Root Cause of Market Failure in Higher Education," *RealClearMarkets*, November 28, 2011.

50 Subsequently, what some: Yojana Sharma, "China: Cutbacks in courses with poor job prospects," *University World News*, November 24, 2011.

51 The McKinsey Global: Diana Farrell and Andrew Grant, "Addressing China's Looming Talent Shortage," McKinsey Global Institute (October 2005).

51 A McKinsey Quarterly: Kevin Lane and Florian Pollner, "How to Address China's Growing Talent Shortage," *McKinsey Quarterly* (July 2008).

51 Documenting his struggles: Randy Pollock, "China's Boxed Itself In," *Los Angeles Times*, May 5, 2009.

52 In 1998, years: Ibid, See 47: Ann Hulbert.

52 In 2001, the: Martha Nussbaum, "The Ugly Models," *The New Republic*, July 1, 2010.

53 "For instance, math": "China's 2020 Education Reform Strategy," *Asia Society*, April 27, 2010.

53 Jonathan Plucker, a: Po Bronson and Ashley Merryman, "The Creativity Crisis," *Newsweek*, July 10, 2010.

54 The story revolves: *3 Idiots*. Dir Rajkumar Hirani. Vinod Chopra Productions, 2009. Film.

55 The English colonial: Lord Macaulay, *Minute on Indian Education*, February 2, 1835.

56 "I am firmly": K. Swaminathan, *The Collected Works of Mahatma Gandhi* (New Delhi: Publications Division, 1958).

56 "In Hindi, the": Anurag Behar, "The making of a rote nation," Wipro's Blog, September 9, 2011; http://www.wipro.com/blog/The-making-of-a-rote-nation.

56 Every year, more: Tim Sullivan, "India cram school town redraws lines of success," *Associated Press*, October 24, 2010.

56 One college, Shri: Tripti Lahiri, "India College Stuns with Perfect Exam Score Demand," *Wall Street Journal*, June 16, 2011; http://blogs.wsj.com/indiarealtime/2011/06/16/indian-college-stuns-with-perfect-exam-score-demand/.

56 "To keep an": Davita Maharaj, "Rabindranath Tagore Vision For An Educated India," *The International India* 16.3, July/August 2009.

56 In a Hindustan: Charu Sudan Kasturi, "The 13th year anxiety," *Hindustan Times*, July 9, 2011.

57 "With a robust": Anand Giridharadas, "A College Education Without Job Prospects," *New York Times*, November 30, 2006.

57 Infosys says that: James Surowiecki, "India's Skills Famine," *New Yorker*, April 16, 2007.

57 "When we are": Ibid, See 57: Anand Giridharadas.

58 The Nobel Laureate: Translated in V. Bhatia, *Rabindranath Tagore: Pioneer in Education* (New Delhi: Sahitya Chayan, 1994).

58 At Tagore's school: Kathleen M. O'Connell, "Rabindranath Tagore on education', the encyclopedia of informal education," Infed (2003); Martha Nussbaum, *Not For Profit* (Princeton: Princeton University Press, 2010).

58 Rabindranath writes that: Rabindranath Tagore, *My Reminiscences* (London: Macmillan, 1917).

58 "Only when our": Ibid, See 56: Davita Maharaj.

58 In December 2011: Meera Srinivasan, "Exam-centric system of education will go: Sibal," *The Hindu*, December 27, 2011.

59 For India's iconic: Rita McGrath, "Failure is a Gold Mine for India's Tata," *Harvard Business Review*, April 11, 2011; http://blogs.hbr.org/hbr/mcgrath/2011/04/failure-is-a-gold-mine-for-ind.html.

59 "The same idea": Vikas Bajaj, "In India, Anxiety Over the Slow Pace of Innovation," *New York Times*, December 9, 2009.

59 "Innovation is not": Dinesh C. Sharma, "System to blame for the lack of innovation," *India Today*, April 28, 2011.

60 "Build products. Build": Sramana Mitra, "An Open Letter to IIT Students," Sramana Mitra's Blog, March 31, 2008; http://www.sramanamitra.com/2008/03/31/an-open-letter-to-iit-students/.

60 Yet, in the: 2009 PISA results: Ibid, See 43: "PISA 2009 Results."

60 Their only real: Joshua Levine, "Finnishing School," *Time*, April 11, 2011.

60 An analysis of the: Reijo Laukkanen (2008).

61 "Parents of newborns": Ellen Gamerman, "What Makes Finnish Kids So Smart?," *Wall Street Journal*, February 29, 2008.

61 For example, at: Ibid, See 60: Joshua Levine.

61 For science, a: Nigel Norris, An Independent Evaluation of Comprehensive Curriculum Reform in Finland (Helsinki: National Board of Education, 1996).

61 Besides Finnish, mathematics: Samuel E. Abrams, "The Children Must Play," *The New Republic*, January 28, 2011.

61 Nearly 30 percent: LynNell Hancock, "Why Are Finland's Schools Successful?," *Smithsonian Magazine*, September 2011.

61 The Finns have: Ibid, See 61: Samuel E. Abrams.

61 "If minus 15": Ibid, See 61: Samuel E. Abrams.

61 The Finnish National: Ibid, See 61: Samuel E. Abrams.

61 Thus, students have: Ellen Gamerman, "What Makes Finnish Kids So Smart?," *Wall Street Journal*, February 29, 2008.

61 Ninety-three percent of: Ibid.

62 Under the current: Ibid.

62 The nation came: Klaus Schwab, "The Global Competitiveness Report 2011-2012," World Economic Forum (2011).

63 "Americans like all": Ibid, See 61: LynNell Hancock.

63 "If you only": Ibid, See 61: LynNell Hancock.

63 We can look: Stephen Jay Gould, *The Mismeasure of Man* (New York: W. W. Norton & Company, 1996).

3: THE CORPORATE TAKEOVER

Interviews: Diane Ravitch, Milton Chen, Arnold Dodge, Alfie Kohn, Deborah Meier, Joe Bower

64 "The educational foundations": D.P. Gardner, "A Nation at Risk: The Imperative For Educational Reform," National Commission on Excellence in Education (1983).

65 "a rise of": Russell Baker, "Beset By Mediocrity." *New York Times*, April 30, 1983.

65 "Computers and computer-controlled": Ibid, See 65: D.P. Gardner.

65 "Reporters fell on": Tamim Ansary, "Education at Risk: Fallout from a Flawed Report," *Edutopia*; http://www.edutopia.org/landmark-education-report-nation-risk.

65 The late Gerald Bracey: Gerald Bracey, "We're a Nation at Risk: At Risk (Happy April Fool's Day)," *Huffington Post*, April 1, 2008; http://www.huffingtonpost.com/gerald-bracey/were-a-nation-at-risk-hap_b_94519.html.

66 A blogger remarked: Dan Sewell Ward, "No Child Left Behind," March 20, 2004; http://www.halexandria.org/dward764.htm.

66 "No Child Left": Diane Ravitch, *The Death and Life of the Great American School System: How Testing and Choice Are Undermining Education* (New York: Basic Books, 2010).

67 A survey concluded: "From the Capitol to the Classroom: Year 4 of the No Child Left Behind Act," Center on Education Policy (2007).

67 "Only two subjects": Sam Dillon, "Schools Cut Back Subjects to Push Reading and Math," *New York Times*, March 26, 2006.

67 Gary Stager, an: Gary Stager, "Why Should She Work For You?," *Huffington Post*, October 29, 2010; http://www.huffingtonpost.com/gary-stager/why-should-she-work-for-y_b_774534.html

67 "Many of the": Joanne Yatvin, "Turning schools into robot factories," *Washington Post*, September 24, 2010; http://voices.washingtonpost.com/answer-sheet/elementary-school/-this-post-was-written.html.

68 "Much of the": Alfie Kohn, "Beware of the Standards, Not Just the Tests," *Education Week*, September 26, 2001.

69 The pupils will: "Why We're Behind: What Top Nations Teach Their Students But We Don't," Common Core (2009).

70 Under NCLB, adequate: No Child Left Behind Act of 2001, H.R. 107-110, 107th Cong. (2002) (enacted).

70 A study found: Linda McSpadden McNeil, "Avoidable Losses: High-Stakes Accountability and the Dropout Crisis," Economic Policy Analysis Archives (2008).

70 Ultimately, another report: Alexandra Usher, "AYP Results for 2010-11," Center on Education Policy (December 2011).

71 "No Child Left": Claudia Wallis, Sonja Steptoe, "How to Fix No Child Left Behind," *Time*, May 24, 2007.

71 When James Arnold: James Arnold, "How Race to the Top is like 'Queen for a Day,'" *Washington Post*, February 2, 2012; http://www.washingtonpost.com/blogs/answer-sheet/post/how-race-to-the-top-is-like-queen-for-a-day/2012/02/01/gIQAhup5iQ_blog.html.

71 On the show: "Queen for a Day," *TV.com*; http://www.tv.com/shows/queen-for-a-day/.

72 University of North: Heather Vogell, "Investigation into APS cheating finds unethical behavior across every level," *The Atlanta Journal-Constitution*, July 6, 2011.

72 Further analysis along: Joy Resmovits, "Schools Caught Cheating in Atlanta, Around the Country," *Huffington Post*, August 8, 2011; http://www.huffingtonpost.com/2011/08/08/atlanta-schools-cheating-scandal-ripples-across-country_n_919509.html

72 The 413-page report: "Volume 1 of Special Investigation into CRCT Cheating at APS: Overview, Interviews, School summaries," *The Atlanta Journal-Constitution*, July 5, 2011.

72 Hall even covered: Michael Winerip, "A New Leader Helps Heal Atlanta Schools, Scarred by Scandal," *New York Times*, February 20, 2012.

73 An explosive investigative: Jack Gillum and Marisol Bello, "When standardized test scores soared in D.C., were the gains real?," *USA Today*, March 30, 2011.

73 "the education Ponzi": Ibid.

73 In January 2003: Valerie Strauss, "Bush Plan to Assess 4-Year-Olds' Progress Stirs Criticism," *Washington Post*, January 17, 2003.

74 "Priority 1: Absolutely": "Race to the Top - Early Learning Challenge (RTT-ELC) Program," U.S. Department of Education (July 2011).

74 "There is something": Valerie Strauss, "Race to the Top: Standardized testing for preschoolers," *Washington Post*, July 6, 2011

74 "Assessment is the": Joy Resmovits, "Education Department Releases Final Race to the Top Guidelines, Stressing Ratings and Assessments," *Huffington Post*, August 23, 2011; http://www.huffingtonpost.com/2011/08/23/final-race-to-the-top-guidelines_n_934493.html.

74 Less than a: Richard D. Kahlenberg, "The Charter School Idea Turns 20: A History of Evolution and Role Reversals," *Education Week*, March 26, 2008.

75 A landmark study: "Multiple Choice: Charter School Performance in 16 States," Center for Research on Education Outcomes: Stanford University (2009).

75 In addition, the National: "A Closer Look at Charter Schools Using Hierarchical Linear Modeling," National Assessment of Educational Progress (2006).

75 In an interview: Steven Brill, *Class Warfare: Inside the Fight to Fix America's Schools* (New York: Simon & Schuster, 2011).

75 With 135 schools: For a great segment on the Gulen Movement, watch the CBS 60 Minutes special featuring it: http://www.cbsnews.com/video/watch/?id=7408418n&tag=contentBody;storyMediaBox.

76 For instance, Williamsburg: Anna M. Phillips, "City and State Move to Shut Down Brooklyn Charter Network," *New York Times*, January 10, 2012.

76 And Philadelphia's charter: NPR Staff, "Investigating Charter Schools Fraud in Philadelphia, *NPR*, June 27, 2011.

76 The New York Times: N.R. Kleinfield, "At Explore Charter School, a Portrait of Segregated Education," *New York Times*, May 13, 2012.

76 Consider a report: Julie Mead and Preston Green, "Chartering Equity: Using Charter School Legislation and Policy to Advance Equal Educational Opportunity," National Policy Education Center (February 2012).

76 Another study identifies: "Choice Without Equity: Charter School Segregation and the Need for Civil Rights Standards," Civil Rights Project/Proyecto Derechos Civiles at UCLA (February 2010).

76 "the kitchen is": Sean Cavanagh, "Some States Skeptical of NCLB Waivers," *Education Week*, January 11, 2012.

77 "We have piled": Barack Obama, "Remarks by the President at Univision Town Hall," Bell Multicultural High School, Washington, D.C., March 28, 2011.

78 "Teach with creativity": Barack Obama, "State of the Union Address," 2011 State of the Union Address, Capitol Building, Washington D.C., January 25, 2011.

79 "In public education": Gary Stager, "Wanna be a School Reformer? You Better Do Your Homework!," *Huffington Post*, October 19, 2010; http://www.huffingtonpost.com/gary-stager/wanna-be-a-school-reforme_b_765199.html.

80 "Below are given": Frederick J. Kelly, "The Kansas Silent Reading Tests," Journal of Educational Psychology (February 1916); Cathy N. Davidson, *Now You See It: How the Brain Science of Attention Will Transform the Way We Live, Work, and Learn* (New York: Viking Adult, 2011).

80 "College practices have": Frederick James Kelly, *The University in Prospect: On the Occasion of His Inauguration as President of the University of Idaho* (Moscow: University of Idaho, 1928).

81 "We do not": Richard Hersh, "Teaching to a Test Worth Teaching to in College and High School," Teagle Foundation.

81 "ideas that are": Alfred North Whitehead, *The Aims of Education and Other Essays* (New York: Free Press, 1929).

81 "The typical English": Matthew Burns, "Learning Facts is a Waste of Time," *Los Angeles Times*, March 16, 1996.

82 First, in 2009: Diane Ravitch, "Toughen the Tests," *New York Post*, August 14, 2009.

82 Intrigued by her: Diana Senechal, "Guessing My Way to Promotion," Gotham Schools, August 17, 2009; http://gothamschools.org/2009/08/17/guessing-my-way-to-promotion/.

83 "Pineapples don't have": The following questions come from the New York State ELA exam.

83 "They feared socialism": Lisa Fleisher, "Test Question Flunks," Wall Street Journal, April 20, 2012.

83 "If your eighth": Alexandra Petri, "Talking pineapples and unanswerable questions," *Washington Post*, April 20, 2012; http://www.washingtonpost.com/blogs/compost/post/talking-pineapples-and-unanswerable-questions/2012/04/20/gIQAZ6M3VT_blog.html.

83 "Is this a": Ken Jennings, "Is this talking pineapple a joke?," *New York Daily News*, April 20, 2012.

84 Apparently, Pearson had: "The Pineapple and the Hare: Pearson's absurd, nonsensical ELA exam, recycled endlessly throughout country," NYC Public School Parents; http://nycpublicschoolparents.blogspot.com/2012/04/pineapple-and-hare-pearsons-absurd.html.

84 In its contract: Sharon Otterman, "In $32 Million Contract, State Lays Out Some Rules for Its Standardized Tests," *New York Times*, August 13, 2011.

84 "The state of": Amy Weivoda, "We hung the most dimwitted essays on the wall," *Salon*, June 5, 2002.

85 "Dozens of scorers": Dan DiMaggio, "The Loneliness of the Long-Distance Test Scorer, *Monthly Review*; http://monthlyreview.org/2010/12/01/the-loneliness-of-the-long-distance-test-scorer.

86 After the passage: Pauline Vu, "Do State Tests Make the Grade?," *Stateline*, January 17, 2008.

86 The annual cost: Jerry Grillo, "One Size Does Not Fit All," *Georgia Trend*,

December 2011.

86 One of the early adopters: Cathy N. Davidson, "The Future of Learning," *Mobility Shifts*, New York, October 2011.

87 An extensive sum: Alfie Kohn, "From Degrading to De-Grading," *High School Magazine* (March 1999).

87 Let's take a: Thom Hartmann, *Thom Hartmann's Complete Guide to ADHD* (Nevada City: Underwood Books, 2000).

87 A 2009 study: Lloyd de Vries, "High School Grades Hit By Inflation," *CBS News*, February 11, 2009; http://www.cbsnews.com/2100-201_162-538000.html.

87 Research has uncovered: Susan Harter, "A new self-report scale of intrinsic versus extrinsic orientation in the classroom: Motivational and informational components," *Developmental Psychology* (May 1981).

87 For instance, badges: Sam Kilb, "Credentials, the Next Generation," *New York Times*, November 4, 2011

88 "a test is": Ruth Mitchell, *Testing for Learning* (New York: The Free Press, 1992).

88 It requires students: "Developing Performance Assessments Tasks," *Prince George's County Public Schools*; http://www.pgcps.pg.k12.md.us/~elc/developingtasks.html

89 The 90-minute performance: College and Work Readiness Assessment; http://www.cae.org/content/pro_collegework.htm.

90 The one-hour outcomes-based: The iSkills™ Assessment from ETS; http://www.ets.org/iskills/about.

4: SO YOU WANT TO BE A BARISTA?

Interviews: Vicki Abeles, Wesley Yang, William Fitzhugh, Zak Malamed, John Katzman, Richard Cao, Paul Von Blum, Priscilla Bremser, Robert Sternberg, Frank Bruni, Kevin Wanek, James Altucher, Sarah Weinstein, Dale Stephens, Natalie Warne, Alaxic Smith, Paul Henry, Joichi Ito, Michael Karnjanaprakorn, Eric Mazur

91 On April Fool's: NPR Staff, "N.Y. Preschool Starts DNA Testing for Ad-

mission," *NPR*, April 1, 2012.

91 It has become: Susan Saulny, "In Baby Boomlet, Preschool Derby Is the Fiercest Yet," *New York Times*, March 3, 2006

91 Slate joked that: Emily Bazelon, "The Getting-Into-Preschool Puzzle," *Slate*, March 15, 2007.

91 Incidentally, the amount: Annamaria Andriotis, "Student Loans on Rise — for Kindergarten," *SmartMoney*, March 28, 2012.

91 The indie documentary: *Nursery University*. Dirs Marc H. Simon and Matthew Makar. Variance Films, 2008. Film.

91 The New York: Susan Dominus, "Cutthroat Preschool Ritual Isn't Like Prison, or Is It?," *New York Times*, November 14, 2008.

92 Plunking down $145: Sharon Otterman, "Tips for the Admissions Test... to Kindergarten," *New York Times*, November 21, 2009.

92 "They'll see how": Maral Kibarian Skelsey, "Time to Kiss Up," *Washington Post*, March 4, 2007.

92 In California, one: Ibid, See: 92: Emily Bazelon.

92 One Manhattan mother: Jose Martinez, "Manhattan mom sues $19K/yr. preschool for damaging 4-year-old daughter's Ivy League chances," *New York Daily News*, March 14, 2011.

92 For instance, in: Joel Shurkin, *Terman's Kids: The Groundbreaking Study of How the Gifted Grow Up* (Boston: Little, Brown, 1992).

93 In fact, two: Malcolm Gladwell, *Outliers: The Story of Success* (New York: Little, Brown and Company, 2008).

93 "I want a": Jennifer Senior, "The Junior Meritocracy," *New York Magazine*, February 8, 2010.

93 "Too much high": Robert Fulghum, *All I Really Need to Know I Learned in Kindergarten* (New York: Villard Books, 1988).

94 "All in all": Kathleen Kingsbury, "Dirty Secrets of College Admissions," *Newsweek*, January 9, 2009.

95 As described in: Amy Chua, "Why Chinese Mothers are Superior," *Wall Street Journal*, January 8, 2011.

95 "Amy Chua is": Betty Ming Liu, "Parents like Amy Chua are the reason why Asian-Americans like me are in therapy," Betty Ming Liu's Blog, January 8, 2011; http://bettymingliu.com/2011/01/parents-like-amy-chua-are-the-reason-why-asian-americans-like-me-are-in-therapy/.

95 "Tiger Mom": Catherine Shu, "Tiger Mom? More like Bat Sh*t Crazy Mom!," Catherine Shu's Blog; http://shuflies.blogspot.com/2011/01/tiger-mom-more-like-bat-sht-crazy-mom.html.

95 "Black folks tell": Jeff Yang, "Mother, superior?," *San Francisco Gate*, January 13, 2011.

95 "Probably the best": Beth J. Harpaz, "Dr. Zuckerberg talks about his son Mark's upbringing," *Associated Press*, February 4, 2011.

96 "Let me summarize": Wesley Yang, "Paper Tigers," *New York Magazine*, May 8, 2011.

96 In her book: Amy Chua, *Battle Hymn of the Tiger Mother* (New York: Penguin, 2011).

97 "For the most": *Race to Nowhere*. Vicki Abeles and Jessica Congdon. Reel Link Films, 2009. DVD.

97 "testing company": Janet Lorin, "Not-For-Profit College Board Getting Rich as Fees Hit Students," *Bloomberg*, August 18, 2011.

98 "There are many": Drew Magary, "What Happens When A 35-Year-Old Man Retakes The SAT?," *Deadspin*; http://deadspin.com/5893189/what-happens-when-a-35+year+old-man-retakes-the-sat.

98 In his book: Carl C. Brigham, *A Study of American Intelligence* (Princeton: Princeton University Press, 1923).

98 Nicholas Lemann argues: Nicholas Lemann, *The Big Test: The Secret History of the American Meritocracy* (New York: Farrar, Straus and Giroux, 1999).

98 "Are talented chess": Howard Gardner, *Frames of Mind: The Theory of Multiple Intelligences* (New York: Basic Books, 1993).

99 "I visited an": Richard C. Atkinson, "Standardized Tests and Access to

American Universities," Eighty-third Annual Meeting of the American Council on Education, Washington, D.C., February 2001.

99 At Chyten Educational: Barbara Matson, "Tutor says practice makes perfect: *The Boston Globe*, February 16, 2003.

99 "His experience covers": Daniel Golden, "China's Test Prep Juggernaut," *Bloomberg Businessweek*, May 5, 2011.

100 "The College Board": Charles Murray, "Abolish the SAT," *The American*, July/August 2007.

100 First, in a: Felice Kaufman, "What educators can learn from gifted adults," in F.J. Monks and W. Peters, *Talent for the Future* (Maastricht: Van Gorcum, 1991).

100 Second, researchers Stacy: Stacy Berg Dale and Alan B. Krueger, "Estimating The Payoff To Attending A More Selective College: An Application of Selection On Observable and Unobservables," National Bureau of Economic Research (1999).

101 A survey of: "2010 Report Card on the Ethics of American Youth," Josephson Institute (2010).

102 Since then, as: " SAT/ACT Optional 4-Year Universities Test Score Optional List," *FairTest*; http://www.fairtest.org/university/optional.

102 "From the moment": "Choose AP," College Board; http://www.collegeboard.com/student/testing/ap/about.html.

103 Thus, in the: "(AP) Participation," National Center for Education Statistics; http://nces.ed.gov/pubs2012/2012026/chapter2_11.asp (2012).

103 More than 850,000: "The 8th Annual AP Report to the Nation," College Board (February 8, 2012).

103 Slamming the A.P.: William B. Wood, *Learning and Understanding: Improving Advanced Study of Mathematics and Science in High Schools: Report on the Content Panel for Biology* (Washington, D.C.: National Academy Press, 2002).

103 First off, a survey: Philip M. Sadler and Robert H. Tai, "The Role of High-School Physics in Preparing Students for College Physics," *The Physics Teacher* 35 (May 1997).

103 In addition more: "College Board Advanced Credit," *Massachusetts Institute of Technology*; http://web.mit.edu/firstyear/2016/subjects/ap.html.

104 "There is little": "Learn About Advanced Placement Program," College Board; http://www.collegeboard.com/student/testing/ap/about.html

104 "A lot of": Michael Winerip, "Teaching Beyond the Test, to Make Room Again for Currents," *New York Times*, May 23, 2011.

106 We will dismantle: This is a reference to President Obama's statement: "We will disrupt, dismantle, and defeat Al Qaeda."

107 "Why is academic": Robert Sternberg, College Admissions for the 21st Century (Cambridge: Harvard University Press, 2010).

107 For the class: "Essay Questions," Tufts University; http://admissions.tufts.edu/apply/essay-questions/.

108 "a privilege reserved": Diane Ravitch, *The Troubled Crusade: American Education, 1945-1980* (New York: Basic Books, 1985).

108 Roughly 40 percent: Camille L. Ryan and Julie Siebens, "Educational Attainment in the United States: 2009," United States Census (February 2012).

108 Still, the country: "The College Completion Agenda 2011 Progress Report," College Board (2011).

108 "A diploma wasn't": Frank Bruni, "The Imperiled Promise of College," *New York Times*, April 29, 2012.

108 Until the early: Adam Davidson, "The Dwindling Power of a College Degree," *New York Times*, November 23, 2011.

108 In the classic: *The Graduate*. Dir Mike Nichols. Embassy Pictures, 1967. Film.

109 The cost of: "Trends in College Pricing," College Board (2011).

109 About two-thirds: Andrew Martin and Andrew W. Lehrer, "A Generation Hobbled by the Soaring Cost of College," *New York Times*, May 13, 2012.

109 For all borrowers: Meta Brown, Andrew Haughwout, Donghoon Lee, Maricar Mabutas, and Wilbert van der Klaauw, "Grading Student Loans,"

Federal Reserve Bank of New York (2012).

109 Average debt for: Ibid, See 110: Andrew Martin and Andrew W. Lehrer.

110 "I readily admit": Ibid, See 110: Andrew Martin and Andrew W. Lehrer.

110 "You get your": *The College Conspiracy*. National Inflation Association, 2011; http://www.youtube.com/watch?v=A75KERKwEQM.

110 "If college is": Jim O'Neill and Michael Gibson, "Thiel Foundation To New Crop Of College-Bound Grads: Don't Go," *Fast Company*, December 22, 2011.

110 "If you add": Daniel Indiviglio, "Chart of the Day: Student Loans Have Grown 511% Since 1999," *The Atlantic*, August 18, 2011.

110 "You will be": Andrew Hacker and Claudia Dreifus, "The Debt Crisis at American Colleges," *The Atlantic*, August 17, 2011.

110 "A true bubble": Sarah Lacy, "Peter Thiel: We're in a Bubble and It's Not the Internet. It's Higher Education," *TechCrunch*, April 10, 2011.

111 "Always use protection": Student Loan STD's. *College Humor,* February 13, 2012; http://www.collegehumor.com/video/6707784/student-loan-stds.

111 In their book: Richard Arum and Josipa Roksa, *Academically Adrift: Limited on College Campuses* (Chicago: University of Chicago Press, 2010).

111 The average student: Philip Babcock and Mindy Marks, "Leisure College, USA: The Decline in Student Study Time," American Enterprise Institute for Public Policy Research, no. 7 (August 2010).

112 In 2007, the: "Trends and Indicators in Higher Education," *Connection XXI, no. 5* (Spring 2007).

112 "It doesn't matter": Daria Hejwosz, "Students as consumers: the commercialisation of higher education in the United States of America," *Liberte World*, May 31, 2010.

112 In college, about: Stuart Rojstaczer and Christopher Healy, "Where A Is Ordinary: The Evolution of American College and University Grading, 1940–2009," *Teachers College Record* (2012).

113 These students are: Jennifer Lee, "Generation Limbo," *New York Times*, September 1, 2011.

113 More than 5,000: Richard Vedder, "Why Did 17 Million Students Go to College?," *Chronicle of Higher Education*, October 20, 2010.

113 With that being: Jessica Godofsky, Cliff Zukin, Carl Van Horn, "Unfulfilled Expectations: Recent College Graduates Struggle in a Troubled Economy," John J. Heldrich Center for Workforce Development at Rutgers, The State University of New Jersey (May 2011).

113 Also, the median: "2010 Census Data," United States Census 2010 (2010)

113 Even worse, the: Nathaniel Penn, "Hello, Cruel World," *New York Times*, March 23, 2012.

113 In April 2012: Hope Yen, "1 in 2 new graduates are jobless or underemployed," *Associated Press*, April 23, 2012.

113 In May 2012: "Employment status of the civilian population 25 years and over by educational attainment," Bureau of Labor Statistics (May 2012).

113 And a report: Stacey Patton, "The Ph.D. Now Comes with Food Stamps," *Chronicle of Higher Education*, May 6, 2012.

114 Again, that argument: Ibid, See 114: Richard Vedder.

114 An online salary: "2012 ROI Rankings: College Education Value Compared," *PayScale* (2012).

114 "In pure financial": William Bennett, "Do we need a revolution in higher education?," *CNN*, June 13, 2012.

114 From a study: Ibid, See 115: Payscale.

115 Unemployment rates are: Anthony P. Carnevale, Ban Cheah, and Jeff Strohl, "Hard Times: College Majors, Unemployment and Earnings: Not All College Degrees Are Created Equal," Georgetown University: Center on Education and the Workplace (2012).

115 "One thing we": Thomas Friedman, "Broadway and the Mosque," *New York Times*, August 4, 2010.

116 "In an information": David Brooks, "History for Dollars," *New York Times*, June 8, 2010.

119 "Let's say you": Michael Ellsberg, *The Education of Millionaires: It's Not What You Think and It's Not Too Late* (New York: Portfolio, 2011).

119 "Does a $40,000": Seth Godin, "Buying an education or buying a brand?," Seth Godin's Blog, April 15, 2011; http://sethgodin.typepad.com/seths_blog/2011/04/buying-an-education-or-buying-a-brand.html.

5: INNOVATE OR DIE

Interviews: Cody Pomeranz, Kathyrn Schulz, Kathy Hirsh-Pasek, Robin Hanson, Steve Strauss, Roger Neill

120 "To be creative": Po Bronson and Ashley Merryman, "The Creativity Crisis," *Newsweek*, July 10, 2010.

121 The finding was: Ibid.

121 "They don't feel": Alex Crevar, "The Father of Creativity," University of Georgia; http://www.uga.edu/gm/301/FeatCreate.html.

121 In fact, Jonathan: Ibid, See 121: Po Bronson and Ashley Merryman.

121 In 1992, we: George Land and Beth Jarman, *Breakpoint and Beyond* (New York: HarperBusiness, 1992).

122 Joanne Rowling is: For the section on J.K. Rowling, I used a number of sources, including her website: http://www.jkrowling.com/; J.K. Rowling, "The Fringe Benefits of Failure, and the Importance of Imagination," Harvard University, June 2008; Marc Shapiro, *J.K. Rowling: The Wizard Behind Harry Potter* (New York: St. Martin's Press, 2000); "Report: Author Rowling considered suicide," *USA Today*, March 23, 2008; Stephen McGinty, "The J.K. Rowling Story," *The Scotsman*, June 16, 2003.

123 "I've always thought": Chuck Salter, "Failure Doesn't Suck," *Fast Company*, May 2007.

123 "were no better": Michael Michalko, "Twelve Things You Were Not Taught in School About Creative Thinking," *The Creativity Post*, December 6, 2011; http://www.creativitypost.com/create/twelve_things_you_were_not_taught_in_school_about_creative_thinking.

123 In life, Reid: Reid Hoffman and Ben Casnocha, *The Startup of You: Adapt to the Future, Invest in Yourself, and Transform Your Career* (New York: Crown Business, 2012).

123 Author Chuck Frey: Chuck Frey, "ABZ: A brilliant approach to life planning," *Up Your Impact*; http://upyourimpact.com/abz-a-brilliant-approach-to-life-planning/.

124 Let's teach kids: "The World's Smartest Companies Take Risks, But Not All Of Them Are The Best Bet," *Fast Company*, October 19, 2011

124 "Play at age five": Peggy Orenstein, "Kindergarten Cram," *New York Times*, April 29, 2009

125 A survey of: Edward Miller and Joan Almon, "Crisis in the Kindergarten Why Children Need to Play in School," *Alliance for Childhood* (2009).

125 In the 1970s: Der Spiegel, 20, 1977.

125 One possible answer: Elizabeth Bonawitz, "The Double-edged Sword of Pedagogy: Instruction Limits Spontaneous Exploration and Discovery," *Cognition* (2010); Jonah Lehrer, "Every Child Is A Scientist," *Wired*, September 28, 2011.

126 "If I teach": "Don't show, don't tell? Direct instruction can thwart independent exploration," *ScienceDaily*, August 5, 2012.

126 "They came close": Walter Isaacson, *Steve Jobs* (New York: Simon & Schuster, 2011).

126 Founded in 2002: I discovered Atlassian's story from Daniel Pink's TED talk; ShipIt Days at Atlassian: http://www.atlassian.com/company/about/shipit

127 "make a broad": Bharat Mediratta told to Julie Bick, "The Google Way: Give Engineers Room," *New York Times*, October 21, 2007.

127 After 280 hours: Belén Aranda-Alvarado, "What Caine's Arcade Teaches Us About Modern Parenting," *Mamiverse*, April 19, 2012.

127 One morning, import-exporter: For the commentary on Steve Mariotti, I used a number of sources, including a brief chat; Frank Rubino, "Leading Economic Educator," *HOPE Magazine*, July/August 2003; Steve Mariotti, *The Young Entrepreneur's Guide to Starting and Running a Business* (New York: 3 Rivers Press, 2000); Jessica Bruder, "A Youth Entrepreneurship Program Goes International," *New York Times*, May 15, 2012.

129 "You were born": Reid Hoffman and Ben Casnocha, *The Startup of You:*

Adapt to the Future, Invest in Yourself, and Transform Your Career (New York: Crown Business, 2012).

129 In the 1990s: Cathy Ashmore, "Why We're So Bad At Teaching Entrepreneurship," *Time*; http://business.time.com/2012/05/23/why-were-so-bad-at-teaching-entrepreneurship/.

129 Indeed, years ago: What's Your EQ? Determine Your Entrepreneurial Quotient; http://diydollars.com/self-employment-news/whats-your-eq-determine-your-entrepreneurial-quotient/.

130 "None of us": Barack Obama, "State of the Union Address," 2011 State of the Union Address, Capitol Building, Washington D.C., January 25, 2011.

131 "Sixth in global": Thomas Friedman, "Can't Keep a Bad Idea Down," *New York Times*, October 27, 2010.

131 The following is: The World's 50 Most Innovative Companies 2012; http://www.fastcompany.com/most-innovative-companies/2012/full-list.

131 Hofstede says that: Geert Hofstede, "The Business of International: Business is Culture," *International Business Review* (1994).

132 The Journal of: CrossCheck: Helen (Yuehong) Zhang, "An Effective Tool for Detecting Plagiarism," Zhejiang University Press (January 2010).

132 "Only 20 percent": Gu Di, "Copycat culture draws down China's IT innovation," *Global Times*, May 30, 2011.

132 "With quick profits": Adam Segal, *Advantage: How American Innovation Can Overcome the Asian Challenge* (New York: W. W. Norton & Company, 2011).

132 What's more, Thomson: Louisa Lim, "Plagiarism Plague Hinders China's Scientific Ambition," *NPR*, August 3, 2011.

132 "...despite the size": "The National Medium and Long Term Plan for the Development of Science and Technology (2006-2020)," State Council of the People's Republic of China (2006).

6: IT'S THE CURRICULUM, STUPID!

Interviews: Kelly Gallagher, William Fitzhugh, Conrad Wolfram, Richard Rusczyk, Frank Noschese, Larry Bock, Shirley Malcom, Jack Hassard,

Chris Lehmann, Eric Mazur, Jeff Hoffman, Joichi Ito, Gever Tulley, Diane Laufenberg, Howard Gardner

134 "It is clear": Ralph W. Tyler, *The Basic Principles of Curriculum and Instruction* (Chicago: University of Chicago, 1949).

135 A majority of: Making Disciples of Oral Learners. *Story Runners*, 2004. DVD.; http://www.storyrunners.com/resources/making-disciples-of-oral-learners.

135 "Homer, Plato, the": Harold Bloom, "Get Lost. In Books," *New York Times*, September 6, 2009.

136 Michelangelo, a sculptor: "The Neglected 'R': The Need for a Writing Revolution," The College Board (April 2003).

136 Thus, only about: Ibid.

136 Experiments over the: Richard Chase Anderson, "Becoming a Nation of Readers: The Report of the Commission on Reading," National Institute of Education (1985).

137 Still, in a: William Fitzhugh, "History Research Paper Study," *The Concord Review* (November 2002).

138 Paul Lockhart, a: Paul Lockhart, "A Mathematical's Lament," Mathematical Association of America (2002).

138 "You expect sitcom-sized": Dan Meyer, "Dan Meyer: Math class needs a makeover," *TEDxNYED*, March 2010.

140 Ironically, M.I.T. graduates: "Notes from the Field," High Tech High; http://www.hightechhigh.org/resource-center/Curriculum/Curric-HTH%20Math.pdf.

140 He found that: Richard Rothstein, "Lessons: Statistics, a Tool for Life, is Getting Short Shrift," *New York Times*, November 28, 2001.

141 Duke University Professor: Cathy Davidson, "Why We Need a 4th R: Reading, wRiting, aRithmetic, algoRithms," *DML Central*, January 25, 2012.

141 Programming language environments: Stephanie Schorow, "Creating from Scratch," *MIT News*, May 14, 2007.

141 For example, Thomas: Thomas Suarez, "Thomas Suarez: A 12-year-old app developer," *TEDxManhattan*, October 2011.

142 In a letter: Ramanujan Srinivasa, *Am Inspiration 2 Vols.* (Madras, 1968).

142 "Is zero divided": Robert Kanigel, *The Man Who Knew Infinity: A Life of the Genius Ramanujan* (New York: Simon & Schuster, 1992).

143 The National Assessment: "The National Assessment: U.S. History 2010 Report Card," National Assessment of Educational Progress (2010).

143 "We're raising young": Brian Bolduc, "Don't Know Much About History," *Wall Street Journal*, June 18, 2011.

143 Citing a 1998: National Constitution Center (1998).

144 In his provocative: James Loewen, *Lies My Teacher Told Me: Everything Your American History Textbook Got Wrong* (New York: Touchstone, 2007).

145 "Not even one": John Goodlad, *A Place Called School: Prospects for the Future* (New York: McGraw-Hill, 1984).

145 A study concludes: Andrew C. Butler, Franklin M. Zaromb, Keith B. Lyle, and Henry L. Roediger, III, "Using Popular Films to Enhance Classroom Learning The Good, the Bad, and the Interesting," *Psychological Science* 20, no. 9 (2009).

147 "They can learn": Ibid, See 144: Brian Bolduc.

147 According to data: "The Nation's Report Card: Civics 2010, National Assessment of Educational Progress (2011).

147 When Newsweek gave: Andrew Romano, "How Dumb Are We?," *Newsweek*, March 20, 2011.

147 What's even more: "Kaiser Health Tracking Poll: Public Opinion on Health Care Issues," The Kaiser Family Foundation (February 2011).

147 While it's easy: Michael X. Delli Carpini and Scott Keeter, *What Americans Know About Politics and Why It Matters* (New Haven: Yale University Press, 1997).

148 "You sit in": Abby Kiesa, "Millennials Talk Politics: A Study of College Student Political Engagement," Center for Information & Research on Civic

Learning & Engagement (CIRCLE) and The Charles F. Kettering Foundation (November 2007).

149 "I cannot tell": Garry Wills, "Play Politics," *New York Times*, September 6, 2009.

149 A 2008 study: "Ready to Innovate," The Conference Board (2008).

150 Some statistics suggest: Nick Rabkin and E. C. Hedberg, "Arts education in America: What the declines mean for arts participation," National Endowment for the Arts (February 2011).

151 Studies have confirmed: Christopher Drew, "Why Science Majors Change Their Minds (It's Just So Darn Hard)," *New York Times*, November 4, 2011.

152 Even forensics science: Mia Sharma, "Why science lessons are boring," *Cosmos Magazine*; November 17, 2010

152 "They learn with": Dudley Herschbach, *State of Tomorrow*; http://www.stateoftomorrow.com/stories/energy/herschbach.htm.

153 "When I teach": Claudia Dreifus, "A Conversation with: Robert C. Richardson; The Chilling of American Science," *New York Times*, July 6, 2004.

153 A majority of: "Science and Engineering Indicators 2012," National Science Foundation (2012).

153 Research from John: John H. Falk and Lynn D. Dierking, "The 95 Percent Solution," *American Scientist*, November-December 2010.

154 Understand, these "high": Ellen V. Futter, "Opinion: The Role of Museums in 21st Century Science Education," *NBC Education Nation*, October 2, 2010.

154 "Science is a perspective": Brian Greene, "Put a Little Science in Your Life," *New York Times*, June 1, 2008.

155 Research conducted over: For research done on lectures, see: http://americanradioworks.publicradio.org/features/tomorrows-college/lectures/resources.html.

155 Then after reading: Halloun and D. Hestenes, "The initial knowledge state of college physics students," *Am. J. Phys.* 53, 1043 (1985).

156 Furthermore, a recent: Gregory Ferenstein, "Move Over Harvard And MIT, Stanford Has The Real "Revolution In Education," *TechCrunch*, May 9, 2012.

156 "has become so": Hemi Gandhi, "Combating the Facebook Index," *The Harvard Crimson*, October 24, 2011.

156 "Khan Academy is": Karim Kai Ani, "Khan Academy: It's Different This Time," *Mathalicious*, February 4, 2012.

157 Author Frans Johansson: Frans Johansson, *The Medici Effect: Breakthrough Insights at the Intersection of Ideas, Concepts, and Cultures* (Cambridge: Harvard Business Review Press, 2004).

158 According to Lakhani's: Tina Rosenberg, "Prizes With an Eye Toward the Future," *New York Times*, February 29, 2012; http://opinionator.blogs.nytimes.com/2012/02/29/prizes-with-an-eye-toward-the-future/.

158 "Today's problems — from": Frank Moss, The Sorcerers and Their Apprentices: *How the Digital Magicians of the MIT Media Lab Are Creating the Innovative Technologies That Will Transform Our Lives* (New York: Crown Business, 2011).

159 "The school must": John Dewey, "My Pedagogic Creed," *School Journal*, January 1897.

159 "wholehearted purposeful activity": William Heard Kilpatrick, "The Project Based Method: The Use of the Purposeful Act in the Educative Process," October 12, 1918.

160 The goal is: Ken Auletta, "Get Rich U," *New Yorker*, April 30, 2012.

160 Based on the: Carolyn T. Geer, "Innovation 101," *Wall Street Journal*, October 16, 2011.

162 "1. Students learn more": Brigid Barron, Linda Darling Hammond, "Powerful Learning: Studies Show Deep Understanding Derives from Collaborative Methods," *Edutopia*; October 8, 2011; http://www.edutopia.org/inquiry-project-learning-research.

163 "'Personalized' learning is": Will Richardson, "Personalizing flipped engagement," *SmartBlogs*, July 2, 2012; http://smartblogs.com/education/2012/07/02/personalizing-flipped-engagement/.

164 "an embryonic community": John Dewey, *The School and Society* (Chicago: University of Chicago Press, 1907).

7: NATION BUILDERS

Interviews: Stephen Ritz, Pasi Sahlberg, Arthur Levine, Tony Wagner, Alfie Kohn, William Johnson

166 "When we don't": Dave Eggers and Nínive Clements Calegari, "The High Cost of Low Teacher Salaries, *New York Times*, May 1, 2011.

166 "Can an education": Michael Winerip, "Teachers Get Little Say in a Book About Them," *New York Times*, August 29, 2011.

166 There was a great: Arne Duncan, "Working Toward 'Wow': A Vision for a New Teaching Profession Remarks of Arne Duncan, National Board of Professional Teaching Standards," July 29, 2011.

167 Of the roughly: John Heilemann, "Schools: The Disaster Movie," *New York Magazine*, September 5, 2010.

167 Only eight universities: Diane Ravitch, "Schools We Can Envy," *The New York Review of Books*, March 8, 2012; http://www.nybooks.com/articles/archives/2012/mar/08/schools-we-can-envy/?pagination=false.

167 In 2008, the: Joshua Levine, "Finnishing School," *Time*, April 11, 2011.

167 A 2010 McKinsey: Byron Auguste, Paul Kihn, Matt Miller, "Closing the talent gap: Attracting and retaining top-third graduates to careers in teaching," McKinsey & Company (September 2010).

167 In fact, according: Martin Gross, *The Conspiracy of Ignorance: The Failure of American Public Schools* (New York: Harper, 1999).

168 According to author: Lynn O'Shaughnessy, "Here's the Nation's Easiest Major," *CBS News*, June 20, 2011.

168 "We recognize that": Ibid, See: 168: Byron Auguste.

168 "You could do": *American Teacher*. Dirs Vanessa Roth and Brian McGinn. First Run Features, 2011. Film.

168 The average starting: Ibid, See 167: Dave Eggers and Nínive Clements Calegari.

168 In 1970 in: Ibid, See: 168: Byron Auguste.

168 Today, including salary: Ibid, See: 168: Byron Auguste.

168 The average income: Annette Witheridge, "Crisis, what crisis? Top 25 hedge fund managers pocket an average of $1 billion in 2009," *Daily Mail*, April 1, 2010.

168 "In Michigan, where": David Z. Hambrick, "Intelligence Is Not the Same as Value," *New York Times*, January 5, 2012; http://www.nytimes.com/roomfordebate/2012/01/02/are-teachers-overpaid/intelligence-is-not-the-same-as-value.

168 Recently, the Organization: Andreas Schleicher, "Building a High-Quality Teaching Profession: Lessons from around the world," Organisation for Economic Co-operation and Development (2011).

169 In Finland, salaries: Ibid, See: 168: Byron Auguste.

169 "Only four years": Susan Saulny, "Voters in Central Florida Want Assurances on Economy," *New York Times*, January 29, 2012.

169 "When you have": Ibid, See 169: *American Teacher*.

169 In 1981, about: Christine Armario, "Teachers, facing low salaries, opt to moonlight," *Boston*, November 11, 2011.

169 Sixty-two percent of: Paul Wolman, "Status of the American Public School Teacher 2005-2006," National Education Association (March 2010).

170 Fourteen percent of: Ibid, See: 168: Byron Auguste.

170 Estimates put the: National Commission on Teaching and America's Future, estimate based on NCTAF Teacher Turnover Cost Calculator applied to the Digest for Education Statistics data for all public school teachers in urban and non-urban public schools and districts.

170 Fortunately, a majority: "Do teachers make enough?," Poll Position (2011).

170 Recently, a study: Raj Chetty, John N. Friedman, Jonah E. Rockoff, "The Long-Term Impacts of Teachers: Teacher Value-Added and Student Outcomes in Adulthood," National Bureau of Economic Research (December 2011).

170 McKinsey polled 900: Dave Eggers and Nínive Clements Calegari, "The High Cost of Low Teacher Salaries," *New York Times*, May 1, 2011.

170 "We want higher": Kennedy-Nixon First Presidential Debate, 1960. John F. Kennedy Library Foundation, 2010; http://www.youtube.com/watch?v=gbrcRKqLSRw.

171 From the beginning: Grace Rubenstein, "Confronting the Crisis in Teacher Training," *Edutopia*, November 14, 2007.

171 Today, these institutions: Personal interview with Arthur Levine.

171 "The dirty little": Jesse Scaccia, "Graduate Schools of Education: 'Cash Cows' says Harvard lecturer," *Teacher*, Revised Blog, March 31, 2009.

171 Traditionally, education schools: Elizabeth Green, "Building a Better Teacher," *New York Times Magazine*, March 7, 2010.

171 A 2006 report: Ibid.

171 Only a semester: Max Bean, "A Better Way to Train Teachers," *Dewey to Delpit*, May 28, 2011.

171 "at least seven": "How to Become a New York City Licensed MASTER PLUMBER," NYC Buildings; http://www.nyc.gov/html/dob/downloads/pdf/master_plumbers_license_exam.pdf.

172 Malcolm Gladwell, in: Malcolm Gladwell, *Outliers: The Story of Success* (New York: Little, Brown and Company, 2008).

172 "The Willie Sutton": Arthur Levine, "How to improve teacher education now (and why Teach for America isn't the answer)," *Washington Post*, August 3, 2011; http://www.washingtonpost.com/blogs/answer-sheet/post/how-to-improve-teacher-education-now-and-why-teach-for-america-isnt-the-answer/2011/08/02/gIQANclsqI_blog.html.

173 In a 2002: Ildiko Laczko-Kerr, David C. Berliner, "The Effectiveness of 'Teach for America' and Other Under-certified Teachers," *Economic Policy Analysis Archives* (2002).

173 "Subject matter knowledge": *John Dewey, Democracy and Education: An Introduction to the Philosophy of Education* (New York: Macmillan, 1916).

174 In the Wall: William V. Healey, "Heal for America," *Wall Street Journal*, September 12, 2009.

174 More than 50: Julian Vasquez Heilig and Su Jin Jez, "Teach for America: A Review of the Evidence," Great Lakes Center for Education Research and Practice (June 2010).

174 Only 11.34 percent: Morgaen L. Donaldson and Susan Moore Johnson, "TFA Teachers: How Long Do They Teach? Why Do They Leave?," *Phi Delta Kappan*, October 4, 2011.

174 "Looking back, I'm": Anna, "Why I Hate Teach for America," *Feministe*, August 23, 2008.

175 A piece by: "My Year Volunteering As A Teacher Helped Educate A New Generation Of Underprivileged Kids," *The Onion*, July 17, 2012

175 Under pressure to: Walt Gardner, "No merit in merit pay for teachers," *Guardian*, March 27, 2011.

176 In 2010, the: Matthew G. Springer, "Teacher Pay for Performance Experimental Evidence from the Project on Incentives in Teaching," National Center on Performance Incentives (September 2010).

176 "no evidence that": Roland G. Fryer, "Teacher Incentives and Student Achievement: Evidence from New York City Public Schools," The National Bureau of Economic Research (March 2011).

176 Decades ago, Frederick: Andrea Gabor, "Why Pay Incentives Are Destined to Fail," *Education Week*, September 22, 2010.

177 "nourishes short-term": W. Edwards Deming, *Out of the Crisis* (Cambridge: Massachusetts Institute of Technology, 1982).

177 In his book: Daniel Pink, *Drive: The Surprising Truth About What Motivates Us* (New York: Riverhead Trade, 2011).

178 "Teachers rated ineffective": Chancellor Tisch and Commissioner King Praise Evaluation Agreement; http://www.oms.nysed.gov/press/ChancellorTischandCommissionerKingPraiseEvaluationAgreement.html.

178 On Friday evening: Leo Casey, "The True Story of Pascale Mauclair," *New York Post*, February 28, 2012; http://www.edwize.org/the-true-story-of-pascale-mauclair.

178 The next day: Jeane Macintosh, "Teachers who got zero ratings," *New York Post*, February 25, 2012.

179 On Sunday, another: Georgett Roberts, "Queens parents demand answers following teacher's low grades," *New York Post*, February 26, 2012.

179 "The current frenzy": Diane Ravitch, "No Student Left Untested," *The New York Review of Books*, February 21, 2012; http://www.nybooks.com/blogs/nyrblog/2012/feb/21/no-student-left-untested/.

179 As the criticism: William Johnson, "Confessions of a 'Bad' Teacher," *New York Times*, March 4, 2012.

180 More than half: "MetLife Survey of the American Teacher: Teachers, Parents and the Economy," *MetLife* (March 2012).

181 Still, a poll: "New York City (NYC) Poll," Quinnipiac University (February 2012).

182 Educator Marvin Mitchell: Larry Ferlazzo, "What's A Good Way For A Teacher To Evaluate Him/Herself?," Larry Ferlazzo's Websites of the Day, March 23, 2009.

182 "No staff members": Peter Gray, Children Educate Themselves IV: Lessons from Sudbury Valley, *Psychology Today*, August 13, 2008; http://www.psychologytoday.com/blog/freedom-learn/200808/children-educate-themselves-iv-lessons-sudbury-valley.

183 "The teacher is": John Dewey, *The Essential Dewey: Pragmatism, Education, Democracy* (Bloomington: Indiana University Press, 1998).

184 "I flew overnight": Matt Damon, Save Our Schools Convention, Washington D.C., July 30, 2011.

185 "You'll never know": Frank McCourt, *Teacher Man: A Memoir* (New York: Scribner, 2005).

EPILOGUE

Interviews: Noam Chomsky, Seth Godin

190 "We live in": Seth Godin, *What Matters Now* (New York: Triibes Press, 2009).

INDEX

ABOUT THE AUTHOR

Nominated for the U.S. Secretary of Education by Diane Ravitch and lauded as an "emerging voice of his generation," at age 17, Nikhil Goyal is the author of *One Size Does Not Fit All: A Student's Assessment of School* by the Alternative Education Resource Organization. His work has appeared in the *New York Times, Wall Street Journal, Fox and Friends, Fox Business: Varney & Co., NBC Nightly News, Forbes,* and *Huffington Post*.

Nikhil has spoken to thousands at conferences and TEDx events around the world from Qatar to Spain and has guest lectured at Baruch College in New York.

He is leading a Learning Revolution movement to transform the American school system. A senior at Syosset High School, Nikhil lives with his family in Woodbury, New York.

Follow Nikhil on Twitter @nikhilgoya_l
His email is ngoyal2013@gmail.com

CPSIA information can be obtained at www.ICGtesting.com
Printed in the USA
BVOW011607140113

310579BV00005B/122/P